D1508848

EARTH IS HIRING

The New Way to Live, Lead, Earn, and Give

For Millennials and Anyone Who Gives a Sh*t

Peta Kelly

Waterside Press

Waterside Press
2055 Oxford Ave
Cardiff, CA 92007
www.waterside.com

FSC
www.fsc.org
MIX
Paper from
responsible sources
FSC® C008955

Tag! You're it!

To my homie _____,

TAG! I'm gifting this book to you because when I think of the world's conscious badasses, you come into my heart.

Thank you for everything that you are for our world.

Thank you for giving a shit.

Thank you for being gloriously and messily YOU.

I'm so grateful to be on this beautiful Earth at the same time as you.

Let's do this. Or more importantly, let's *be* this.

Love all around the galaxies and back,

From _____

For Sol,

My beautiful, brilliant daughter who was in my womb at the time of writing this, and will be in my arms at the time you're reading it.

Sol, you inspire me more than any person on Earth.

I hope our generation makes you proud. X

Contents

When I first discovered Peta Kelly...

I scrolled through her Instagram page like a kid in a candy shop. Wide-eyed at her posts (aka mic-drops of wisdom), I could hear her voice through the screen—so fierce and powerful yet so inviting. I remember being in disbelief at not only the way she spoke so high-level, but that she did it in such a bad-ass way. Not to mention with 100% humility; NO spiritual 'better-than-thou.' I instantly felt a deep respect for Peta and the way she serves the world.

By the time I met PK in person, I had been channeling Delighted By Hummus—my 'chief entity' as PK calls it—for over a year. I had the privilege of being connected to her event, *The New Way LIVE*. As I dished out dessert hummus for her attendees, I listened in the back awe-struck at what she was rapping about on stage. Her words reflected the exact theories I'd been applying to Delighted By since inception....but because I had never heard anyone else speak/write about them, I was shocked to hear them come out of her mouth. I had in fact only been introduced to these trinkets of wisdom through dozens of Ayahuasca ceremonies. In these ceremonies I was invited to see my entity (Delighted By, a 'her') as separate from me; to get out of my own way and simply 'be the channel;' and to remember that abundance is my divine birthright. I had been applying these concepts to my entity, but to be truthful, wasn't speaking about them publicly because my head was down—focusing on the business itself. What Peta calls 'the New Way of business' was already *really* working for me, so to hear her bring these messages to her tribe left me with 'thank god someone is talking about this.' Not only did PK bring it all to the next level for me; she also gave me the freedom to keep doing what I was doing—to stay focused—because now I knew that Peta was getting the real message out there.

As my friendship with PK developed, my respect continued to increase. The way she connects to her tribe so authentically and humbly is next to none. She is a daily invitation into being more thoughtful, compassionate, big-thinking, and wild. How can someone up to so much 'epic shit,' also be *so there* for her loved ones, while also staying radically committed to her own happiness? Peta doesn't get up on a platform to preach; no, she stands up tall and asks *'how can I serve today, in the way I speak, write, nourish my body, and circulate resources?'* You can count on Peta to not just envision change, but to *be* change; count on Peta to not shame the current issues, but to *co-create* the exact world she desires; count on Peta to do her 'magic' by simply recognizing her own responsibility in it all. Last but not least, you can count on Peta to be the first to claim her humanness and imperfections; I love the way she can recognize it, bring it forward playfully, and remind us to not take ourselves too seriously.

It's hard to find the words to explain just what Peta means to me. She is the voice of our generation. She is a true initiator. She has been trusted with one of the most important messages of our time. We are all listening to Peta, and for good reason. We trust her because we can feel that Mother Earth trusts her. When I tap into PK's old soul, I feel a brilliant, extra-terrestrial, galactic goddess that united with an indigenous, tribal Earth-shaman—who then morphed into a thought-leader with extra swag and humor. I love her fierceness that she has for the planet, for humanity, but above all for *herself*. PK gives us permission through her example to live a super badass, abundant, FUN life, while also making a difference. I know it wasn't easy, however, being the one that went first—which is why I bow down to her courage.

Peta hasn't even hit the tip of the iceberg of what she is bringing through in this lifetime. It's pretty insane to think about, when you recognize the thousands of lives she has already impacted.

One time I asked Peta if I could be the one to introduce her to stage at a future event of hers. I just wanted the chance to publicly announce just how epic this human really is, especially now that I had seen her realness and alignment 'behind the scenes.' Peta is honest AF; she is committed to her own alignment no matter what people think about it; she is open and authentic about her real-life experiences; and she has boldly said yes to speaking up. When PK asked me to write the foreword to her book *Earth Is Hiring*, I bawled my eyes out on the beach. And I'm crying as I write this now, because to me, *Earth Is Hiring* is the most important book ever written. To give my 'blessing' to PK's big, beautiful, aligned voice in this way is one of the top honors of my life.

All that is left for me here is sincere gratitude to my lion twin, Peta Jean Kelly. PK—you are one in a trillion. I have taken on you and your life-mission as personal commitments and top priorities; which is why I am infinitely grateful to Erik as well, for his unconditional love and presence in overseeing the Earth-angel you are (you deserve the best). You constantly teach me and inspire me, and above all you leave me/my Soul with the constant message 'keep going.' Thank you for being my family; thank you for being a guardian and cheerleader for my entities; thank you for connecting the dots for so many people by simply spreading your beautiful wings and flying. I am so fucking proud of you.

Makenzie Marzluff
Badass.Conscious.Millennial.Entrepreneur
Founder and Chief Breath Taker of Delighted By Dessert Hummus and Kakao Ceremonial Drinking Chocolate

My little Starseed,

When I was 9 months old, my mum took me to get the routine check up to make sure I wasn't deaf. My ears were the same size as Mickey Mouse's so I'm not quite sure why they needed testing. My poor Mum had to take me back five more times to have the same tests, because every time I went, I wouldn't cooperate with the nurses. I'd wriggle around and ignore their prompts. Don't ask me how I was so badass back then, I just was. On the final visit they gave up. They said to my Mum, "Christine, we can't tell if Peta is deaf, but we can tell that she has attitude."

Attitude, is the greatest piece of equipment (other than a love of Backstreet Boys and The Parent Trap), the Universe could have placed in my DNA back in 1988. Attitude is the greatest piece of equipment the Universe could have placed into the DNA of all millennials. Attitude is what I like to call **divine intolerance.**

Divine intolerance is the greatest gift we have to gift to you, your generation and to our entire planet.

Divine intolerance is why we work all day long at stand up desks, wearing our ripped levi's and no shoes, to build conscious enterprises that replace those that are abusing our Earth. Divine intolerance is why we don't watch TV or listen to the radio cos we can't believe Big Pharma still tries to trick us out of our innate health with their "If you take this medication for a common cold you will grow three boobs and acne on your eyeballs." Divine intolerance is why we change our minds about old dogmas and teachings that we may have learned in school, cos they just don't make sense in our souls. Divine intolerance is what some people call ADD, but is simply an intolerance for being told to sit at a desk all day when our minds are simply too brilliant and adventurous. Divine intolerance is why we don't buy into the old models of success that tell us that a mortgage and a daily traffic jam, and sucking up a boss's butt is what's will help us 'reach the top' (There's no top). Divine intolerance is why 95% of millennials don't want to work for a company that puts profits *before purpose. Divine intolerance is how our generation teaches the world what is needed, relevant and required for us to evolve in a way that has ALL people, ALL countries, ALL beings thriving.*

Baby, my generation's divine intolerance for what's no longer working is what's gonna ensure we give this planet to you with a whole new book of standards. You didn't choose to come to planet Earth in 2017 to do what everyone else is doing, to say what everyone else is saying, or to tolerate what most people are tolerating. And that's why I don't have a worry in the world for you coming down to Earth during this crazy time.

I know that you and your little buddies are equipped with powers and magic that nobody on Earth right now can comprehend, and that you're coming with your greatest piece of equipment ever— divine intolerance.

Whenever I have moments of, **Oh God, they're actually drilling into our sacred lands for more oil!** *I look down at my belly and see that you're not worried. You're smiling with your rad, evolved, specially-wired DNA saying, "Don't worry Mum, you should see the equipment I have!"*

And I say, "But baby do you have your—"

"—Yes, Mum. I have my divine intolerance. Don't worry. I wouldn't come down to Earth without it."

I love you so much.

Love Mum. XX

Homie,

And in the early 1980's, before millennials descended upon Earth, God gathered them in a team huddle.

> *'Alright guys, the population is about to grow, we're gonna hit an intense point in evolution where shit feels really dense and chaotic, and the Earth and all of her creatures are gonna need you more than ever. So listen up! I've put some very specific equipment inside your DNA. Some of it's really cool, and some of it's gonna be really annoying to your parents. You'll know what to do when you get there. It will be natural for you. Make me proud, but have fun. Okay—fist bump. And don't worry, you'll be rewarded with Tamagotchis. Good talk. See you out there.'*

Start here. Do not pass Go until you read.

"Change the world," they said.

"Ok," we said. "We'll change the world."

And now we can't stop saying it.

World Changer, Change Maker, Game changer. Three terms we use as commonly as we roll our eyes at plastic wrap and companies with no social cause. Three terms that feature frequently on our Instagram bios or in our conversations about our high performing friends. Three terms we hashtag so we can find other people who wanna #crushit #changetheworld #bethechange.

We're obsessed with changing the world, and we feel it's what we're here to do. But what does that even mean? Doesn't every generation change the world?

Yeah, but it's our turn. We are the millennials, and I am *so proud* of millennials! I do wish we had a better, newer name for our generation though. Millennials sort of makes us sound like video game-loving, bubblegum-popping, *Spice Girl* shoe-wearing brats who are still rocking those NYE glasses from 2000. But for now, fuck it. Millennial it is. Millennials we are.

What is a millennial? Theoretically, it's a word used to describe the group of people on Earth, born roughly between 1981-2001. It's not written in stone. It's not something slapped on your birth certificate. It's not something that gets put under your name on your driver's license. It's not a tattoo you get at birth so the rest of the world can recognize you and know to stay away from you and your gang.

There is no mark to indicate millennial, but nonetheless we know who we are.

We grew up on *Fresh Prince of Bel Air*, Backstreet Boys, Tamagotchis, butterfly clips, Sony Discmans, Nokia 3310 (and snake), Pogs, MSN messenger, Koosh Balls, the theme song to 'The Nanny', Home Alone, The Macarena, (and how we butchered that spanish chorus, *Dale a tu cuerpo alegria macarena*) Hanson? Omg Taylor—Drool. We collected Pogs and traded Pokemon at our local markets. There was the graphics calculator that we used to write 8008 on, which meant BOOB. And choker necklaces, hoop earrings, *Saved By the Bell*, MC Hammer, Neopets, Sims. Remember those little string fringes we let hang around our face while the rest of our hair was gelled back? So sultry. Or the way boys spiked their hair like Scott from 5ive? Hot.

Oh, and most importantly, we grew up with digital technology, although some of us were born into analog (WILD!). We were the first group of kids ever to be able to use the internet! Dial up. So slow, so painful, but those 37 minutes of scratchy sound were so worth it to be able to finally get on MSN or AOL chat and ask 'A/S/L?' (Hit me up petabum_888).

Older generations often refer to us as: *selfish* or *the ones always on those bloody devices* or *spoilt and entitled* or *silver platter kids* or *selfie lovers* or, as I most recently read *generation snowflake*. Millennials are the most studied, analyzed, talked about generation yet. This has been suggested by the US Chamber Foundation and Forbes, but you only need 10 minutes on Google to discover anything—from where millennials prefer to live, to how many sleep with their phones beside their bed. People are desperate to understand millennials cos we're just so… *different*. It's as if we're an alien species who accidentally came falling out of starships in the 1980s. "Oops! Better keep 'em!"

Simon Sinek, author, speaker and marketing consultant (and someone I hugely admire and respect), recently shared his explanation of millennials. I love how Simon takes highly intelligent ideas and breaks them down by using straightforward language for the masses to understand. Millennial was his latest highly intelligent idea.

Here are his key points:

○ tough to manage

○ result of failed parenting strategies

○ don't know how to form deep and meaningful relationships

○ told they were special and could have anything they wanted in life

○ can't handle rejection.

○ growing up with lower self esteem

○ super impatient and rely on instant gratification, thanks to the digital age in which they grew up.

The world leapt at it, gobbled it up, shared it around the interwebs like crazy, millions of times over, and people commented the likes of 'makes so much sense'. People were just so damn happy to finally have some reasoning to explain how on Earth an entire generation could possibly be different from the one before us. I struggle to read the comments on videos like that, as well intentioned as they are. Just like I struggle to watch Steve Jobs documentaries. I feel fiercely protective of Steve Jobs and I feel fiercely protective of millennials—for similar reasons.

Steve Jobs came to Earth genetically equipped to be different than most people, because he was assigned to do a specific job. He did that job, and now the world rejoices in his brilliance and the wild conveniences he allows us all through the never ending gifts of Apple. When he died, people tried desperately to understand him. Why wasn't he nicer to his wife and kids? Why was he such an outcast? Was he autistic? Why couldn't he just be the complete package? Apparently he was a dickhead to his staff.

People sometimes are unable to see people for the unique genetic gifts they're given, for their contributions to this Earth. That's why I get so pissed off when people spend so long focusing on all of the 'shit parts' of his vision, turning a somewhat blind eye to the fact that *he did his job*. He did his best. He fulfilled his mission. If he tried to please the entire population on Earth and have everyone understand him, like him, praise him, then you wouldn't have that slim device in your hand that enables you to take your vital signs at the same time as calling your Mum, paying your bills, counting your calories, and seeing what your friends 4,000 miles away are doing. He came to Earth with a purpose and with the exact genetic gifts he required to fulfil it for us and to leave us with a long lasting contribution.

He didn't need to be understood, in order to take his turn and gift this world his brilliance. He just did it. When I feel into the heart of the millennial generation, I feel that that's what we're trying to do, too.

What I want to do, is remind the world that they can trust us. And rather than scrutinize this generation, I want to shine a light on the things we do well, how much we care, and how we're doing our very best with the tools we have. We're often misunderstood, regularly criticized, sometimes praised, definitely analyzed, but we are here for a very specific reason, carrying with us very specific genetic gifts, in order to take our turn to change the world.

I watch videos, I read articles of people all over the world trying to explain this generation, and I have not yet heard or read one that truly hits the nail on the head.

"It's their parents fault."

"It's their phones."

"It's just their attitude."

Perhaps, all of the above. I mean, we do love the occasional Insta scroll, while sitting on the toilet, and we do roll our eyes at a lot of things… like too much carbon dioxide in the air, camouflage pants that zip off at the knee, and water bottles that still have BPA in them. But seriously? I want to save everyone the time and energy spent on trying to figure this crazy ass generation out. Could it be that a generation of people could actually, simply *evolve*?

Do you want to know why millennials have brought standards, methods, and attitudes that are so new and foreign that the world has little panic attacks over it? Let me give you a one word explanation, and the only one you need.

Evolution

Evolution is the reason our generation doesn't do a thing the same way as our parents. When it came time for God, or Source or the stalks or whatever you believe, to create millennials, he scrolled Instagram and pulled out the Maya Angelou quote "Do the best you can until you know better. Then when you know better, do better." Which is a nice, eloquent way of saying that the world required some *new* people, with *new* equipment, with *new* standards. So he created them.

I was watching *Shark Tank* the other day, and one of the pitches shared that they "have a social cause attached." (I think it was to save the elephants.) Lori Greiner asked, "but what's different about your product? Every company has a social cause attached to it now." And it's true. Because that's what evolution demands of us. We were born different, because the world requires different. It doesn't mean that the world before us was broken. It means that in order for the world to evolve in the direction of increased consciousness that the people being born on Earth needed to be born fitted with the appropriate equipment.

And we were.

> ○ There is still poverty on Earth, so we were gifted a new genetic wiring that allows us to have the highest collective sense of genuine empathy that the world has known for centuries. We're equipped with a 'but of course' approach to building social causes into our companies as if they're meant to be there. We're equipped with an inherent mission and a collective goal to see every person on Earth be able to access their basic needs by the time we exit this Earth.

○ There are still remnants of inequality—racism, sexism, religion-ism—so we were gifted with a new set of DNA that allows us to be the most civically minded generation since the early '30s and '40s, caring more about society as a whole than us as individuals.

○ There are now more people on Earth than ever, and the environment is at its most vulnerable in history, so we are gifted with an inherent intolerance for environmental abuse and a non-negotiable commitment to raising the standard for all policies, companies, and practices that impact our planet.

○ Workaholism has been glorified to the point that it is a deadly disease, so we were gifted new ideas that allow us to evolve the traditional working day, environment and pressures and yes—have bean bag office chairs and work from home policies.

○ The world is still divided. So we were gifted with a greater sense of unity, oneness and an increased sense of global mindedness. There are still broken systems, corruption, and shit that just doesn't serve the world anymore, so here we are, gifted with our greatest gift ever as a generation— our divine intolerance.

No. Not anymore.

Divine Intolerance

Divine intolerance is my way of explaining this 'attitude' we have. Yes, we do have an attitude, and it's real, so damn real. It was gifted to us at birth along with our Tamagotchis, hoop earrings, and the big lungs that we use to blow the dust off our Sega Mega drive games before we'd plug them in and play. But even though it looks like attitude, smells like attitude, and sounds like attitude, it's so much more than attitude. It's *Divine Intolerance*.

Divine intolerance is a genetically wired piece of equipment that was placed in us by God himself with instructions that read, "Do not tolerate anything that doesn't support the life and the world you're here to create. Got it? Ok, go".

Divine intolerance applies to anything that doesn't align with how we know the world can be. We didn't come to this planet to cruise along and leave this place exactly as we found it. We came with a vision for better. Our vision is a thriving planet, taken care of by all who are lucky enough to call it home. Our vision is a world where all people have their basic needs met, and no more tippy-toe excuses for why some people are starving and some are spending $60k on a teaspoon of caviar. Our vision is a world where people really freaking thrive. Not the workaholism that has families torn apart and people collapsing due to heart disease.

And this vision is why we won't buy from companies who don't do business ethically and sustainably. This is why we can't stay in jobs where we're expected to wear pin striped skirts, baggy suits, and stare at a computer for 10 hours in exchange for two weeks of vacation—total. This is why we collaborate so abundantly in ways that used to be pretty much illegal in the old competitive world of *you gotta beat their ass!*

We are different, because we *need* to be different. Our world can't change, unless we change. If the world kept going the way it's always gone, and humans were being put on Earth with the exact same genetic equipment as before, then how would we ever evolve? Thrive? Grow? Heal?

We millennials are so deeply respectful for every generation that has come before us, how they have led us, raised us, given to us, taught us, and for the world they created for us. I tell my Mum regularly how much I admire so many things about her and her generation—their courtesy (how they *always* call to RSVP), how they won't leave anything unanswered (even if it's a facebook comment by a random person in Japan), how rich in tradition they are, how important belly-to-belly community is, how their word means *everything,* and how hand-written cards will always trump a text message.

Everything was perfect then, and everything is perfect now.

So to the world, hello. We are millennials. Please trust us.

We are progressive.

We are conscious.

We are compassionate.

We are creative.

We are bold.

We are courageous.

We are nomadic.

We are diverse.

We are accepting.

We are collaborative.

We are adventurous and yes…..

We are impatient.

We are impatient, because we were fitted with a set of genetic equipment that has us super clear on how we know the world can be. We question everything and argue anything that makes us want to vomit up our Kombucha and superfood version of Coco Pops. We attach a social cause to all of our companies because purpose is a million times more important to us than profit. We do want bean bags and more fun working hours because we know that workhaholism and unflattering suits just aren't the way anymore.

We might be on our phones all the time, but chances are we're creating a gofundme page, setting up a new company, posting something dope on insty, or doing something that's trying to make the world better. We laugh a lot and spend more time creating and playing than generations before us did, but not because we're lazy, but because we know we *all* need to lighten up.

Work needs to be done here. Things need to be upgraded. It's how evolution works.

We don't need to be understood, we need to be trusted. We are simply using our upgraded genetic equipment to expand and excite this beautiful world and make it a planet worthy of housing the next brilliant generation. We are divinely intolerant—of anything that doesn't work for our collective anymore.

To the world, my message is *Trust us.*

To millennials, my message is *Earth is hiring you.*

To the next generation, my message is, *We know your genetic equipment is going to blow our freaking minds, so we're doing our bit to prime this beautiful planet in time for you and your brilliance to take your turn.*

Why This Book

For the last half of a decade, I have had the privilege of working with some of the most conscious, influential, heart-centered millennials on Earth. I have a deep, deep love, respect, admiration and understanding for what lies in the heart of this generation. In the beginning, this book was going to be solely for millennials, because, well, I get them. Seriously, I feel like a protective mumma bear when it comes to our generation. Yet, as much as I wanted to write a guidebook solely for my beloved generation, resistance kicked my butt—again and again and again.

Every time I'd get to around chapter 10, I'd go travelling or get caught up in my work and events, which meant that I had to put the book off 'til I got back,' which meant 'til whenever I got inspired again.' I'd start the book, stop the book, start the book, stop the book. It was like I was getting whiffs of inspiration and big fat clock-blocks—one and then other. After three failed attempts at completing a manuscript, or coming up with any sort of structure that resembled a book, I became pregnant with our first child. That changed everything, because there it was—all of the clarity and inspiration I ever could've wanted, delivered to me in the form of a baby growing in my womb. I was being clock-blocked all those times trying to write this book, because this book wasn't meant to *just* be for millennials.

As I write this, I am a millennial who is carrying the next generation in her womb (by the time you read this, she will be here!), and I realize that soon it will be my child's turn to light up the world like we're doing now. I don't think I've ever felt more inspired to contribute to our planet as I do now. I want my kids to know how we felt when we were contributing to their world, and that we cared. I want them to know that when it's their turn to lead this beautiful collective that we'll be cheering them on all the way, honouring their new equipment and how they've evolved from where we are now. I want this book to unite us as a team and help lighten the load that so many of us feel when we think of our role to 'change' or 'save the world'. I want this book to be a gift to the world of all that I've learned from being yet another human with the privilege of walking this Earth at this brilliantly, badass time.

And so it is.

This book is a **conversation** about The New Way to Live, Lead, Earn, and Give. It is a **collection** of insights and ideas about how we can, and how we are, changing the world. It's an **invitation** to the New Superheroes—the people all over the world who give a shit about each other and our Earth—to lighten up in our work as Game Changers. It's a **time stamp** so that our kids and their kids can read it and say, "Oh, so that's what you were growing through back then..."

Finding My Way

I'm 28 years old as I write this, born in 1988.

I was born and raised in Fremantle, Western Australia by a single mum who is my *hero*. I was one of four kids, and I kicked butt at school. I was an overachiever when it came to academics and a sports and fitness fanatic. By-the-way, "sport" is the way a single mum successfully raises four kids. Mum always said that routine was her saving grace and the reason our home and life had order. So going to sport every night and every weekend, always being part of a community, and having a clear schedule for all of us for the week ahead, *that* was her secret sauce.

Work ethic was never a problem for me. I saw it in my mum and it was embedded in my cells. Since the age of 13, I worked over 20 jobs throughout high school, some of which earned me $5.15. I worked at the bakery, slicing cold meat at the deli, leading horses around fairs, doing the paper drop in my neighborhood, the check-out chick jobs, a 'sandwich artist' at Subway... I had a goal. I was going to become a doctor by the time I was 25 years old. I loved the human body, and I loved helping people. Promptly after graduating high school with a TER of 94.5, several soccer championships, and academic awards that had the nerd in me smiling from ear to ear, I began my science degree at The University of Western Australia. I had my sights set on a PhD in Exercise Physiology. Upon completing my undergraduate degree, I was awarded a spot in the honours program in exercise physiology. My thesis on 'The Effects of Dehydration During Exercise on Subsequent Appetite' was published with first class honours and I was given a PhD scholarship. I was 22. There I was crushing goals and breezing along my chosen path. Less than three years and I could write "Dr." in front of my name. *Dr. Peta Kelly* by the time I was 25. That was my goal, and I was crushing it.

It wasn't until I was a semester into my PhD studies that I started to notice what I'd been pretending not to notice. I was struggling to get out of bed each day. *Ugghhhh* was all I could think when it was time to go to the lab. I found myself counting down the days and hours to… *to what?* That's when it hit me. I was 22, blasting forward toward my goal, and going through the motions. I hadn't stopped to consciously check in on what my soul wanted me to be doing. Then again, at that point in my life, I was quite unfamiliar with the term "soul." Regardless, I was faced with an ugly truth. I wasn't happy. In fact, the only reason I was continuing my PhD program was because of the *shoulds* it carried. You *should* finish it, because you're so lucky to be where you are, Peta. You *should* finish it, because everything takes hard work and not everything is meant to feel good. You *should* finish it, because you set it as a goal and you must complete every goal. You *should* finish it, because "Dr. Kelly" is the pinnacle of success. There were so many *shoulds* that *should* was taking up the majority of noise in my head. I couldn't hear anything else. It felt like there was a boombox in my head blasting only one channel—*what Peta should do.*

One morning, I was lying in bed, having that few minutes of con-templation before getting up. Rather than do my usual scan over all the things I *had* to do that day, and give myself the 'get up and move' pep talk, my tummy dropped and it went quiet. The *shoulds* got so loud that it felt like I must have blew the speakers blasting inside my head. Everything went silent. I had clarity. I could hear.

"You're done, Peta. Leave your PhD. Honours was enough. There's more for you. Happiness is the way, not the result."

It was like my soul finally got the chance to speak and spat out what she wanted to say in the 20 seconds of quiet she had to reach me. In those brief 20 seconds I gained courage. That same day, I walked into my supervisor's office and told her that I was going to defer my PhD. I was a mess, crying myself through a mix of relief and mega anxiety. *What had I just done? What was I going to do?* My family had no business background. Sure, my mum was a hard working high school teacher who gifted us with amazing work ethic, and I knew my dad to be pretty smart with money, but I didn't know anything other than science and school and sport.

I had no idea what I was gonna do, but I knew that I just wanted to feel happy and free. Freedom was what I craved the most. I didn't want to feel how I felt rolling up to my PhD or rolling up to train a PT client—that *just gotta get it done, can't wait til it's over* feeling. I knew that life wasn't meant to be made up of days where we count down the hours until they're over. There was just something about this *slog it out all day for (you name it) amount of money* that didn't feel good to me. I knew how to work hard, but my cells were singing a different song, asking me for something different. I wanted to work hard for something that would reward me more than just a few days off and a limited pay check. And what about my dreams? How did people live these big dreams they posted about on Instagram with the hashtag #ifonly? Did people honestly just wait to win lotto?

One of my dreams, was to soon retire my mum from her 40 year career as a school teacher so that she could relax for the first time since we were born. She worked her ass off every single day, not just as our mum, but as a full time English teacher, the woman who handled the bullies and tough kids at school, the soccer coach, and the chairman of our athletics club. She gave and served and gave, and she never complained about it, but it was exhausting her. When I was young, I used to say to my brother and sisters, "You need to help with the dishes, Mum is so stressed can't you see?" She sold her cars so we could go on our soccer trips. She slept on the couch for a few years too, because we didn't have enough bedrooms in the house. I slept in the garage we converted into a makeshift bedroom. We were surrounded by love and grew up feeling like the luckiest kids on Earth, never going without a thing, but my mum deserved a break. And I took responsibility for giving it to her.

I had planned to do this by becoming a Dr. Peta Kelly, because my relatively big income post PhD would allow me to pass some onto mum. But the Universe had a different plan for me and for my mum, and looking back what I realize is that the Universe was definitely paying attention to my dream and guiding me right to it. Although, as is typical of humans, I took my sweet-ass time to notice.

Sans PhD route, I started thinking. Maybe I could start a metabolism business? I'd start a traditional small business and just expand it, working for myself and nobody else. I had personal training clients too, so I could always expand that for the time being. Or I could get a job as an exercise physiologist for money until I got my shit sorted and set up a business that allowed me to be in control. I wasn't super clear, but I also wasn't worried. So I did what any wise 22-year-old does in between jobs. I moved my stuff out of my share house with my friends and moved back into my mum's place. Good ol' mums place, always there when I needed a little comfort pause throughout early adulthood (and a pantry full of the snacks I'd only eat 'if mum bought them'). Then I went travelling with my friend Jo around Southeast Asia, and it was Jo who introduced me to the solution and the next step that the Universe had in store for me, and it was not what I ever would have expected.

Network Marketing.

Hang on… Don't think you are about to read a book about network marketing, but it's an important part of my story, so listen in.

Network Marketing? What is that? I'd never heard of it before. Is that the Tupperware thing? A pyramid scheme? The words 'network marketing' didn't resonate with me at all. I was a scientist, a free spirit. I wanted freedom, and I absolutely wanted integrity. I didn't want to sell things to my friends. Is that what I'd have to do? Or is network marketing a techy thing? Until Jo explained it to me, I had no idea.

This was a business model attached to a product. If you love the product, you share it with people. The product was a wellness system called Isagenix which means 'balance' in ancient language. This business model and 'word of mouth marketing' just sounded too airy-fairy for me. I was a scientist, and I didn't see any evidence of this actually working, at least not for young people in Australia. I bought the product happily but I ignored this 'network marketing' thing.

When we got home, I came to personally love the product. I felt *really* good, so naturally I began sharing the product with my clients, family and friends. Boom! Without even realizing it, I was actually doing this 'network marketing' thing pretty well. How had this business model just woven its way into my life without me even wanting it to? I paid attention. I learned about this business model, and I realized how well it fit into what I wanted for my life. Bigger Boom! I wanted to help people, I wanted my hard work to go further than just a pay cheque and a few days off, I wanted an income that allowed me to travel the world, give bountifully to charities I cared about, afford organic food and a new pair of runners when I wore the tread off my old ones, and…. I *really* wanted to retire my Mum. I learned this business model and I went to work to build it, my way. The good thing about there being no young people in Australia doing this network marketing thing was that I had to create what it actually meant for my generation. And what it meant for me, was so much bigger than just a product or a business model.

I had discovered a way that my generation could live life on our own terms. I saw it, and I made it my mission to cast this vision for as many young people as I could. People didn't know that there was any other way, other than their 9-5 or the path their parents had laid out for them. I'd give presentations to hundreds of people weekly to cast this vision and one of my favourite slides had the words *What does your ideal day look like?* I'd get everyone to close their eyes and really think about it. Some people opened their eyes teary. Some opened their eyes looking at me as if to say, *Are you off your head? This is real life, we don't get to just live our ideal days.* This idea of living your ideal day every day was new to my generation, but it was what we wanted, what we craved. We wanted freedom from the restraints that limited our parents. We weren't here to travel the same path as our parents did. We were here to do things a new way, *The New Way*.

I began to travel the world and started working from a laptop. I was ignoring the common and normal ways of living and earning. It was a huge leap, but then (as always) a net appeared. I had the realization that my generation was battling advice that wasn't working for them—for us—at all. We were called to live in a "new way." It was something that so many people my age were feeling, but something that so many of us were struggling to make real. This new way extended far beyond working independently from an office, choosing your own hours, following your bliss (and not following what looks good on the resume). The New Way was a paradigm shift. It was created by my generation—the millennials—and as exciting as this new way was for us, it came with a lot of pain, push back, and judgement from the generations that preceded us. They called us "selfish," "lazy," "ignorant," and "entitled," just because we didn't want do things the way they did. Because we didn't believe in sitting at a desk for ten hours a day just to earn enough money to live a little on the weekends. Because we didn't believe in following the traditional route of success to establish a career. Because we didn't want to answer to an unappreciative boss who didn't value our contributions. I began to realize that the kids of my class were simply wired so differently from our parents. We had different equipment. In some cases, we were physically unable to tolerate the patterns of life that came before us—and that's just the way of evolution.

I was watching animal planet the other night and I saw a mongoose eat a cobra. *Whattt??* The coolest part was that the mongoose wasn't even scared of the cobra. The voice over told us that mongoose has evolved to be resistant to the venom of cobras, which can actually kill a human. They have developed this over time so they can attack and eat cobras to survive. I also read the other day about a new type of house mouse that all of a sudden has immunity to warfarin, which is the poison used to fight infestations. Animals change as their circumstances change so they can be better adapted to their new environment. And so do we. We were born on a planet that requires an urgent upgrade of respect and care, and so our generation was born with a collective and innate responsibility to ensure we take care of it. It's no mistake that sustainable practices are normal and required when it comes to the companies millennials build. I've come to learn that the "attitude" that many say we have is a divine intolerance of a way that doesn't work anymore, and it extends far beyond time and financial freedom.

By the time I was 25, I was earning a million dollars a year. Me, a girl raised in one of the most isolated cities in the whole word, who grew up sleeping in the garage of our cozy but way too small family home. Perth, Western Australia is in the southwestern part of the country. The population is about 2 million, and the closest city is Adelaide (2200 km away). There are over 12,500km of coastline along Western Australia. It's a BIG place. It's easier for us to fly to Bali from Perth then to any other Aussie city. Me, a kid raised by a single mum raising three other kids, a used to wanna-be-a-doctor with zero business experience. Yeah, *me*. I was making my own money running my own business. I was in my early twenties, and my sole purpose had become teaching young people how to get out of the rat race and begin to live their highest visions for themselves. It was time and freedom of location, but it was also so much more than that. I was showing them how to live in The New Way, and I was learning along the way.

In 2014, we celebrated Christmas in New York City as a family. It was one of mum's life-long dreams. We'd never been able to go on family holidays growing up, so it was a real moment of 'wow,' and then in April 2015 my brother (also building a network marketing business) and I retired my mum. We did it together.

One of my biggest goals in the world had been ticked, so *how does it get any better than that?*

Over the next few years, I achieved a lot. I was speaking on big stages, leading a big beautiful team from all over the world, being featured in magazines, and travelling the world non-stop. I was young and making millions, but all of a sudden my schedule was all monstrous 16-hour days. I was moving at such a pace that my brakes were nowhere to be seen, zooming down a hill in the world's fastest car and with broken brakes. I didn't stop much to look up, take a pause, and tune in to where I was in my life and how I was feeling. I believed I was here to help more people, speak on more stages, do more good work, give to more charities, kick more goals. I was young and making millions, but similar to my PhD years, I was carrying around the old models of success, which screamed *more more more,* trapped by the collective pursuit for *more more more!* I was burning out giving money to charity, creating content, training and mentoring millennials across the globe, but each night when my head hit the pillow I was empty. Sure, I wasn't sitting at a desk for ten hours working for a boss who pissed me off, but I still wasn't modelling a kind of success that felt good. I was flying when I didn't feel like flying, and I was saying *yes* when I really meant *no.* Social media had me feeling the fear of "never doing enough," and "hustle" became my most frequently used word, because "hustling" was the only way to go about getting what you want. My life was long days and late nights. I was doing it *all,* but my dissatisfaction kept me acutely aware that there was more to this paradigm shift.

Eventually, I moved to the United States to be with my now husband where I was thrust into the collective pace of the American lifestyle, which further showed me what The New Way was *not.* I had just spent the last few years defending the burgeoning ideals of millennials, and I continued to wake up every single day to be a voice for them. Now I realized that I had to be the voice for this new way, because it is so much deeper than we had ever defined. I had been completely missing the point. It was time to evolve from network marketing and into a new phase of my life. My message had evolved. The New Way wasn't just about working from our laptops all over the world and 'being our own bosses'. No, that was freedom 1.0. and that song had been sung. It was time for a new song, a new evolved mission, and a new awareness.

Now, I create communities, mentoring programs (like The Supercharged) and events which are part of Jeaniius—a global hub of nakedly brilliant people mobilized in The New Way to create epic shit. I create events like The New Way Live which celebrate all things the new way, unite a generation, and take the heavy and serious charge off this changing the world stuff. I am in love with building and creating and supporting conscious enterprises, not for profits and studying the spirit of these entities.

Is 'hustle and grind' really the message of The New Way? Is financial freedom really what it's about? Is 'living life on our terms' really the summit of this mission? Is The New Way about becoming more successful than our generations before us?

No, no, no, and no.

We've evolved. The New Way is not just about having more money at the end of the month. Success as we'd been taught isn't sufficient. Success to our generation looks and feels completely different to what it looked and felt like to generations before us. The religious separation that our parents' generation know is torturing our hearts. Our planet isn't a place for us to holiday, but a place of permanent residence with the requirement that we nurture and love our Mother Earth as our one collective mother. There is no 'top' when it comes to leadership, but instead we're all about the power of tribe. We don't care to move forward at lightning speed, but would rather stop and go back to our indigenous roots and ensure that ancient wisdoms are never forgotten. Taking care of our brothers and sisters who are without basic necessities is the only way we all win. Play is everything.

We're here to change the world, but we've gotta stop taking it so seriously. We're here to use our talents and abilities to create epic shit, but we've gotta stop missing the point along the way. It's time for us to thrive like no previous generation. It's time for us to show the world how good it's really meant to be. Because we've evolved into living what The New Way really is. Hence, this book.

It wasn't until I was growing one of the next generation of conscious custodians in my own womb that I realized what my real intention was for defining The New Way to Live, to Lead, to Earn and to Give. I wanted to create a timestamp, a way to document this time on Earth so that it can be enjoyed as both a nostalgic gift and as a reference to how this generation navigated our time here.

I hope that my daughter in my womb, and all the beautiful humans yet to come, are proud of me, and of us, for doing our best for each other and for the world they're inheriting from us.

Now read this, then we'll begin.

Earth is Hiring

At age 22 I rolled up to work at 5:15 a.m., and my boss berated me at for having a slightly off centre top knot. "God, could you at least have done your hair today?" while looking me up and down in disgust. It was then that I decided I didn't want to have a 'boss' ever again. At least not a boss who walked, talked, and wore shoes. So when I started creating my own businesses in my early twenties, we'd always say, "I am my own boss." and "I work for myself." Think of it as language that comes in the entrepreneur's starter pack.

But the truth is, we do have a boss.

And her name is Earth.

Now imagine that no matter what you're building or creating, no matter who you are working for, you've just stumbled upon the greatest job posting of all time. *And the recruitment agency that found you?* God, Universe, Divine, Infinite Spirit, Lord, Divinity, Creator or in my words—Source. *The job?* Be The New Superhero. *Your boss?* Mother Earth.

The New Superhero

No, you're not going to receive a cape in the mail with "Captain Planet," written in glitter on the back, but you can wear a cape or distressed jeans or yoga pants or whatever you want. No, there is no preferred race, body shape, IQ, religion or sexual orientation—just you as you are, please! And no one is going to require you to go about knocking on doors declaring that you're here to "Save the Earth," but you kinda are….

Job Responsibilities of The New Superhero

> *The New Superhero will help others stop taking this 'change the world thing' so seriously, by encouraging other people to lighten up, to care and not worry, and to stop moving so fast that you miss the point. This position will be responsible for revealing his or her own humanity and encouraging others to do so; for giving a really big shit about the Earth and about other people; for rewriting the world's money story (ideally by rewriting his or her own); for creating conscious enterprises that surprise and delight us all; and for putting pleasure higher up on the to-do list than 'should.' As an ambassador for Earth, The New Superhero will always find play in the profound and fun in the important and remember that one of the greatest powers is being human, the messy, OMG, I fucked up, but I reeeeeally give a shit about the world humanity.*

You've got this book in your hand. You care. You give a shit. You're human, ready to play, get a little messy, and of course—make some change. Chances are you're a millennial, so you already have all the qualifications and credentials to be The New Superhero. You were born with them, and what you hold in your hand is actually your training manual.

Congratulations, you're hired!

The New Way to Live, Lead, Earn and Give.

This book is not a bible-like set of instructions or a bold claim of 'this is *the* way and it has to be *your* way.' God, no. Talk about an attitude that will stray us from unity. It is a guideline for how our generation—and all those who give shit—can Live, Lead, Earn and Give differently than what we have been. I call it The New Way. But much of it is ancient ways, made fresh and relevant.

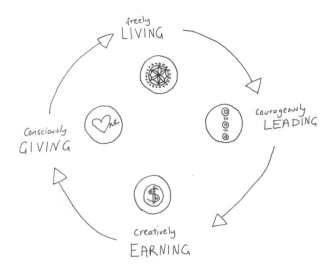

Pause here.
We reserve the right to change our minds.

My greatest challenge in writing this book was to not put in everything I know *and* everything I'm learning on the pages. Perhaps there will be more, second or third editions, but in writing *Earth is Hiring,* I became acutely aware that our views change, our thoughts evolve, and that as a writer my integrity is not limited to having the same beliefs forever, but my integrity expands to letting go of what might be my truth in the future so that I can gift the world with what my truth is now.

So I reserve the right to change my mind, as do you, *always*.

How to Use This Book

That's just one tip for getting the most out this book, and here are some others:

○ Take what feels good and leave the rest. This isn't gospel.

○ Read it in order: Living, Leading, Earning and Giving. It will make more sense; however, if you're particularly hungry for business and money, skip straight to it. I won't stop you.

○ It gets better as you go. It crescendos and then does a full circle.

○ Earning has a particular section for entrepreneurs. If this doesn't apply to you, skip straight through that bit to page 229 where we can rejoin and talk about money.

○ The book goes full circle, meaning how it begins links up with how it ends. Be sure to finish it, unless you can't stand it. Then don't finish it.

○ My intention for this book was a more playful format, with little surprises and goodies thrown in. My intention is to have it feel like a playground for you—fun and light with some 'oh wow' and 'haha' thrown in. So if at any point you're like, "WTF, why is there a stick figure drawing of a consciousness police car here?" Just roll with it. Surprise is good for the soul.

○ You'll find some letters to my daughter Sol (In my womb at the time of writing. Out of the womb by the time you read!) in these pages. I just had to. It helps us to remember that there are beautiful little people watching us, thanking us and depending on us..

○ With The New Way comes new words and phrases. If you see one that has you lost, just page your way to the back of the book where you will find a Glossary. I know, so OG, right? Words that are included in the Glossary will be in **bold** throughout the book.

○ I hand drew all of the chapter drawings, you'll be able to tell. I kept them raw and in my hand writing because *raw* is very The New Way.

Connect with others reading this book (and me!) by using the hashie #earthishiring on IG, FB and twitter. Also check out earthishiring. com so you can join me online or in person.

Tag! You're it!

Give what feels good. I believe expanding our consciousness is a game of "Tag, you're it!!" We're all just lighting each other up along the way. So I encourage everyone to gift one of these books to yourself and one, or two, to your friends who you feel are fellow Game Changers. I've included a section at the front of the book where you can write their name and what you love about them. Once they receive it, "Tag, they're it!"

On Instagram someone asked,

"In three words, what will change the world?" People commented...

Stop being stupid	Love, Faith, Empowerment
Love kindness acceptance	Love consideration empathy
No ego preference	A new generation
Becoming yourself authentically	A reset button
Ban all religion	Stop killing animals
Stop climate change	Impeach Donald Trump
The second coming	Smoke weed everyday
Divine feminine awakening	Put God first
Love thy neighbour	Kindness without expectation
My new granddaughter	Equality, peace, love
Understanding each other	Respect for all

What are your 3 words? Write them down

_____   _____   _____

LIVING

Choosing your alignment and raising your vibration are your greatest gifts to this planet—Period .

"You don't have to worry about not being of value to the world when you're in tune with Source. Because Source is always of value to the world."
—Abraham Hicks

Freely Living is the element of The New Way that is all about YOU and how YOU can raise your vibration to live in radical, glorious alignment.

Stop Missing the Point

Your vibration is your greatest gift to our planet.

Before we get cranking, if you're anything like me, you often skip past the preface and introduction of the book and hurry straight to the chapters. If you did that with this one, please turn back. My husband read them and said 'This could be the whole book! That's scary because usually I skip past the intro and preface!'. I promised him I'd make sure you didn't miss them.

Ok, so shall we dive straight in?

How ya doin?

Most people in the world aren't having a very good time. Here we are at such a beautiful, privileged, exciting (albeit at times challenging, sad, and sometimes scary) time for our planet, and the majority of the people you meet on the street are not enjoying themselves all that much. They aren't feeling good at all. In fact, when you ask someone the question *How are you?* how often do you think you would get an answer like *Brilliant, Magical, Wonderful, Happy, Fantastic...?* Not often. You get a lot of *"fines"*.

Before I go on, let's get one thing clear. I am not referring here to the people who are suffering—due to geographical, cultural, economic situations—or those who are incredibly under-privileged. I am talking about asking the people who are so freaking blessed to live beautiful, wonderful, privileged lives in free countries, the people who have the house, the job, the partner, the vacation time. These are the people I'm concerned about, these are the people who are still *not having a very good time*. And, yes, even those super-duper spiritual people who have dedicated their lives to fighting for our planet and our people are often *not having a very good time*. And the people who live their life preaching about success and motivation and winning don't feel that good if you ask them. Many of those who have achieved "the American dream" rarely answer the question with "Magical" or "Happy" or "Brilliant." There exists a collective dissatisfaction and constant yearning for more, more, more, and, to me, that feels a bit like a big slap in the face to this all-providing, all-nourishing Universe and our ridiculously nurturing, patient, and generous planet we call home. *Right?*

So why-oh-why aren't most people having a very good time?

The answer: Because most people on this planet are completely, entirely, utterly, and disgracefully missing the point. *We are missing the point*. It's that simple, and the good news is, we are in luck, because a divine and timely shift is here. "A tilt," we shall call it. We've reached the time of our human evolution where we are experiencing a shift from the very masculine world to a more feminine world. You can find teachers globally, across all fields, who are arriving at the same conclusion, as if the same message is being sent to us all. Just check out the works of Jean Houston, Deepak Chopra, and Matt Kahn, to name a few.

Nikita Mor (Personal Growth Aficionado) says it best.

The divine feminine is rising. The masculine and feminine energies are realigning and returning to a proper cyclic balance of ceaseless motion to bring about peace, harmony, and a new world order.

We are moving from the world of.... *Do this. Achieve this. Win this. Decide this. Act like this. Analyze this. Do more. Achieve more. Be more. Earn more. Have more. Compete more. More and more and more until you die!!!...* to a world of... *Slow down... Take a pause... Breathe for a minute... Look around.... Trust your gut... It's enough... Play today... Turn your phone off... Chew your food... Let life in... Say no when you mean no... Say yes when you mean yes...*

It's time to welcome the rise of the divine feminine, because it's here. It's time to tune in, take a pause, and pay attention to how you're really feeling.

The Age of Doing

As a millennial, I caught the tail end of the masculine times. For a long time I was entrenched in the mentality that life was about doing. "How grand can my resume look?" "How many goals can I kick?" "How much more can I fit into my day?" "Relax? Really? Who has time to relax? I'll sleep when I'm dead."

My age of "doing" was valid and very much supported that phase of my life, my work ethic, and my pursuit for excellence—all of which earned me a first class Honours degree and a seven-figure income by the time I was 26. No argument there. However, I got to a point in my life where I had two businesses, shared a beautiful life with my husband between the U.S. and Australia, and we enjoyed every freedom and privilege in the world, but every single day was spent racing around as if I was absolutely worthless if I was not racing around. I lived in a state of constant action—can't stop, won't stop (get it, get it). Whether it was spending my hours and energy teaching The New Way, or exercising my passion for the planet, or contributing to my many philanthropies, I was always on the pursuit for more.

So what's wrong with that? you ask. Well, nothing. Except that I was missing the point. I was eating my food with my phone in my hand. I would eat a meal without taking notice of one single taste or texture of what I ate. I barely chewed my food. I read pages of books and I couldn't have told you one single thing I read. I would say "bye" to my husband in the morning while doing something else— preparing my workspace, feeding the dogs, working out. I'd smooch him mid shoulder press, meanwhile mentally processing every one of the 22 things I wanted to get done that day. I scrolled through Instagram while I talked on the phone with my friends. I told people that "I'm too busy." so much that it got to the point that everyone in my life began their messages to me with "I know you're busy, but…" I counted down the minutes to the end of my workouts, throwing weights around just so I could burn more fat, so I could consume more calories, so I could eat more of the food that I wasn't even chewing. I would raise hundreds of thousands of dollars for a charity I love, but I couldn't stand still long enough to enjoy the feeling of giving. I was always, always on to the next thing, and there was always a next thing.

Yeah, I was achieving big things—a thriving organization, keynoting right and left, crushing my goals, and being asked to be in movies. Sure, I was, but every night as soon as my head hit the pillow (no matter how early or late), I would lie in bed and count the many, many things I did that day, making a mental record of all that I had achieved, and all that I had given. I felt empty every single night, so I had to keep going, because something was certainly missing. It wasn't until 2016 when the Universe showed me exactly what it was. I was in the gym—blowing through my workout and burning calories—when my soul gave me the nudge.

"Babes, why the fuck are you doing this workout if you don't enjoy one second of it? Isn't that whole point of creating this life and teaching these people all of this exciting stuff? Aren't you supposed to be enjoying your days?"

I didn't have an answer then, but in the months to follow in almost every single one of my journaling sessions my soul would remind me of something. "Babes (she calls me Babes, because she's rad), just put your to-do list down for a minute. Your **Vibration** is your greatest gift to yourself and to the planet and its people. How you're *feeling* matters more than what you're doing."

Toward the end of the year, when I was preparing to host The New Way Live (TNWL) in Sydney, Australia, I knew I had my theme—*Stop Missing the Point*. This was the new message I was going to deliver to 500 young, conscious entrepreneurs, those who are the ones to show the world how good it's really meant to be. *Be the one to show the world how good it's really meant to be.*

If you've ever received an email from me, you'll see that line at the bottom. It's my truth, and I believe it in every cell of my being that WE are the ones to show the world how good it's really meant to be. YOU are the one to show the world how good it's really meant to be. I am the one to show the world how good it's really meant to be. Because being born in these times means that you are of the generation made of DNA and cosmic wirings that equip us to do this exact job on Earth—present the world with a new, exciting, astronomical vision and example for how differently we can live, how we can take the lead on our own lives and stop answering to 'superiors', how many offices we can have on beaches around the world, how we can completely change the story of money and how it works in our communities, how we can redefine success and ditch the old model, the endless capacity we each have to create epic shit, how we can create conscious companies and organizations and art that surprises and delights the world, how we can stand up and fight for our Mother Earth with more fierceness than ever—and most importantly, how we can push the boundaries on human potential like never before (Think Elon Musk, 2.0).

And right there, within this message, the one I'd been sharing for years, is where I checked myself. I could absolutely show the world how good it's really meant to BE, but could I show the world how good it's really meant to FEEL? Yes. I had to. Because I was done missing the point, and there was no way I was going to let my fellow generation of rad, badass, ridiculously wild, and heart-centered game changers miss the point either. When we feel good, we raise our vibration, and when we raise our vibration, we are more like Mother Earth.

Raise Your Vibration

Many of us know that Mother Earth needs us now more than ever. Climate change is real. Our indigenous tribes and native land is being threatened. Land is being dug up for the purpose of profit. It's snowing less where it used to snow more. Species of animals are becoming extinct. Islands are sinking. Forests are disappearing. There are more people than ever right now fighting for our planet. And rightly so. She is the mother of all mothers with billions of devoted, loving, and adoring children who want to protect her. Humanity is evolving and figuring out how to unify after centuries of separation. We want to act, move, do, create, conquer, and challenge. We feel that *action* is our greatest gift to our Mother Earth, yet Momma Earth is patiently, but urgently, commanding that we do things differently for her. Our gorgeous, Momma Earth is a 5th dimensional being. If that just got too woo-woo for you, look at it this way. Earth is vibrating on an entirely different level than most of us, and in order for us to help and heal our planet, we must collectively raise our vibration to meet hers.

Changemakers, remember this. Our action is invaluable, but when action is not coupled with our alignment and our good feels, it's not half as powerful as it can be.

Action + Alignment is the secret sauce.

Whenever any action is out of alignment, then we are missing the point and living at a lower vibration. In your pursuit for harmony out there, don't forget your pursuit for harmony in here (taps chest). As much as we are in pursuit for harmony with our planet, we cannot lose the pursuit of harmony with each other. Judgement, animosity, blame, and jealousy and are all lower vibrations that separate us from our Mother. When we judge people because they don't eat like us, we drop. When we overwork ourselves to the bone and it doesn't feel good, we drop. When we go an entire day without actually noticing the sky or the grass or our own breath, we drop. During our fights, our pursuits, and our endless charges for change, we are dropping our vibration. History shows us how that makes sense. Here we are holding on to so much masculine residue that still feels good to many parts of us. It's still in our blood. But, as we move into the divine feminine, what the planet really asks of us right now is to *raise our vibration*. Our opportunity to thrive and align is purely energetic.

All of the solutions we're looking for to make the world better are 'up there.' The harmony we want between humans and the Earth is 'up there.' The humility to truly all be on the same team, that crazy sick conscious enterprise idea, those divine orchestrations that literally flip our world in an instant… they're all 'up there.' So much of what we're looking for, wishing for and wanting for ourselves and for the planet is just on a different energetic altitude to us right now.

Let's move up.

> *"You want to be a solution to this planet? Then don't let anything you see in the world rob you of your smile."*
> —Matt Kahn.

When we remind ourselves that our greatest gift to our planet is our vibration, it makes it a lot easier to smile as if it's our job. That doesn't mean that you spiritually bypass the fact that you feel hurt, sad, or totally raging when those emotions come, but for most of the day when those emotions are not there, where's your vibe at? Are you getting the point, or are you missing it?

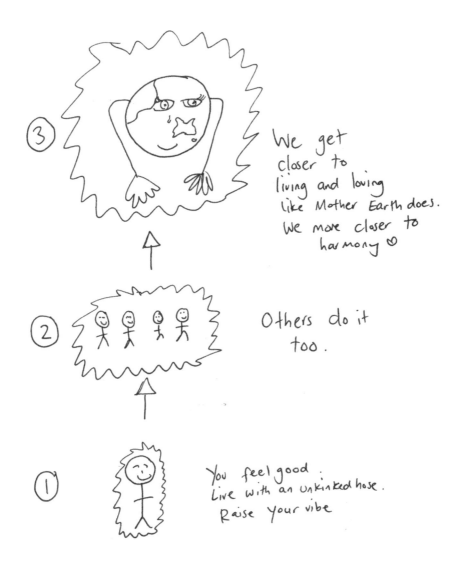

③ We get
closer to
living and loving
like Mother Earth does.
We move closer to
harmony ♡

② Others do it
too.

① You feel good.
Live with an unkinked hose.
Raise your vibe

Feel Good, I Dare Ya

Feeling good is the way, not the result.

How you feel is more important than what you do. I repeat. How you feel is more important that what you do. I'm going to say it again. "How you feel is more important than what you do." One more time... Hey, I like the sound of my own voice. Don't you? Hear yourself. Say it out loud with me.

"How you feel is more important than what you do."

Feeling good is just as much our job as doing good. Feeling good is what raises our vibration. The moment I learned this truth—the power of feeling good—was the moment everything about my life changed. It all started with a cup of cacao. I had a cup of cacao every single day. And what on Earth was the reason for this? Drinking warm cacao drinks made me feel very good. That was it. That was the only reason. At around 10 a.m. each morning it was like a ceremony. The warmth, the ritual, the little jolt of 'you are the most creatively badass mofo on the planet so text everyone you love and tell them you love them' that comes with the first two sips. It was a little daymaker for me—every day. I had always been so disciplined, and sometimes it was at the expense of feeling good or it was in pursuit of feeling good, later. But not anymore. Feeling good was my new favourite priority, and it caught on like a wildfire, which was sparked by a warm cuppa' cacao.

For years upon years society has looked at feeling good as the end result, the end and not the means. Lose weight, and you'll feel better. Meet Mr. or Mrs. Right, and you'll be happy. Make this amount of money, and you will feel worthwhile. Sign up for this program, and you will achieve something. Do this, that, the other thing, all the things, everything and only then will you feel good. These are the rules about happiness that we have been following for centuries, rules that have been supported by people who have completed all of the actions in the effort to incite good feelings. If we do something, then we will feel something good. That is until that decidedly temporary good feeling subsides and we are left empty. Next thing you know it's back to the crazy pursuit and back into the rat race for the next feel-good thing we can do.

But, oh how we have gotten it so very wrong. We take an action, then we seek a feeling. We act, then we feel. First act, then feel. Act, feel. Act, feel. This cycle puts us on a wheel like a hamster, running ourselves into a tizzy in search of the next action we can take to create something good we can feel. Round and round and round—it's a sick cycle. Is there any wonder we're waking up to the fact that this work all week doing something that doesn't feel good, so you can earn two days on the weekend that do feel good is a damaging model of success that teaches us that we have to earn our basic right to feel good? We have to burn out in order to feel like we're working hard enough to earn feeling good. We have to overwork in order to feel accomplished enough, and then we can feel good? We have to quit travelling for five years straight so we can get a mortgage and buy a house, so then we can feel real good? It's no surprise that people lose their love for food when they follow a strict eating plan for six days a week so they can enjoy a cheat meal that 'feels good' on the 7th.

We are taught that feeling good is the reward and the outcome. Feeling good has become embedded in our goals, but I have some very good news. You do not have to complete an action—score the goal, get a promotion, buy the car, win the lottery—to earn it. You can feel good right now—right this very second. Now that you know this, feeling good best become your numero uno priority. Let nothing else come before it. In fact, stop and ask yourself what you can do that would make you feel good right now. Could you clear your schedule, call your friend, walk your dog, kiss your kid, stop doing those brutal workouts?

> *"Always leave enough time in your life to do something*
> *that makes you happy, satisfied, even joyous. That has*
> *more of an effect on economic well-being than any*
> *other single factor."*
>
> —Paul Hawken.

When you feel good, you've found your vibration, your alignment. You'll live in that sweet spot where you're not floating on an oblivious cloud of 'I am a fairy, real life doesn't apply to me,' but you're grounded in reality, making choices that help you thrive and feel good *ta-day*, not next March. I'm sure you've seen "Good Vibes" on a singlet worn by hipsters and yogis—even anyone who wants to get in on the trend. "Good Vibes" aren't just two hipster words that you say after nailing some barrels in Margaret River. "Good Vibes" is the result of you choosing to feel good and choosing to design your life around what makes you feel good. "Good Vibes" is high vibration.

First Feel

Before you kick back and think the hard work is over, like all you have to do is find the time to sip on your favourite warm beverage (though you can do that!), I'm here to tell you that the feeling good is not laziness or entitlement or anti-effort or anti-work. Bingeing on a Netflix series could be a lazy pleasure, *or* it could be 'feeling good' cos you require some time out from all your wild, fun, creative projects. Actually, acknowledging and celebrating when and how you feel good is a level of work that becomes necessary in order for your actions to generate the most good. Here we are asked to shift the paradigm. Out with the old ways. No more acting and then feeling. We are here to feel.

First feel the good feeling, and then take an action.

First feel, then act. Feel, then act. Feel, act. Feel, act. Everything we want, wish, or aim for—including harmony on Earth—comes zipping at us at lightning speed when we are feeling good. Feeling good becomes the point, all of the time. I didn't say feeling 'elated' or 'ecstatic' is the point, it's simply, feeling *good*. Our feeling good is like a highway. Everything that travels on it is swift and moves fast and goes in one direction.

I'm sure you've had those days that start off feeling good. You take the time to put on some oils, your favourite music, and you make yourself your fav breakfast—oatmeal with banana and cinnamon. As you get ready for your day, you're humming and bopping about to music. Music is always a daymaker for you. You look in your emails just before you leave the house and see a subject line of 'Good news!'. The traffic on your way to work is surprisingly light and you get every green light there is. You listen to a podcast on the way there and you hear the *exact* thing you felt like you needed to hear. It's not even 8:30 a.m., and you're feeling good is leading to more feeling good. At lunch time, you find a new, funky cafe with the best menu and they have a vegan caesar salad—no way! The afternoon is pure fire, you crank through your work at the café, having so much fun with it. You don't even think to check your phone, not like some other days when you can't write two sentences without an insty scroll. Sitting next to you in the cafe is a woman who leans over and asks what you're working on. You tell her, and she says "Oh wow! We were meant to sit next to each other today, I'm looking for someone like you to collaborate with!" You get home and the sun is shining, so you go for a walk with your phone off—with no guilt. Later that evening you just feel so spacious, so you watch a documentary without that usual remorse you feel when you do something that makes you feel good when you 'should' be answering emails. Everything is good.

Can you see how good feels invites good? When you're on the highway of feeling good, you are on your way to more good. Your world and the world responds to you. How does the domino effect begin? By you choosing and prioritizing the little things that make you feel good. Music in the morning, waking up a tad earlier so you can cook breakfast rather than eat on the run, leaving your phone off for a couple hours in the morning so you don't have to be distracted by others, reading, taking the time to set your goals, workout, walk barefoot in nature, have sex, do yoga. Whatever it is, when you choose things that make you feel good, your vibration is sending energetic requests and instructions to the Universe to say, "This is what I want, more of this, please." And the Universe is more than happy to cooperate, cos well, that's how it works. Good attracts good, shitty attracts shitty. We can move with momentum—in either direction.

The Universe doesn't judge you for feeling good. The Universe does not think it's a short cut. When you choose feeling good, the Universe is on your side, giving you a standing O, just like a mum at her 10-year-old's dance recital, clapping feverishly and thinking "Finally, she nailed it."

The Unkinked Hose

Your alignment is everything.

"When you're in alignment, everything rendezvous for you"

—Abraham Hicks

Picture a garden hose connected to a wall. At one end is a supply of water and at the other end is the spout where the water comes out. Turn the tap on. If you turn the tap on and leave it on, the water can flow freely and uninterrupted. That's just what water does. Pick up a bit of the hose and fold it or twist it, the water slows or stops. You've kinked the hose. Now the plants have gone thirsty. *Dammit!*

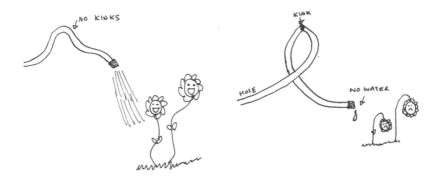

Imagine that you have a hose running through you, not a rubber garden hose, but a shiny, light-filled, magical hose that runs from the

sky right down to the roots in the Earth and up through your body. At the very top, it's not just connected to *the sky*, but it's connected to God, the Universe, Source, Spirit, the Divine—whatever feels best for you. Up there is everything—all the resources in the world, all the colour in the world, all the light, all of the ideas, insights, and solutions to your problems, all cosmic gifts, new opportunities, and exciting loves. You will find your clarity about what to do next up there. Your ideas that take you from this stage to that stage are up there. *Everything* you need is up there, and it all naturally flows down to the Earth and through your shiny hose so that you can use these resources however you choose. This is a tap of divinity with the sole purpose of nourishing your joy, your adventure, and your brilliance. You know how water flows through an unkinked hose unhindered? Well, it's the same with your hose, which we call **The Tap**.

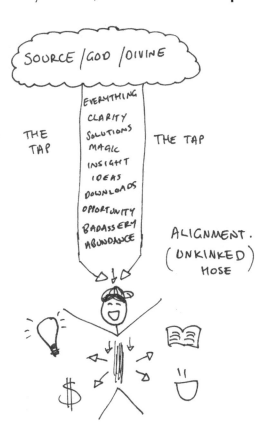

Everyone has one, and your tap's default mode is to flow through you unhindered and infinite. It is always on and the Source will never run out. To be living fully in your tap means that this divine cosmic magic is flowing through from this greater Source without obstruction. This is your life force, your natural energy. Living in your tap is what we call "your alignment." When we're here, things just happen. Opportunities surface. Ideas makes sense. People show up. Creativity comes. Worlds collide. We feel good, as if we are effortlessly floating downstream in sync with the flow of the Universe. Living in the tap is when there is no rush and there is nothing stopping us.

Living in your tap is when your ideas are so frequent there aren't enough notebooks in all the stores in your suburb that would capture them all. Living in your tap is when issues and problems that you've tried to figure out, just get cleared up magically as if it was all in your favour all along. Living in your tap is when you can write and speak about the shit that lights you up without second guessing how 'good' it sounds to a single other soul. Living in your tap is when you say yes when you mean yes, and no when you mean no and that's the end of that story. Living in your tap is when there is absolutely nothing in your schedule or life that makes you screw your face up in angst. Living in your tap feels like you have somehow found yourself attached to a big party keg and the funnel is always flowing through you—Only the keg doesn't have beer, it has boundless creativity, your next moves, energy to support your highest vibe, clarity, delight and surprise, and it shines a light through your being that makes your vibration say "HEY LIFE, GIMME ALL THE EPIC SHIT!!" And life does. And you think to yourself 'this must be too good to be true!' Life smirks and in it's best movie voice says 'the glory of the tap belongs to those only who stop kinking their freaking hose.'

Kinking the Hose

But what we little humans tend to do with our tap is exactly what anyone can do to a garden hose. We kink it. We don't mean to, it's not on purpose. Often we don't even realize we're doing it. It just happens, and soon all of this infinite energy and cosmic magic is struggling to flow through us. Overtime, if we don't find the kink, we begin to feel undernourished, losing any sense of ease or alignment. Our soul wants one thing, and we do the other thing. We begin doing, saying, being, and venturing into situations that are *not* in alignment with our soul, our highest self, or our vibration. That's a kinked hose. That's misalignment.

You'll notice how humans everywhere have been taught that misalignment is noble and selfless. We receive praise for doing something that we don't want to do. We celebrate after forcing ourselves through something that doesn't feel good. "No pain, no gain." is one of the number one motivational phrases. How about, "No guts, no glory!" Or "Strength and growth come only from continuous effort and struggle." That last one from Napoleon Hill.

There are many places we humans force ourselves into misalignment:

○ *We borrow others' ideas of how it should be.* How happy we are entitled to feel, what we 'should' do to be a good person comes from someone else. Mum, Dad, husband, wife, friends, everyone has their ideas of right, wrong, good, bad, noble, or whatever, but when we adjust our lives to fit into someone else's ideals, one kink after the other.

○ *We push forward on projects and commitments past a point that feels good.* We feel *ugh,* we feel heavy, and often we are moving at a pace that isn't our own to keep up with. Success and wins on someone else's terms is a kinked hose.

○ *We accept others' projections, expectations, and demands of us.* That feels easier than standing up for ourselves, saying "No," or "I choose this for me…" And immediately, we are energetically punished for that decision (cue, tiredness and resentment), but continue with what's easier—again and again and again. Cue, kinked hose.

○ *We feel endlessly obligated.* We say yes because, "well, I really *should*…" even though our soul is screaming at us "Can you please just have this night off to snuggle up with a cup of tea and watch that TV show 'Suits'?" Obligation often comes from people to whom we are emotionally connected, and they put pressure on us, so we put pressure on ourselves, and the pressure kinks the hose. Obligation is a word that drops my vibe and sucks energy from my hose just looking at it.

○ *We people please*. Choosing to make sure others are okay, over ourselves. Yes, we all care so genuinely for people and want to always be there in whatever way they request from us, but then we forget this big truth: *We cannot choose for other people. We can only choose for ourselves*. Choose over you, and you kink your hose.

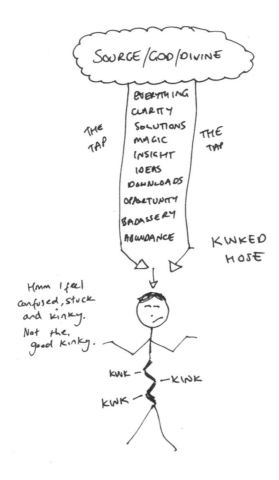

Unkinking the Hose

"So how do I unkink my hose?" I get that question almost daily, along with "Where do I begin?"

My simple answer is "You just do it." You don't need advice on *how* to unkink your kinks. After all, they're your kinks so you're the master of them. If you kinked it, you can unkink it. When you pretend you don't know what you need to do to unkink your hose, chances are it's because you want to buy time until you have the courage. And that's ok, I get it. But the longer you wait, the kinkier the kink.

The more important question to help you begin is, "*Where* are the kinks in your hose?" That's a good place to start, and here is a little exercise to help.

List all things, people, and commitments in your life that are kinking your hose. What parts of your life make your energy go down, you dread, avoid, or just make you feel less you? What do you do purely out of obligation? These are the little kinks.

This one can be fun, but do it in private. You never know if one of your kinks is sitting next to you. Write down a name next to the word *kink,* and Debbie rocks up to your desk with handcuffs. "Um, Debbie, you're a kink in my hose, I don't want to *get kinky* with you. Big difference, babes."

Here are a handful of mine:

- ○ commitments after 6pm

- ○ shopping malls

- ○ calls, emails, social media before I've had my creative, peaceful time

- ○ scrolling Facebook, Instagram mindlessly.

- ○ gossiping

- ○ working with people who are super slow, inefficient or incompetent (sounds brutal but think about it, is it?)

- ○ going to bed late (9 p.m. waddup?)

○ loaning money. (I prefer to just give)

○ overcommitting out of obligation or guilt

○ when I don't see my chiro for a few weeks

○ getting on too many planes

○ having house guests too long

Of course, there are some bigger kinks too, the one's that feel impossible and suffocating. As if this one kink could be cutting off your whole Source. When I moved to Scottsdale and missed Australia like mad, I found my big kink.

○ living in a city where there is hardly any healthy, plant-based food, clean air, a vibing cafe culture, and access to the ocean.

I felt like my soul was sad, and all I wanted to do was turn around and come home. I thrive when I can walk down the street, visit cafes full of healthy, plant-based food and high creative vibes, like in Aus. I missed the beach culture, super relaxed but very creative, like in Aus. I live for feeling a part of a community of people who share the similar values and views, like in Aus. These elements of life were not a reality for me in Scottsdale. I unkinked this kink by acknowledging my life in Scottsdale and working with my husband to create a life where we could both thrive in our work and in our marriage between the two countries and all around the world. And now we are. We have a home in Bondi Beach, Sydney that we spend time in each year and where we will give birth to our starseed, Sol. Geographical location can be *a big kink,* that takes time, but with recognition and commitment, you can unkink.

Write down your biggest kink.

I have had people run up to me at events and send me emails saying "My whole life is a kink! How do I unkink it?" I always remind them of their power—because they know their kinks better than anyone. It helps to answer two questions. What is the greatest, most pressing kink, and how can you slowly unkink it? Which kinks require the most courage to unkink? Now, take a step back. Plan out the unkinking for the bigger kinks (like moving cities, dumping your bf/gf, buying out your business partner).

First, work with the smaller kinks. Just rip the Band Aid. Unkink them right now! It will take courage, but it's all in your power. Your yoga studio is moldy? *Try out the new one.* You eat too much sugar at night. *Eat something different.* You don't want to learn Japanese online anymore? *Find a human to teach you (if you must learn it).* Ain't nobody got time for kinks.

Because when your hose is unkinked, you can water more plants. When your hose is kinked, you can't water anything. Remember that. So now that you know, can you uh, unkink your hose a little bit?

> *You have access to absolutely everything you even think you need. Your tap is your supply of infinite resources and it's not your job to wonder if they're there for you. It's your job to get into the tap, stay in the tap, and intentionally unkink any kinks that slow your flow. P.S. Kinks will happen. Sometimes we're meant to be kinky for a long while, but as long as you know how to unkink, that unkinking will get you back into the tap. In the tap you're all good. You have access to everything.*

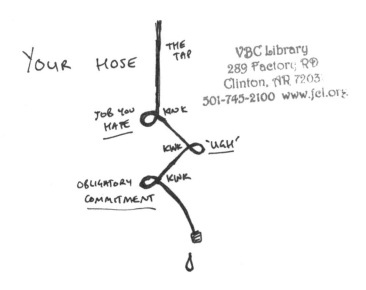

YOUR HOSE

THE TAP

JOB YOU HATE — KINK

KINK — "UGH"

OBLIGATORY COMMITMENT — KINK

POP OUT: An unkinked hose feels like....

The freedom to know your version of enough. Take a pause, any kind of pause at any kind of time and not beat yourself up for it.

Light speed clarity.

The freedom to not set huge radical business goals just cos everyone else is, cos it's just not your time to over-hustle.

Spaciousness.

The freedom to politely decline the request in your inbox in two short sentences and zero guilt, even though the person is _really_ nice and 'I should just do it'.

Knowing without second guessing.

The freedom to evolve on from a business that just isn't vibing with your soul anymore, because your soul doesn't need to justify it any more than that.

Crazy good ideas and downloads coming out of nowhere (but somewhere—your unkinked tap).

The freedom to post on facebook and without needing to check your phone afterwards for 6 hours to see who commented (and approved).

Effortlessly clear guidance and intuition, and the knowing that you can trust it.

The freedom to be in the gratitude and joy of your life without worrying about when it's all gonna turn to shit.

It feels like you had a scoop of creative, connected, charismatic badassery in your morning smoothie, delish.

Know Your Gatekeepers

Your values and boundaries are the gatekeepers to your alignment.

Whether it's on a big scale, like speaking at an event, or on a very small scale, like going out on a cold night when you're already snuggled in your PJs, you have to follow your honest-to-goodness, deep-down-in-your core *Yes*. In most cases no one means any harm requesting things of you, sharing their opinions with you, or telling you what you should and shouldn't do. It's not even a case of bad vs. good. It's just that their alignment is not matching up with your alignment—at that moment in time. And this is exactly why you must be the advocate for, and the protector of, your own alignment. Finding your alignment is the most important thing you can do for yourself, because there is no one else on this Earth that can ever know what your alignment is.

Nobody, I repeat, *nobody* can choose your alignment for you. That's why it has to be your job, and choosing your own alignment doesn't come easy. Don't let the smoothness of the word alignment throw you off the ruthlessness of it. Living in full alignment is the ballsiest thing you can do. In a world where everyone is moving, speaking and requesting from their own vibration and perception, unless you prioritize your own alignment, you will be living according to others' needs. Alignment requires courage, and radical alignment requires the biggest set of balls around.

Saying no to someone in your family when they're asking you to go on a family trip that you just do not want to go on. Saying no to a friend who asks you for money for the eighth time, even though they "really need it." Telling your business partner that you are "not taking calls before noon," because that's your creative time. Leaving the job, ending the relationship, moving from the city, turning your phone off. Every single one of those actions takes courage. And every single one of those actions puts you in your tap, in your alignment.

Right about now, some of you might be thinking… *So I just get to do what I want all the time? Like, I don't have to brush my teeth, or go to work before 10 a.m., because I want to go surfing instead?* To which I say, that yes—to some degree—you get to do what you want to do. However, I want to add that doing what you truly want, what is in your alignment, what puts you in your tap, is only possible when you are clear on your values.

Your values are the gatekeepers of your alignment. They are the security guards that keep watch over your hose and say "Yes!" or "No!" to choices. For example, you may not *feel* like going to work before 10 a.m., cos the waves are pumping and #YOLO, but you believe that practising commitment, loyalty, and doing a great job is living in your alignment. *Yes, I will go to work.* Or, you may not *feel* like eating a delicious salad for lunch when someone offers you a fried burrito with seven pounds of cheese on it, but you believe that energizing food during the workday is far better than a momentary taste bud orgasm. *No, I will not eat that burrito.* I really don't *feel* like speaking at an event, because I'm a hermit in the evenings, but I value (see, there it is!) community and connection highly. *Yes, I will speak. It will feel so in alignment once I get there.* You may not *feel* like spending the extra $20 to buy the same tee but ethically sourced and made from bamboo, but you really value sustainability and conscious enterprise. *Yes, it's always worth the money.* What you feel like doing in the moment and what is in alignment with your values may not always be the same thing.

This is why it's so critical that you know what's important to you and what you truly value. Your values do two big things: They act as your swift and efficient yes-or-no guide when making decisions, big and small. They protect your alignment—your smooth unkinked hose. Small decisions are the hardest decisions, because the conglomeration of those small decisions is what becomes powerful enough to pull you out of alignment. Going to dinner with people you don't vibe with, drinking water from plastic bottles while cringing at the thought of BPA's, packing your schedule so full you have no time to quiet down and read are seemingly little decisions in the scope of life, but they are ruled by very big and powerful words. *Fear. Justification. Doubt. Lack. Envy. Judgment…* are just a few. Me, personally, I can sum up the root cause of my misalignment in one big fat word, starting with the letter O. *Obligation.* When this word—this mentality—becomes the ruler of my little (or big) decision making world, then misalignment has an open invitation.

Having clear values is as essential as having courage to unkink our hose. When we do not have clear values, we have no gatekeepers. When we have no gatekeepers, our hose is available to the general public and we run out, we run dry. There is a fine line between forcing ourselves to do something we aren't into and the duty of choosing something that let's our tap flow.

Get clear on your values.

Don't just choose values that sound good, pulling from something you see on someone else's mission statement, or copying words from your company's manifesto. Sure, words like *integrity, honesty, creativity* are fabulous and make great values, but pause and think. What do the words mean to you? What means the very most to you? Everyone has different gatekeepers.

Some people value play more than they value organisation. If you value play more than you value organisation, when your tax bill needs to be finalised by next week, you may say yes to the weekend trip to Napa with your friends and take care of the tax bill next week, easy! Whereas the person who values organisation, would say no (Or, have it done 3 months prior) and feel happy to stay at home, with plenty of space to get it done. Our values say Y or N for us, that's why it's so critical to know them.

True values are independent of external circumstances.

"Everyone liking me," "having as much money as so-and-so," or "winning all the time," will not make for good gatekeepers. To be in tune with your alignment, your values must be unconditional and independent of external circumstances—and those grey areas are tricky and the reason why so many struggle with radical authenticity.

Let's look at *Honesty as a value*. You can choose to be honest at all times regardless of anything (unconditional and independent of external circumstances). Something arises and your choice is, *Do I tell the truth or not*? Your answer is clear, "Yes!" You tell the truth regardless of whether the other person will like it or not, because *Honesty* is your value. Now let's look at *Making Others Happy* as a value. Your decision is affected by other (external) people's reactions (conditional). Something arises and your choice is, *Do I tell the truth or not*? Your answer is, "Um, maybe…" You tell the truth if it doesn't hurt someone's feelings, because *Making Others Happy* is your value. Which gatekeeper does a better job protecting your alignment?

Think about how good it feels to choose for you, to be able to have more access of the life force that's running through your tap—specifically for you. When we honour our values regardless of anything external, we have more energy to do what matter most. Remember that the people around you might not always love your alignment as much as you do, but that's because *your alignment* doesn't always equal the alignment of others. Lucky for you, you can choose your values, and have "having other people feel stoked at my alignment" doesn't have to be one of them.

Four of my highest values are:

Alignment. Making choices based on my soul's desires and the instruction I feel from my core. I know that when I am in my alignment, I am nicer, kinder, more efficient, more generous, more creative and everyone around me benefits.

Health. Making choices that honour my body and show appreciation for her relentless service to me every single day.

Community. Surrounding myself with those who nourish me and my family, and being of service to those I am here to nourish.

Authenticity. Speaking as I speak, writing how I write, being how I be without tailoring anything to suit an audience.

Redefining values is not easy at first—it takes courage, just as it does to unkink you hose. You might cancel dinner with some friends, because Tuesday nights are now Salsa nights (*Dance*) and said friends might get all "ugh" on you, but it fades. You will see that living by your values will show you who and what should be in your life. The more aligned you are, the more quickly the Universe can rearrange your life so that your environment supports it.

If you're anything like me, the people around me respect me more and appreciate me more when I honour my boundaries. *Why?* Cos they care about me and they want me to thrive, more than they want me to be a yes person to every request. *And those that don't agree with my alignment?* Well, they're fine too. Because my alignment isn't dependent upon anyone agreeing with it.

Ready to choose your gatekeepers?

Ask yourself these 5 questions. Maybe even write them down. Let's get into The Tap, your tap.

1. When are you the happiest?

2. If there was no right or wrong when it came to planning your schedule, what would be different about your day?

3. If you got a FREE PASS to cancel any commitment in your life, would you need to use it? If so, what on?

4. What do you most value? Write as many as you want, but choose only the 5 that are non-negotiable.

5. Now picture your values standing at the gate, protecting your alignment. What in your life is no longer allowed in? e.g bad eating habits, scrolling your phone late at night, a relationship.

A little PK aside:

Boundaries are your gatekeepers, too.

I feel this is an important add on. Let's talk about family and alignment.

It's not uncommon for people to leave a family event and feel shittier than when they got there. Families can bully people, guilt people, and force them into doing things that are not in their alignment. But, it's family, so you show up—every single time. It's family hierarchy, and we are bound by DNA and conditioned like a rule book. It's too bad we can't have it our way. We could change the relationship and have a connection with our family that feels good on our terms.

Wait, why don't we have it our way? Two words: Ruthless Alignment. Yes, that would mean gathering up the balls to always choose ruthless alignment over guilt and obligation to family.

"Yeah, but you don't understand *my* family dynamic." I hear that a lot. To which I say, "No, I don't." But choosing your family dynamic over your alignment is your choice. And if it's your choice, then you have to own the kinks that that choice is creating for you and stop complaining. I might have lost some friends on that one, because it's pretty harsh. However, I repeat… Stop complaining about the things you are not willing to change. *Yes, your relationship with your family counts as one of them.* You can recreate and re-choose how you participate in your relationship so that it feels good for you.

"But that goes against all my morals!"

Tough love again. That depends on if your morals are something you put before your alignment. Again, this is 100% your choice. For most of us, family is the toughest place on Earth to practise our alignment. Here is where we are bound by DNA, by unwritten rules, and years and histories of stories and shoulds. If family is a kink for you, explore how you can unkink it. Do whatever you need to, and then you can return and you will notice how differently you feel about your family when you are operating from your open and healthy tap. You can love your family, and still be in your own, very important alignment. This was game changing for me when I learned it recently.

A couple of years ago when I first moved to Arizona from Perth, Australia, my brother came to visit for 4 weeks. 'Great!' I thought. I love my bro, he's so funny, super easy to be around and one of my best friends. But soon into the four weeks I was thinking 'Great? Really?' My brother had done nothing (except scroll his phone a lot). But having him in my space for so long turned me into an annoying nag. The type of nag that would definitely piss me off if I were on the receiving end.

"Ben, don't park the car like that the sun gets on the seats."

"Ben, why put a carton back in the fridge if the eggs are all gone"

"Ben, who are you expecting to wash your plate?"

I was the same when my Mum and sisters visited with Ben too. I turned into the freaking home police. "Whose charger is this? Don't forget to turn the TV off. Don't use all the vegan shakes cos the new ones don't come til Tuesday." Yep. I wasn't that 'don't worry guys I'll clean it up' kinda host when it came to my family.

I hated being in nag mode. Here my family was, visiting me in the USA all the way from Australia and I was more concerned with whether or not they put their shoes away. I was never as laid back, happy, and present as I would have loved to have been. The worst part was my guilt that went to bed with me every night they were there. Every single night during their visit, I'd go to sleep and promise myself that I'd be more chilled, present, and less annoying the next day.

When it came time for them to leave and fly home, I felt nauseous, guilty and just awful, like I didn't give them the best of myself while they were there. (You know the feeling of regret that makes you bite the inside of your mouth and not want to eat? I had that.) As soon as they'd leave, I'd text them all frantically telling them how much I loved them and how much I miss them already. And it was totally true. I did miss them. I'd beat myself up for a solid three days after they left seeking approval from my husband "I should have been more present. I should have been more relaxed, right?" I so badly wanting to be that chilled super fun house guest host with my family.

One day, in my 'beating myself up for being a nag when my family was visiting' episodes, I actually arrived at an answer for my response. I felt on edge having my house full of family, because we grew up in a *very* small home. It was the five of us—my three siblings, myself and Mum. I shared a room with my two sisters before moving into the converted garage—the one I had to access through my brother's bedroom. I used to study at the kitchen table while everyone was eating and get so bothered by their chewing that I'd…. yep, NAG! "Shhhhhhh can't you see I'm studying?" They'd snap back "Peta it's the fucking kitchen table! We're allowed to eat!!"

I *craved* space as a kid. And then as an adult, I finally got that space.

That's why having my family all up in my space had me feeling anxious. It felt bloody good to figure that out. Suddenly I wasn't so hard on myself. I just really enjoy my space and there's nothing wrong with that. I communicated this to my Mum. She said "Yes Peta, we know that and we totally respect this. We can stay at an airbnb when we visit. We just want to spend time with you."

I would never have my family stay in an airbnb when they fly all the way across the world to visit me. And here's the thing, when I check in with my alignment, I don't want them to. I love having them stay with me. But I couldn't arrive at this until I explored my alignment and acknowledged the fact that for me to feel aligned, I require limits and *boundaries* around how long I can have house guests, and I have to be honest about these boundaries or else it will become tension in my body, and tension for those around me.

Phew. What a relief. Now I own it. I'm not a 'house guest for weeks and weeks' kind of person, no matter how much I love my family. But because I can now own that, I can set boundaries around it and how long guests are welcome to stay before I start feeling like I'm sacrificing my own peace and space. When I do have house guests now, I'm fine and I can enjoy it (introvert alert) because I have boundaries that protect my alignment. My family is grateful too, cos I can just be funny AF with them and not an uptight tosser. Relationships work better when we're in alignment.

◇◇◇

○ When you are in your alignment, you let people off the hook.

○ When you are in your alignment, you don't need people to be/act a certain way.

○ When you are in your alignment, you aren't needy.

○ When you are in your alignment, people around you get the best of you.

○ When you are in your alignment, people affect you less.

○ When you are in your alignment, you're more free to choose for you

○ When you are in your alignment, you're clear.

○ When you are in your alignment, others respond to your alignment.

○ When you are in your alignment, you aren't projecting onto other people.

Choose your alignment first, then be in relationship. Everything will appear different when you are in your alignment. Your heart will be more open, you won't be as easy bothered, you will be more sure of your choices, you will say yes or no and mean it.

Relationships just work better when you choose for you first—everything does. Let me tell you about a rule of the Universe. The Universe is made of energy and is able to read everything you feel and everything you don't feel from cosmic light years away, and your goal is to always be traveling on your highway of alignment, in your free flowing, divine tap—feeling good.

The Universe cannot be tricked if you say, "I'm in alignment," when, in fact, you and the Universe both know that you are not. You can't hide your misalignment from the Universe. You can't hide it from yourself, or from your family, or from your tribe. Living in your alignment is your greatest gift to all around you. Your values are your tools for navigating life in a way that let's you feel good.

My little starseed,

May you always wear yellow undies and crip walk to the fridge. Sometimes, when I begin to write these little reminders, I LOL at myself, especially this one. Because when I think about the people on our Earth who absolutely nail what we're going to talk about next, it's most definitely you. The children. You little ones are the masters of this one, and I'm getting so excited for you to be here, because I know how much I'm going to be able to up my game when it comes to circulating energy.

Circulating energy: DANCING OUTRAGEOUSLY AT INAPPROPRIATE TIMES!

Okay, sorta. What it really means is acknowledging that you are an energetic being and that energy can never be destroyed, but can only change forms. This is easy for adults to forget. We sit at a desk with a pen and paper for days or weeks in a row, trying to force clarity to just appear from the sky. We write pros and cons lists, we mind map, we do all the fancy brainstorming techniques we learn from the internet. We sit in the same spot, at the same time of day, trying to force something brand new to emerge. A lot of the time, our forcing of it, blocks it, and it doesn't come. It just makes our head feel full and confused. When we ditch the desk on a random Tuesday afternoon and go surfing, head to a new coffee shop, or turn our phones off for a weekend of camping, then 'uh huh, whoa! Omg I've got it!'. The ideas, the clarity, the solution, the insight, it's all right there. Why? Because we did what you brilliant kids do when your energy feels stuck, we moved it around and did something different. I know that if I was a brilliant idea I wouldn't really want to flow right down into an energy field of stuck-ness. Ew, no thanks. Ideas come to you when you ditch the desk for the day and go and jump in the ocean, or walk down the street to a new coffee shop and grab a muffin.

It's so true, huh? My generation, baby, creates memes like: "I wish there was a waterproof notebook in my shower." Or "I can't stay in yoga for 60 minutes without wanting to run out and write down all of my epic ideas." We millennials know that when we are out of our

I-must-think mode that we are open and accessible to everything. Yet, there are still so many people living today that don't know this fact. They are out there trying to change their life by doing the same thing every day, every week, every month, and every year, and expecting all this brand new stuff to show up in their field. It just won't. Newness needs space. Everything you want is there but, it can't come to you if you're not clearing out the old and welcoming the new. You so get this.

When you feel 'ew,' you flip your arms around and chase after butterflies. You wear tutus with gum boots until you get bored, and then you switch to a hat back to front and a leotard with wings. You're masterful at recognizing when something is stuck and you have no tolerance for boredom. You're masterful at circulating energy. I think you, you wildly amazingly brilliant children of the Earth, know that this is the way. Oh how wise you are. Don't ever stop randomly flapping your arms about and chasing butterflies, you're into something.

Love Mum. XX

Circulating Energy

Shake it up

I'm here in a brand new café writing these words. When I first tried to write this book, I would sit in the same desk at my house and just tap, tap, tap away at my computer. Same time, same place, every day. And almost every day I was hitting what felt like creative blocks, or more like creative boulders. I would sit and try so hard to write. Every day was a routine. Sit. Struggle. Get frustrated. Do a little bit to say you did something today. Get up and do what I do at 11 a.m. What an ugly pattern I was creating. I had my routine, but I was so stuck when it came to writing. So, of course, I had to learn the lesson of circulating energy, which came in the form of a Matt Kahn video I happened upon.

Matt Kahn's insights always land very powerfully for me. I feel that he is one the most relevant teachers of our time. In this particular video, he was talking about "the one reason that people are not manifesting what they want" and "feeling how they want to feel." I remember thinking: *Wow! There is only one reason, just one? If this one single reason is really the reason, then people are gonna be real happy. Oooooh… gimme!* And he was oh so very right. Since the day I watched that video his one reason has become my not-so-secret weapon.

The reason: Circulating Energy.

"And what the heck does that mean?" you might ask. Circulating energy is intentionally changing things up to clear out stagnant energy and allow space for new, wild, exciting, rewarding energy. Circulating energy is doing things differently, shaking up routines and patterns so that our cells can release energy that has become stale. When we circulate energy, we invite the newness into our lives that's been unsuccessfully trying to make its way to us.

Out with the old, in with the new!

I started working in all different spots all over my house—my office, the lounge room, the kitchen bench, and even outside on the days my laptop wouldn't overheat in the Arizona heat. On the days that I chose to sit at my round table in our great room, I rotated my seat so that each day was a different view. Somedays I got out of my house and started doing my work in new cafes. And when it came to writing—that work I'd previously been plugging away at—I started to give myself some flexibility and forgiveness, which is exactly what landed me here, in this café in San Antonio writing these words that will surely become the content for a chapter in my book. I was beginning to witness how the power of circulating energy was critical for my creativity. But it wasn't just critical for my creativity, it was critical to every single thing in my life. I started seeing all the areas in my life where I felt stagnant, bored, and stuck.

One of them was my tried and true morning routine. Wake up, have probiotics, meditate, journal, work out, sit down in the same spot as yesterday, open google docs, write, scroll Instagram for a bit, continue writing. Lately, I was just going through motions, but it was beginning to feel boring and I was becoming attached with no place for newness. Solution: I started waking up and doing something different every day. I would draw if I felt like it. I would dance on most mornings, because that is when I felt my energy really circulate. I would write in different places and use different coloured pens. (Seriously, it can be that minute—writing with a different colored pen! It truly is the smallest things we can do that are new to us that help us circulate energy.) I stopped just walking to the fridge and I started dancing my way to the fridge. Why had I been walking my whole entire life to the fridge? *Boring.*

What newness could I invite into my life if I changed even the most normal, ingrained habits I had? Two stepping while I was brushing my teeth, there's another one. Standing while brushing was *so* 1988-2016. Oh and my calendar… my calendar full of so much same, same, same. Time to rearrange things. I started working out smack-dab in the middle of the day. I went for walks in the morning. I left my bed, my room, to go and read. It was all so simple, but so wildly exciting to find ways to switch up my own normal day.

As my energy changed and felt so much more free, open and exciting, new stuff started showing up. It became addictive—circulating energy. I stopped wearing my workout clothes every damn day. Working from home has its perks, but I was just dressing by default. There I was with a wardrobe full of clothes, yet I was wearing the same yoga pants, Jeaniius Tee, and hair scrunchie top knot every damn day. Time to wear the clothes I'd never worn, just because! I felt refreshed. Paying more attention to my clothes led to something else that shifted my energy level. I have always given away my clothes in bundles, because I just love the feeling of minimalism (and giving), but I was reaching a whole new level. I realized that every single thing in my home had its own energy—even my clothes. So if there was something sitting around that was not getting used or giving me any joy or excitement, it was time for it to go. I felt I had space for so many surprises to show up, and of course, they did.

I was addicted.

Create New Structure

Circulating energy has professional advantages, too. I changed the structure of my programs to give them a new invigoration (obviously I don't do this too often, just when my tribe needed me to, when energy started to border on the verge of stagnant!), and I changed my mentoring style so that my tribe was also experiencing the circulation of energy just like I was. It's infectious. Even my travel schedule was contributing to this positive shift. I realized how truly alive I feel when I land in a new city. My energy goes wild. I feel instantly refreshed. Just like now, when I'm in San Antonio Texas writing, working on this book. I've been all over the world, but I've never been here. Admittedly San Antonio is not my style of city, but it is new to me and that newness is moving my energy around and inviting in new thoughts, new perceptions, new ideas, new insights, so much new.

Circulating energy is why I feel so giddy in London. There is just so much going on, so many funky little cafes to visit, parks to sit in. There are so many dynamics present in one city, so many cultures, so many different energies, so much to do. The fact that I walk everywhere when I'm in London too, that circulates energy like sitting in a car doesn't. I LOVE the newness everywhere in London. When I was there just recently, my tribe commented "Whoa! Your energy! You're so giddy!" I can't even tell you how many new ideas and downloads came to me while in London. I made a note to visit new cities even more regularly purely for this reason.

Now you, shake it.

Look around and you will see so many opportunities to circulate your energy—personally and professionally. Every day we can do this. Whether it's on a micro scale like dancing when you get up in the morning to release and circulate any energy we stored over night or whether it's moving to a new home, a new city, a new job, because you need a big shift. It does not matter how we circulate energy, it simply matters that we do. And we must do this over and over and over again.

Yes, routine is important. Routine has its place—absolutely. Without routine my mum would have a helluva time raising four children close in age, who all played an average of five different sports each. But, I've come to learn that routine is not *the most* important. Circulating energy is. Make *that* a part of your routine.

If we want to attract newness into our lives in any way, then we need to become masters of circulating energy.

Changing things up, shaking up our cells. When we invite newness into our field, stagnant energy moves and our life force turns on.

Getting stuck just thinking about where to circulate your energy in your life? Try to change a few things with me. Just shake it up. You'll get addicted.

Change your outfit. Do you have a default outfit? See what happens if you let your soul choose your outfit today. Cropped Michael Jackson tee with high-waisted jeans on a Tuesday? *You go Glen Coco.* Can't because, work requires your duds? Wear some crazy, sexy underwear!

Recreate your workspace. Work in a new space every day or every week. Somewhere new in your house, somewhere new in your hood, or if you're in an office—do something different with it. Buy a plant or a bubble gum machine. Get wild. Laptop screen saver? What do you look at every day? Surprise yourself. Change your password. *Whoa.*

Switch up your schedule. Don't do the same thing at the same time every day. Re-jig your morning routine so that there's something new, spicy, exciting in there (and repeat). Dance. Do a headstand. Walk your dog a different direction.

Get rid of what you don't need. There's nothing that says 'gimme some new energies!' like physically getting rid of old ones. Go through your home and ditch (give away) anything that doesn't bring you joy—in each room. Clothes you've had for yonks (do not throw out the vintage though, that shit is gold). Gifts from people whose energy isn't what you want to bring into your life (don't feel bad). Let go of all that "stuff" that is taking up space and bringing no new juju into your world.

Find a new workout. If you walk in the morning, try yoga, Pilates or a 20 minute HIIT sesh. If you usually work out at lunch time, try working out in the morning. If you never walk, try walking. If you never swim, try swimming.

Shake up your evenings. If you watch Suits every single evening without fail, turn the TV off. Read a few nights, learn a language, play guitar, go for a walk, call your friends.

Don't be a regular. If you're like me when you find a good thing you stick to it. Now we're in Sydney, and I have my fav few Bondi hangs and I go to them—*all the time*. But just last week I said to hubs, "Ok, next weekend we're trying two new places." Sure, I don't like to risk a shitty meal, but it's worth the risk for some new, delightful energies.

Meals you eat and when. Do you have soup on Sundays, spaghetti on Tuesdays, Postmates or Deliveroo on Wednesdays, out on Thursdays, Pizza on Fridays, Burgers on Saturdays and repeat? Change it up. Go out on a Monday, have soup on a Thursday. Take lunch some days, eat a new breakfast once a week. Be a little frisky.

Shuffle the apps around your phone. I know, really PK? *Yes, really.* Make it a little treasure hunt on your phone so that you don't automatically click on the blue FB icon without thinking about it at 8:07 am every day (and 150 more times after that).

> *Circulating energy is a magical tool and it's not just a tool we 'can' have, it's a tool we 'need to have' in order to keep attracting the new and evolved experiences and people and opportunities and feelings. We are our own solution to our stuck-ness, and when we can circulate new energy as a daily habit, newness falls in love with us and we're forever open to expanding delights. Circulating new energy doesn't have to be huge—it can be in the smallest things, like how you move to your fridge, how you brush your teeth, what underwear you wear, how you do your hair, what time you read, your morning routine, the plates you eat from. It's all new. Go forth and let the magic in.*

Play

I get my clarity so much faster when it's fun.

Last year, and all my years before last, I would never have been described as "someone who knows how to play." And I definitely didn't dance my way to my fridge. I was quite serious, the get-it-done type of woman, always on some sort of mission. It's been like this since I was a little girl. Once, in primary school I got a report back and the teacher had written "Peta is intelligent and bright. Her grades are great, but her sense of humour is so dry. Sometimes I don't understand her." Well, that has summed me up quite perfectly. I carried this mentality with me into adulthood, and although I've travelled the world and had my fair share of benders, I was never fully able to relax, and I rarely would say that I was having fun. Sounds crazy. Actually, it was very crazy.

But now here I am, age 28, and writing to tell you that play is not a distraction from the important stuff. Play *is* the important stuff. And understanding play has profoundly changed my life. Before I begin to explain why and how to add play to our lives, I'm going to share something that's super sacred to me. I'm going to share a story that is quite taboo, and talk about a subject that's often easier to just shut up about. But, here we go anyway.

A disclaimer: I'm not prescribing, or suggesting you do anything by sharing this story. I'm sharing it because it's authentic for me to do so.

Last year I sat for my first **Ayahuasca** ceremony, and it was one of the most profound experiences of my life (says everyone ever). But seriously, it was (I know, I know). Truth is, I had been called to this ancient Amazonian plant medicine for a couple of years. I'd been invited by my more spiritual friends, one after the other, and each time they shared their experiences with me I was more intrigued. It felt almost like Ayahuasca was sending smoke signals to me through different people. What I knew was that Ayahuasca (Aya) allows you to access more than just what your five senses show you, which enables you to go beyond your normal thought patterns. You begin to *see* beyond your sight, to see what she wants to show you, what you *need to see*. But more importantly, what you need to understand and feel. It's like an installation, an upgrade.

But "my time" was in 2016, and as soon as I made the decision to go to the mountains and commit to the ceremony, the spirit of Ayahuasca started working through me. Ayahuasca is both a sacred plant medicine and a spirit that I now know to be divinely feminine, beautifully powerful, and boundlessly loving. Everyone has different experiences, and I'm not here to write a whole chapter on Ayahuasca herself. I'm here to show you that my Aya (what we'll call this divine, feminine, and oh so loving energy) experience was particularly profound when it comes to PLAY.

The entire month before I sat in the mountains with Aya, she began slowing me down, lightening me up, and loosening my reins. I just felt like I was moving slower, like my nervous system was unwinding. Then came the evening I sat with Aya. It was magical, my God. I was with my soul sister Makenzie, Makenzie's Aunt Amy, and her partner Mish. We all sat with a shaman whose energy was that of pure divinity. I couldn't contain my excitement.

The first 90 minutes of the ceremony Aya simply taught me to breathe. I remember thinking 'I know how to breathe! Let's get to the good stuff!', to which Aya responded 'No you don't. And we're not moving on until you *really* breathe.' I remember lying down, breathing, and having her widen my breath as if it was as wide as the Pacific Ocean. It was like she was showing me how much replenishment I could feel with just one breath. She showed me what my breath looked like when I breathed, like really breathed, how big and wide and healing my breath could be. Every inhalation wasn't just about me filling up my lungs, it was about getting in sync with the Universe and everyone in it, and being instantly reminded of what mattered, and what didn't. Every breath made me feel like I was breathing with the whole world. An hour and a half of just breathing and I fell in love. I fell in love with breathing, and I finally understood *why* I needed to breathe more deeply. Eventually, when I looked up at the wall in front of me I saw the word *RELAX*. Of course. And only once I'd started breathing properly, did she let me move onto her real lesson (gift) for me.

Once Aya has shown me my breath, then the real work could begin—PLAY. Her whole purpose was to introduce me to the importance of play, but she couldn't do that until I was able to slow down, breathe, and relax. Only then could I be one with the high vibration of play. This was more than a lesson. This was instant embodiment. I started downloading crazy, wild, colourful, images—lively animations of what play actually looked and felt like. I wasn't just being shown, I was being gifted play like a piece of software being installed in my cells. I was in a 5-D playground. Everything was coloured in a way I had never seen. Colours that I didn't even know existed. There were swings everywhere, rides. It was what I imagine Disneyland times a billion to look like. I wasn't hungry, thirsty, yearning, impatient, scared, or jealous. I felt only one vibration—play. I sat there with tears streaming down my face, so grateful to be in that spot, right there, in my life to be shown this so vividly and viscerally what it was to play. It felt like a new program was being inserted into my cells, and an old rusty one was being taken out. PLAY was in, and WORRY was out. I was swimming in the vibration of play and it was embedding itself into my cells. I remember having tears streaming down my face because I just felt like I was being gifted the greatest gift, while simultaneously dissolving my stupid worries that up until that point had consumed me. I started to not only know how powerful it was for me to lighten up, loosen up, laugh, and smile, but I was learning how to embody the vibration of play—for the first time ever, at the age of 28.

We must all make play a priority. At least, that's what Aya was telling me. When I got home, I started dancing for no reason. I started enjoying my workouts and only moving my body in ways that felt good to me. I dropped dragging myself to do weights circuits that just had me throwing weights around like a chimpanzee until the 40-60 mins was up. I started doing Pilates and walking (moving at a pace which allowed me to actually notice my body and enjoy movement). I started cutting projects out of my agenda, so that I had more room to breathe. I'd never felt so deeply calm and relaxed, yet I was still getting all of my work done. All month long I felt so good, so different, so in harmony, and so okay-so-this-is-how-it's-meant-to-be. This was when I finally stopped missing the point. It was one of the most profound months of my entire life.

My Mum used to call me Paranoid Pete, because I've always had a wild imagination, but for a lot of my life I used it to worry. I'd worry as if it was my job. I'd worry even when I didn't have anything to worry about, you know, just always doing my job. If 'worrying' paid a 'by the minute' salary, I'd have been as rich as the Sultan of Brunei. I thought that because I wanted to change the world, I needed to worry about everyone and everything, all of the time. I'd create imaginary scenarios in my head and think about them over and over again until I believed I had real cause to worry about them. I was teaching people about success and freedom and designing their own life from the inside out, but here I was ol' Paranoid Pete not really nailing this 'freedom on the inside' thing. I couldn't relax. I couldn't turn off. I was charging at a million miles an hour acting as if I needed to carry the weight of all of the galaxies in a backpack on my shoulders all day every day. I look back and my nervous system was *so tired*. During Aya, my nervous system unraveled from its tight bind of 28 years, and I was given new, cellular space to play and to breathe. Paranoid Pete was gone. Playful Peta, was in…

There are many people out there—some who have sat with Aya, others who have not—who call this a "trip." But I'm here to tell you that I was acutely conscious throughout my entire journey, and therefore, instead of calling it a trip, I see my experience as insight—a crystal clear showing of what I couldn't see before through the noise and clouds of everyday life. I didn't know it was ok to breathe, until now. I didn't know it was ok to play, until now. I didn't know how much I needed to learn how to do both, until now. On that playground I saw Jeaniius (my vision, my boss, my 'chief entity', the company I was working for) everywhere, and Jeaniius kept telling me the same thing. "Peta, teach your entire generation this, they need to play, urgently."

In the morning, as we were leaving, I asked the Shaman if he wanted my help packing up. He looked me in the eyes and said "Peta, it's your job now to relax and have fun." Now if that wasn't the bow that was tied around the most magical gift in the world, I don't know what is. I went home with a renewed sense of purpose, which felt a hell of a lot better than mobilizing the next generation of conscious leaders. Rather that strategize and mobilize, I was here to help us all lighten up and loosen up.

> *Personal growth and creativity and conscious enterprise and leadership and saving the planet can be so damn serious, and our generation needs to do something much different than the generations before us if we are going to change that.*

Time to Play

Play is the way back home, the way to our innocent, worry-free, blissful inner child that isn't endlessly distracted by life, but playing the game of life as it was intended. Play is the fastest way I know to cut through all the shitty vibrations we collect throughout a normal day of #adulting and rise up to a vibration that is where our soul is hanging out. Play is how we clear toxic residue from our cells that's been accumulating from every FB scroll, every horrific news story, every long day on our computer copping damaging EMF (electro-magnetic field) left right and centre. Play is how we clear out the crap, and jump on an escalator that takes us straight to clarity.

Do you ever feel shittier after you dance? (Breaking a leg table dancing doesn't count). Do you ever feel shittier after you take a step back from the computer and go and dunk a few hoops? We do so, so much work to get back to our vibe when things go south or when we feel in a funk that we have tricked ourselves into thinking that any kind of play is a distraction from our deepest work. Play is our deepest work. For me, play has the ability to cut through any of my low vibrations and the power to restore and rejuvenate and realign me. Play can do that for anyone. Play is one of the most powerful ways to heal our planet, and it is part of my purpose to take play out of the *Immature, Distraction,* and *What's the Point?* boxes and place it back into the box where it belongs, *Absolutely Necessary.*

Your turn

When you think of the word 'play', what do you see? Do you see colour? A new vintage outfit and one of those dope technicolour Reebok tracksuits from the 90's? Dancing in the middle of the day? A Playground? Skateboarding? Riding a razor scooter even at age 30? (I do). Splatter Painting? Wearing costumes to the movies? Baking in the kitchen? Being on holiday and waking up at 10am to a cocktail? Re-arranging flowers? Chasing children around playing tag?

This is where you take a look at your life and see where you can add more play. Making time for play, is not just an 'add on' that we should 'do if we have time'. Play can be how we do things. It can be laced through everything we do. Our email signature, our work, what we wear, how we move around our house, the music we listen to on our drives, how we cook and bake, how we decorate our homes, our conversations. Play is a vibration that we can choose at any time of day. Some questions to help you get grooving:

What does play look, feel and taste like to you?

What are some things you do that make you feel playful?

How can you weave play throughout your day?

How can you add more play into your week?

How can you do something SUPER playful this year?

And a spicy one. After you play, do you usually feel more clear, or less clear?

We must consider play as some of our deepest and most important work. This is not just a tool but a reminder that hardly anything that we worry about really matters. You can stop doing absolutely anything you don't enjoy and shift to teach, work, create, and live in a way that never ever moves play away from the top of your priorities list.

So homie, when you're asked to write your goals, please have PLAY as #1. Write it into your spirit routine. Tattoo it on your notebook—or yourself—unable to ever be unimportant.

> *I saw home during my Aya ceremony. And more importantly, I saw the relevance of that amount of joy on our Earth right now. I experienced, saw, and now know play. Play shifts your vibe, elevates your spirit, and takes you home. Play is not just an activity, it's a vibration. It's healing, invigorating, rejuvenating, and one of the most spiritual acts of all. Playing does not mean to ignore all adult responsibilities, but it means to not ignore your #1 responsibility of all—your vibration.*

The Magic Question

How does it get any better than this?

There's this question, that my mentor V has asked me multiple times a month for the last four years. It's changed my world.

My God, I wish I could articulate to you—to all of you, all of you my fellow millennials, to all people everywhere—how powerful this question has been for me. I ask it in all situations. It's constructive. I ask it when I'm stuck, when I'm in a tough spot. It's also expansive, so I ask it when I'm so over the moon about something that all I want to do is dance. You know, those times things feel so good that you're equal parts grateful but also looking over your shoulder to keep an eye out for that thing that's gonna wreck it? I ask it then.

When it comes to constructive versus expansive, my work has shown me that it's the expansive bit that's most important. It's what I used to struggle with and with which I see many young people struggle. As soon as our wildest dreams manifest in reality, our old stories kick in. There you are spinning, arms wide open, and a little voice is warning you, "Enjoy this, because there is no going up from here! This is as good as it gets!" These thoughts flip a switch and soon you begin to worry that things could get worse, that this joy will peter out. You begin to claw back. Why get that excited in the first place, right? At some point the other shoe will drop. All good things come to an end, as the cliché goes.

Don't Claw Back

Joy is a skill. Humans are able to feel such a great amount of joy (I'm talking that natural, euphoric high of happiness), but many times humans do not allow themselves to be in that joy, to experience it, to live it—at least not for very long. Soon it's all about the noise, the stories, the misery of others, and all the external factors that lead to the feelings of joy being replaced by guilt or fear or something else that is not joy. We are now at the point where we have to convince ourselves that we deserve our happiness—and we work really hard at that! Even so, in comes that joy and it ends up feeling wrong, as in we don't deserve to be that happy. This is self-sabotage, and it's a bad habit that many millennials, really, all humans have acquired. When you feel like everything is working out perfectly and you are expanding into somewhere new, that's when self-sabotage kicks in. You justify your actions. You explain your feelings. You defend your joy.

But here is the truth: Joy is your home. Expansiveness is your state. There is no need to explain, justify, or defend yourself. Instead of the sabotage, the best action is to ask the magic question.

How does it get better than this?

With this question, you will invite in more of all that is good. You'll invite in more love, more success, more abundance, and more happiness and joy. You'll keep yourself on your super highway to alignment and in your flowing tap.

I can think of times in my life where everything has just been so rad. You know, days full of sunshine, everything I'm working on is so fun, no obligations on my calendar. I'm cooking new foods, feeling spacious in my mornings, everything is simple and enjoyable and there's nothing to worry about (ah, the simple things are the most joyful). So I'd pause in the morning, to sit in gratitude for all the good, and mind would start to reel: *Ok, well, what about the next 3 months coming up? You have lots of flights coming up... this project is gonna require you to work your ass off for longer each day... have you answered all of your emails from last week?... What are you going to say to Deb about next Thursday night?... Is the book-keeper still coming over on Wednesday?.... Shit, I've got a call at that time....* And then, just like that, I'm out of my joy and feeling anxious. It can be that swift.

And now, when I've been feeling all the good feels, I go up to my little zen room and intentionally and purposefully ask, "How does it get any better than this?" I sit quietly with the question, letting my mind and my heart explore—"How does it get any better than this?" I'll tell Source, The Universe, that I want to know and see the answers to "How does it get any better than this?" Later on, I'll notice that the emails that land in my inbox are pleasantly surprising, I'll get invited to collab with a conscious leader I've been following on Insty, and my hubs books us a surprise weekend away. It's getting better. It's getting better all the time if we allow it, if we ask for it.

The Universe will answer any question you ask, so be mindful of which questions are you asking. Why me? Why is this happening? What was that person thinking? How did I get here? What did I do to deserve this? You'll just be asked to dive deeper into those situations and the frustrations and fears will grow. How does it get better than this? Make 'How does it get any better than this?' your go-to question. For all the times. For when things are great. For when things are just cruisin.' For when things are *uggh*. For when things are so freaking epic you can't even handle it. When you ask yourself this question, you will leave no room for self-sabotage and only invite room for expansion.

Calling it the magic question, might feel a little woo-woo voodoo for you, but the truth is that it's a very intentional and purposeful question. It puts you in the driver's seat and reminds you that you are leading your life. You get to choose: consciously expand or subconsciously sabotage. Watch things get better than this or stick with this, because this is eh, fine, good enough, right?

You decide.

Step into the Magic.

"The answer's in the question."

—Bob Seger

Magic questions can be a thing. Make them one. "The answer's in the question." What is the question you want the answer to? Ask the right question, and you'll get the answer you're looking for. Here are few to get you started.

Where are the solutions I'm not seeing?

What does 100% clarity look like?

What could I do with just 5% more courage?

Who and what can contribute to this project?

Where are there resources making their way to me?

What are my choices here?

What energy do I want to be in?

What are the possibilities for this?

The Universe happily makes infinite goodness, love, alignment, success, abundance, and joy available to you. Most people never think to ask for it. Instead, they think they stop at a certain place because of X-Y-Z crazy reason that humans come up with to fight for limits. Explore your infinity, let the Universe wow you, and ask "How does it get any better than this?" Ask it ten times. Ask it while looking up at the sky or while closing your eyes. Ask intently. Ask purposefully. Then, let it get even better than this. I dare you.

Ask this question every day 10 x while looking up.

Pause & Play

I made this crossword for you so you can pause and have a little fun. I did it by hand, can you tell?

1. CUTS THROUGH SHITTY VIBES.

2. UNKINKED HOSE

3. SHAKE IT UP! _____ ENERGY!.

4. OBLIGATION DOES THIS TO YOUR HOSE.

5. YOUR GREATEST GIFT TO EARTH.

6. YOUR WATERFALL FROM SOURCE.

7. STOP MISSING THE _____ .

8. ASK A _____ QUESTION .

*POST A PIC OF YOUR CROSSWORDS
& HASHIE #EARTHISHIRING ♡

LEADING

Lead yourself. Lead your tribe. Be led by your vision. Then together let's lead the world.

"True belonging is the spiritual practice of believing in and belonging to yourself so deeply that you can share your most authentic self with the world and find sacredness in both being a part of something and standing alone in the wilderness. True belonging doesn't require you to change who you are; it requires you to be who you are."

—Brene Brown

Courageously Leading is the element of The New Way that is all about how we lead ourselves by being human AF; how we lead others by being radically honest ; how we let ourselves be led by our vision to do important work; and how we together lead the world by going high, when everything seems to go low.

Permission to Screw Up

Leading is not only for lightworkers (Leading YOU)

When I think of what is really required of our generation, it's simple—to be the new superheroes, which is what this book's all about. Originally I had the word 'lightworker' written in place of superheroes, but I scratched that. Lightworker felt too limiting. To be a superhero, you don't need to be a Kundalini yogi or wear crystals around your neck or read from the deck of spirit animal cards by your laptop or know which star system you came from. You don't even need to know what a chakra is. *Feeling some relief?* I mean, you can be and do those things, but they are not required of a new superhero. The new superhero is the adventurer, the rap lover, the tattoo obsessed, the eclectic introvert, the new mum, the self-educated, the formally-educated, the yoga lover, the yoga hater, the doting dad, the surfer, the crappy speller, and (you!) reading this book. The new superhero is a leader of a new kind.

Whether you consider yourself a leader or not, you are a leader. There are so many ways to lead. Leading is not limited to the person at the front of the room, the Prime Minister, the president, the CEO, or the captain of the team. Leading is choosing your alignment, following your own divine intolerance of what doesn't sit right, navigating a big and scary vision. You are leading you own life. You are leading even when you don't know you are leading, and that is where we begin. So, can we lighten up on the word "Leader" and just learn what it means to lead?

First, you must learn how to lead you. Once you lead you, then you will lead others. Once you lead others, then all together we are able to lead the world, the collective, the generations here and to come. And to lead you, you must first and foremost learn how to lead you from a place of radical alignment. When you choose to lead from alignment, you've got to be willing to flex. What is true for you this year, might not be true for you next year. What is rewarding for you today, might not be rewarding for you next week. You must always lead you from a place of impeccability and integrity, and the highest form of impeccability is honouring your humanness, and the highest form of integrity is honouring your alignment.

Impeccability

Impeccability is a word that gets used a lot when it comes to leadership. When I think of the word "impeccable," I think "clean as a whistle." No dirt, no mess, no mold, just squeaky clean, cleaner than the plate you eat off. Impeccable also happens to be one of Miguel Ruiz's four agreements. It's the first one.

> "Be Impeccable with your Word: Speak with integrity. Say only what you mean. Avoid using the Word to speak against yourself or to gossip about others. Use the power of your Word in the direction of truth and love."

It's the one that I know I have tried to practise ever since reading his book, *The Four Agreements*, many years ago. It makes sense, right? Speak words in private that you'd be comfortable having people hear in public—I agree. Nobody likes a two faced Tommy. However, being impeccable with your word is one thing, being impeccable with yourself is another. Being impeccable with *your word* means that you won't speak about Todd when he's not around, differently than you'd speak to him when he is. Being impeccable with *yourself* means only doing and saying what is true for you—even if it doesn't appear 'squeaky clean' by other people's standards. Your truth, is more beneficial to the world, than acting as if you were born wearing mala beads, with no party history, no mistakes, no destructive relationships, no fuck bombs. You are human. You are clean and you are dirty, and we (the collective) want to see you as both because that's what makes you glorious. We want to see your mistakes, your struggles, we want to know what you've learned from your dirty past.

There is the 2017 story of Tiger Woods getting pulled over for a DUI with a most horrendous photo attached. My God, I cringed when I saw it. His eyes are puffy, he looks half-asleep, and yeah—he also looks high. He later pleads guilty to reckless driving and tests revealed that he had five drugs in his systems (a cocktail of mood enhancers, sleeping pills, and painkillers). The internet was busy making memes using that most-unflattering photo, while Tiger was at an obvious low point, having to share it with the entire world. He's a person, a dad, a guy kids look up to, a pro. Yet, famous as he may be, his responsibility above and before all of those things is being a freakin' human. I wish he could have silenced the whole word with this kind of a statement.

"Hey world, yeah, I fucked up. But guess what? I'm human. I'm clearly going through some tough times right now, so I could use your prayers more than I could use your memes."

Tiger could have given the world a gift. He could have opened up, revealed himself and been brutally honest about the low point in his life (I think he may have to some degree). Sure, it's not his responsibility to please the public when he's going through shit, but radical honesty so often warrants compassion. I find it so beautiful when people show their humanity, it makes me feel more bonded and connected to them. I just want to hug people so tight when they admit stuff, when they apologise, when they ask for help. It's like when their walls come down, the magnet in their heart pulls my heart in. They remind me of how vulnerable we are, they inspire me to own all parts of myself, and to choose 'here I am, love me anyway' over shame.

> *"If we can share our story with someone who responds with empathy and understanding, shame can't survive."*
> —Brené Brown

Impeccability is being radically honest and authentic about our humanness and revealing that to the world—not a hyped up, squeaky clean more 'appealing' version. Both when it's easy, and when it's not. Impeccability is unconditional transparency. It's when we are honest about the good, the bad, and the ugly—no matter who our audience is.

Impeccability is you leading you.

Integrity

Integrity, as most of us understand it, is to "do what you say you'll do," and to live in alignment with your beliefs and values. What it doesn't mean is to live a perfect life without any contradictions. Like impeccability, integrity is necessary for radical honesty and alignment. Integrity is being okay with the fact that we may change our mind, that our beliefs might change, and that we might change our course of action. I am here to tell you that you have the permission to pause, stop, and even quit with the most honest explanation there is, "I changed my mind."

Sometimes we are so obsessed with being seen as committed and "in integrity" that we ignore the fact that our truth is changing—when, in fact, the height of integrity is being able to say, "I just don't believe in that anymore, even after 20 years of preaching it." To live in alignment, we don't need to make up BS excuses and spend a week beating around the bush trying to find the words to say the simple four words that we really want to say. *I changed my mind.* Changing your mind doesn't mean that you are any less impeccable or have less integrity. It does not mean you have a to share every single breakdown or be less committed. Changing your mind is simply you choosing to lead your own life.

Here are some other high integrity statements.

○ *I don't feel good following through with this project, even though we're so close to a return on investment.*

○ *I'm no longer excited about this, even though it was my everything for the last five years.*

○ *I actually agree with him now, even though I used to hate his guts for the last year.*

Integrity is you leading you.

> *Impeccability and integrity are two buzzwords when it comes to leadership, but if you're not careful they can take you away from your greatest commitment—our alignment. Impeccability doesn't mean being squeaky clean and having no 'dirt' in your life. It means being radically honest and only doing and saying what is true for you—no matter what. Integrity doesn't mean believing the same thing forever because you believed it once. Your highest form of integrity is honouring your alignment, even when it means you may surprisingly change your mind.*

Success 2.0

There is no 'top'. (Leading YOU).

Time Macho isn't cool anymore.

"Time Macho," the term I first heard used by Arianna Huffington in her book *Thrive*. I fell in love with it, because so many people are Time Macho. I used to be. I was just so damn proud that I worked 16-hour days. I would run this story in my head that I didn't have time for anyone, and before long it became true. Whenever a friend would invite me to do something during the day, I'd respond with, "I can't, I'm working," accompanied by a little smart-ass tone and a face that read, *What on Earth would make you think I wasn't busy?* I was almost offended that someone could think I had any free time.

Can you relate? *Why would I have free time when I have work to do?* My mind starts spinning: *I am a hard worker and I take pride in being a hard worker. You should work more like me.* That was my attitude. I started to notice that it became my script, my story. I never had time for anything but work. I'd go to family dinners, but I still had that nagging feeling, so I'd say, "I have to check and see if I have calls." I would completely shun my friends and others building the same business as me when they'd suggest we could do lunch. "What do you mean? Why aren't you working?" I was really, really proud of my work ethic and I couldn't let it go. Time macho had become my identity.

I was the perfect example of what Success looked like out there— speaking on big stages, traveling the world, doing all the suc- cessful kinda things—going for more, more, and more. Until the never-ending pursuit for more started to wear thin. It started to become irrelevant. I was helping others have a freedom that I wasn't allowing myself. People stopped inviting me places. I was missing the point, because there wasn't an income I could reach, a number I could hit, a stage I could speak on that would ever make me feel more successful than my alignment with my soul could.

I had to drop the never ending, misaligned pursuit for more. I no longer wanted to feel like I could never stop and smell the roses or feel like I couldn't take a day off to freaking breathe or bake or turn my phone off. I wanted to save my generation from this endless pursuit for the top, from being so time macho. I had to go deeper. I decided to take a success holiday. During the first few week of not giving a fuck about success (as it was so defined), I felt like I actually was on holiday, like I had just pulled myself out of a marathon I'd been running in without even realizing it.

I looked at my schedule and got ruthlessly honest with myself. I asked myself some questions:

○ What during my week feels like crap to me?

○ What have I committed to in pursuit of success 'out there' and not success 'in here'?

○ What needs to change for me to feel fulfilled and at peace tonight?

And yeh, I even got deep....

○ If I was to only have a year left to live, which of this would feel worthless to me?

○ If I was to only have a year to live, what would I want to start doing right now?

It all changed. I was still putting in a lot of hours during the day to create epic shit, but they were MY hours that I'd chosen and they were being spent on new and exciting things and not 'ugh, that commitment'. They weren't 'cos I had to' hours. They weren't 'cos that's what successful people do' hours. They were 'cos it feels good' hours. When my head hit the pillow each night, I felt different. Each night felt like I was celebrating another beautiful choice filled day on Earth, rather than going to sleep just so I could fast forward to the next one and get more shit done. I felt incomparable. I felt incomparable because my greatest measure of success wasn't comparable to my peers or to my mentors. As long as I did what my soul most wanted to do, I was nailing each day. And I didn't have to prove, defend or justify this to anyone. There was no ranking system, no 'top 25 entrepreneurs' list I could make that would have me feeling more successful than me fist bumping my soul as my head hit the pillow as if to say 'we chose for us today'.

In a world as beautifully ripe for success and accomplishment as ours people are *doing* more than ever right now. Even though people are *doing* more than ever right now and becoming more 'successful' than ever right now, they're not *feeling* any better. In fact, they're feeling worse, which is why the old model of success of so ov-ahhhhh. Yes, sing it with me now. OVAHHHH!!

But we can't just throw out success all together. We have to redefine it, homie. So, tell me, how do you feel about these three *current* definitions of success, three which pop up right away on Google.

Success: the accomplishment of an aim or purpose

Success: the attainment of popularity or profit

Success: a person or thing that achieves desired aims or attains prosperity

OLD SUCCESS

"See you at the TOP"

Accomplishments, attainments, and achievements are the big words we use to define and describe success. These words drive the current models of success, models which are currently driving everyone on Earth right into the ground. Humans are exhausting themselves in the endless pursuit for more. But before we throw out the old and bring in the new, let's question these definitions. Let's see how we *feel*?

Success: the accomplishment of an aim or purpose

> *Ok cool, but what if it doesn't feel good?*

Success: the attainment of popularity or profit

> *Ok cool P-diddy, but what if it doesn't feel good?*

Success: a person or thing that achieves desired aims or attains prosperity

> *Ok cool money bags, but what if it doesn't feel good?*

Success wasn't wrong before, it's just changed. Everything changes. That's evolution. So we've got to press pause and collectively let out a big, "Hold up," which will give us some time to redefine success for future generations, because the old model of success of *go to school, get a degree, get a good job, get a mortgage, start a family* feels so ancient now. Our generation has very quickly interrupted that advice with our divine intolerance for systems, and we've started to mould our own version of success, which involves a whole lot more freedom, creativity, travel, and sometimes a big ol' flip of the bird to a mortgage and student debt. Why would we bust our balls so we can get a job that we don't enjoy so we can bust our balls to pay off the years of school (where we busted our balls) so that we can buy a house we can't afford and keep busting our balls to pay off said house so we can start a family and then keep busting our balls to support them? We are doing so much ball-busting that we have no time to spend with our family. *That's success?* That doesn't make any sense to us.

There is more to defining success these days. Success that doesn't feel good, isn't success. We have evolved to a new kind of success, and its measurements and vital signs are something that Forbes 500 can't measure.

Success 2.0: the state at which you and your soul fist bump when your head hits the pillow each night.

The state at which "you and your soul fist bump each night when your head hits the pillow," recognizes that success means your soul is the deciding factor when it comes to a win or a no win—not the bank, not the client, not the boss, not the book, not even your parents. You're either smiling, feeling fulfilled, aligned, fabulous (success 2.0) or you plunk down and feel like "bleh," just going through the motions of gotta get up and do it all over again.

You don't have to look far to find the memes on the internet to support this, like the one by Charles Bukowski that I've seen re-posted a jillion times.

"How in the hell could a man enjoy being awakened at 8:30 a.m. by an alarm clock, leap out of bed, dress, force-feed, shit, piss, brush teeth and hair, and fight traffic to get to a place where essentially you made lots of money for somebody else and were asked to be grateful for the opportunity to do so?"

Success is feeling free, feeling good.

There is something else rising—a new revolution, and it's been building in the last five years. I know you are aware of it. You have this book in your hands. I'm talking about the **Freedom Lifestyle**. Freedom allows your creative brilliance to start a brand or a company, your job allows you to travel the world or move your office from the beach to the café. These are not the angry face Bukowski memes, but the memes that have pictures of laptops in paradise. Collaborate with other homies, go through the hustle and grind together, couch surf if it means you don't need to work for a mean boss; just follow the dream of freedom. Live and lead life on your terms.

Organizations that know that the revolution is real are catching on, as employees are demanding better work from home policies and free dress codes and more time off. Suits and ties? High heels and pin skirts? (What sorta creative work do you expect me to get done in that?) Two weeks off a year? Ten hour work day? (What kind of energy and motivation to you expect me to have?) Less strict dress codes, more holiday leave, and better life conditions are just some of the answers to the demand of us millennials. Success, to us, is not so much about climbing a corporate ladder or having an income that's bigger than our sense of fulfillment or following the cookie cutter life that was presented to us at school. Success is feeling good in your cells, feeling free.

My first few years in entrepreneurship were working with young people to awaken that sense of freedom and success in them, but the last couple of years I've found a success within the revolution of freedom that extends far beyond 'not being on someone else's clock.' because even though I was living the Freedom Lifestyle, every night my head hit my pillow, I was drowning in un-fulfillment. I wasn't strapped for cash or under anyone else's pressures, but I was over obligated, overscheduled, and overcommitted. It didn't matter that the outside world saw a girl in her twenties who was earning, giving, crushing, and flying around the world. It didn't matter that she was retiring her mom, leading her cause, creating epic shit, and blowing up on social media. It didn't matter because the people looking in were not there to take the pulse of my soul each night when my head hit the pillow.

How much of it was a *yes* to my soul and a *no* to obligation? How much of my day was my own? My answer was tough to admit. 30% of my day was a yes to my soul, 70% of my day was a yes to obligation. *Ouch.* Only minutes of my waking day were my own. *Double-Ouch.*

2015 was a year of too many *yeses* for me, so I told myself that 2016 had to be different. I would like more months in one spot and less months feeling like I had a spare room at the airport. It turned out, with some planning, I would have all of September to November in Phoenix. I was so very excited for these three months to honour my commitment to myself in my US home, and then a test came. I received an email in August asking me to speak at an event in September on leadership alongside John Maxwell, which came with the opportunity to create a legacy leadership program with 10 other millennial leaders. I love and respect John Maxwell so much, so what an opportunity, right? *Do you really want to fly again?* I was just arriving home from London after a year chock-full of travel. I was so looking forward to my free months and peace and quiet. My soul was begging me to sit still. Staying at home during this time is what would have me feeling the best when my head hit the pillow each night. But John Maxwell? *Ahhh! What an opportunity! Think of the opportunity, the exposure. Shouldn't you jump at it regardless of anything?*

"Babes, is exposure really your greatest measure of success right now? My soul was standing firm. "It might be the measure of success *out there,* but what about *in here?*"

After a week of internal to-and-fro, I responded to the email. I said *No.* I felt relieved. Sure, I'd passed quite an opportunity, but not everything is about growing big, getting exposure, and gaining opportunities. Sometimes opportunities are cleverly disguised as distractions. They're a knock on your door, wearing the most beautiful coat, looking just like opportunity when opportunity knocks, but all you really wanted to that night is stay in and watch *Suits*.

When your alignment with your soul is your measure of success, it's easy to say either a *full body yes* to an opportunity that keeps you in your alignment, or a *no thank you* to anything which distracts you from alignment. Even though it may take you two weeks to respond with a 'no thank you' email, you know your answer the minute the email comes in. Trust that. Usher in Success 2.0, and its new models that go beyond attainment and accomplishments, and its new ways that go beyond the Freedom Lifestyle.

There is no top

I was climbing the Echo Canyon Trail on Camelback Mountain a few months back (pre-preggo, that thing is a beast!). It's the type of climb where you wear hiking shoes, you take water and snacks, and you get your freaking game face on. Going up, I was seeing people stopping one-third of the way up, two-thirds of the way up, at different viewpoints just to look out over the city. "Let's just stop here," I'd say to my husband. "Nah, let's go to the top," he'd say. Naturally—we are climbing to the top. That's what you do when you climb a mountain, you climb until you reach the top. The top, the summit, the peak is always the goal. But I did not really care about getting to the top. We were 45 minutes up and it would be another 30 minutes to get back down. A little over an hour workout, and even right at the elevation we had reached, the view was *amazing*. This high up was high enough for me. I was so happy to stop here. *Why do we always need to get to the top?*

Hiking puts me in my tap, and I always have epic downloads about my keynotes and work projects when I hike. Isn't this mountain so much like success, as we know it? *Everything* is about getting to the top. *I'll meet you at top. See you at the summit. I'm going straight to the top. He peaked. Rise to the top.* It's as though success is something we must ascend, because there is a definitive top and bottom. Well, maybe that was Success, but Success 2.0 has no top. Success 2.0 is not a ladder, a line, or a triangle. It is not something vertical. Success 2.0 is round, and it represents your happy, fulfilled, and cycling ecosystem.

What makes you feel successful when your head hits the pillow each night? Put it in.

SUCCESS 2.0

"How does it feel to me?"

I feel so LIT by my work!

I love watching docos at night guilt free

My schedule excites me

my soul fist bumps me each night :)

I have so much juicy time in the mornings!

Its ROUND. There is no TOP

Where are you chasing success in a model that doesn't fit our generation anymore? More importantly, where are you chasing the kind of success that is making your soul cringe? Are you climbing and clawing your way to The Top? Are you too Time Macho with your long-ass days filled with achievements and attainments? Your true success is only measured by the relationship between what you do and what your soul wants you to do. That is Success 2.0. So knowing this, take a breath out. Stop chasing, and tune in. What state are you in when your head hits the pillow?

"You cannot compare your insides to someone else's outsides."

~ Elisa Romeo

Beware the Shiny Goals

There are real goals, and there are BS goals (Leading YOU)

Goals!!

It's make your goals or bust, ya'll!
Four keys to nailing your goals every time.
Goals—the bigger the better!
No goals no glory!
Get your goals—How to win in 5 steps.

Really, though?

Success talks and motivational speakers on the subject of "Goals" come a dime a dozen these days. Goals have always been one of the hottest topics, even long before Cecil Alec Mace carried out some of the first studies on goal setting in 1935 that found that people are motivated by the accomplishment of goals—ground breaking at the time! Since then, there has been no shortage of scientific papers that have been published to prove the validity of goals and how great of a tool they are for helping us achieve what we want in all aspects of life.

Goal setting, while being a wildly useful tool for setting a path, following it, and kicking some mega butt, can also take us out of presence and have us constantly leaping from one arrival point to another and another and another. There is a dichotomy that exists. Setting a goal can be rewarding and also non-rewarding. A goal can take you to a higher vibration or knock you down to a lower. Following a goal can lead to alignment or further from the path. As you can see, I have a love-hate relationship with goals and some real hang-ups with all these goals, goals, goals, goals!

Some are bullshit, some are borrowed.

At certain points in my life I've been raring to get after my goals. Take for example, moving through university. I had very clear, non-negotiable goals, because I was after my PhD. I was going to be Dr. Peta Kelly. I would: score over 85% on each assignment; score over 85% on each exam; obtain an average of 85% across all subjects; and receive 80% or higher on my Honours thesis. I set these goals and I achieved them—every single one. I set bigger and higher goals, and that continued to serve me well. I set a goal. I crushed a goal. Years later, even after walking off my PhD path, I set similar goals to grow my network marketing career. I was on a mission, and a mission as big as mine was only possible with big goals, intentional actions, and a strict timeline—I was going to retire my mum. Financial goals and business growth goals were very relevant, and remain so today. I now have the goals I set for The New Way Live—attendance, dates, and details. I also set goals that focus more on intention than financials or business.

Intentional Goal Example:

> *"People will feel ten times lighter than when they walked in, and they'll hear one or two things that will completely change the game for them. They will feel calm and light and not overwhelmed by the content. It will all land in their cells while allowing their energy to remain excited and clear. They'll leave the event with a new re-wiring and a new set of subconscious instructions that upgrades their lives in all areas."*

These intentional goals are the kind of goals that have been rewarding—both for my progression toward my pursuits and for keeping this little lady laser-focused. They might be bold broad, but they are *real* goals. I have set some crazy records for jumping through the ranks in the network marketing organisation I built, because my soul just knew what was possible and my inner fire was unstoppable. I was lit. However, I have also learned that there is a fine line between the outrageous (real) goal and the fantasy (bullshit) goal. The outrageous feels good in my soul. The fantasy goal feels like I pulled it out of my ass. I know, that's crass, I'm sorry. Fantasy goals, or bullshit (let's keep it crass) goals come from all sorts of places and in all sorts of forms: our desire to appear a certain level of 'motivated' to those around us; the way we subconsciously 'copycat' our peers so to not get left behind as they make a run towards their goals; and the on-going game of comparison and competition.

We develop *bullshit* (BS) goals when we do not take the time or find the courage to tune in and get clear on what we really want—what's in our alignment. When life moves fast, it is easy to be clouded by what others want and what others want from us, and the focus shifts from internal to external. Soon we are so turned around that we have no flippin' clue what we want. It becomes easier to just throw down whatever "sounds good" or looks "progressive," than to take some time without a goal. We live by numbers and dates, which add to our anxiety. We set goals to double our income, even though all we want to do is take time off to write a book or be with family. We set goals to get more clients, but in truth we'd like less. Bigger is better, obviously. I mean, we can't be without goals, right? Might as well just make some up that will suffice. At least you have some goals on paper that look amazing, even epic. Yet, you can't derive any sensation in your body when you think about them, write them down, read them out loud, or make plans to move them forward. That's because these beautiful goals are—pardon the phrase again—goals you pulled out of your ass.

Alongside the bullshit goals are the *borrowed* goals. There was a point when my peers wanted to hit more zeros, but my soul didn't. I wanted to generate and create more with what I had. But since I didn't have a real financial goal, I tacked on some zeros and matched someone else's number. As the months passed, I never hit that number. My soul didn't give a shit about that goal, because it was one of the shoulds. It was borrowed. She wants to become a New York Times Best-selling Author, so I guess—if I'm writing a book—I probably should want that, too. What's-her-name wants to be a guest on Oprah, so I should want to that, too. My Bestie wants to be married by the time she's thirty… I guess me, too, right? My soul sister wants to travel the whole world by the time she's 45, then I guess I should, too. So-and-so is getting six nipple rings, well of course I want that. Right? Look how easy—and dangerous—it is to borrow goals.

Stay the Course

Arbitrary numbers and other people's' goals are fantasy goals. They are not yours, not born from your soul, and not something you can achieve. They are not going to get you anywhere, but off your path of alignment.

Anytime you set a real, aligned, OMG-whole-body-yes goal, you feel excited by your goal and not drained by it. BS goals and borrowed goals are like jumping on a train traveling the other direction—far, far away from your alignment, and you're just a sad sack leaning on a window (you know the movie scenes like this) watching your soul wave at you from the platform. "Bye-bye," she yells. "See you when you get back." She will be there with open arms after you return from your detour, because of course, in the end, you arrive where you're meant to arrive. Of course, there are no mistakes in the Universe. Of course, sometimes you're meant to go the long way because you end up finding a new journey and seeing some gorgeous flowers, both of which are liable to change your whole direction. The danger is being in the pattern of setting one fantasy goal after the other, to the point that your entire life is based around borrowed and bullshit goals, and every day moves you further away from your tap.

Real goals will only ever support or accelerate your alignment, and at the very least will not disturb it or interfere with it.

Think about it. If your soul wants to leave your job, take 6 months to go to Asia, and create online programs, but yet you set a goal to become a director at work, what do you do? You work 12-hour days to sprint up that ladder as fast as you can. And you're exhausted, greeting every morning you wake up with an "ugh." You don't have to be a rocket scientist to figure this one out. You are sprinting further away from your alignment. Just listen. Get real with yourself and give yourself permission to drop whatever heavy goals are dragging you away from your tap of alignment.

Let's take a moment to check in with your current goals.

Write them down—all of them—from easy to outrageous.

Cross out the goals that feel heavy.
Cross out the goals that you are not enjoying pursuing.
Cross out the goals that you made up.
Cross out the goals that you borrowed.

OMG! What if you have no goals left?

You don't actually have to have a goal right now.

I know! *The shock! The horror!* I hope the success and motivation coaches reading this don't spit on this page. But it's true. Sometimes your focus can be on no more than presence and direction.

In recent times, I've become looser with goals, and the lighter and looser I get, the more I've learned about the artistry of setting goals and how much more there is to the goal than reaching the actual goal. I used to set a goal and focus on nothing but reaching said goal. I was completely discounting all the work I did to get as close as I did. I would have a pile of goals, one for every aspect of my life— my body, my impact, my financial abundance, my location, my philanthropy, my spiritual journey, and other personal goals like 'Learn Norwegian'.

There came a time when these goals didn't fit, because once I realized that I was happy with my body, I didn't want to lose anymore body fat. A few years ago, in an annual 'transform your body' competition I joined, we were asked to set goals for our body. This is what I chose: Peta is going to grow her eyelashes longer. What? You might be thinking. But, you see, I didn't want to create any body goals that would take me away from that happiness I was currently feeling in my own body. I didn't want to throw down a number: get to 12% body fat. I didn't want to borrow something from someone else: lose five pounds. I was already achieving my goal of feeling totally harmonious with how I ate and moved. Why set a goal that would take me away from that? Eyelashes it was.

My intention is always to expand into health, abundance, happiness, and soul success. But intention and direction are so very different from solid, nose to the grindstone, hit the bullseye or you fail GOALS. As I grow into a longtime goal setter (setting goals since I was 7), I've come to understand that there are phases of my life where goals are not necessary. These were the phases of my life that asked for radical presence, going inward, and paying attention to the direction life wanted to move me in, not so much the direction in which I wanted to move. These are times for listening, observing, and being present. Times to allow yourself to shift from the conscious creator to a humble child of the Universe who is patiently waiting for guidance. It is those times that call for setting intentions and directions rather than goals.

So, ask yourself: What does life want from me? It's a little lighter than the question: What do I want to get from life?

Pause with this question. It's juicy.

You are a masterful creator.
You know that, right?

So now we know that it might not always be time for an inflexible bullseye goal—especially if you feel you need to pull one out of your butt. But it's *always* time to be consciously creating. You don't need a specific goal to do that. There's a difference between:

   a) Setting a goal because I feel like I need to set a goal. Pursue this goal even though it doesn't feel good. Ignore all of the other opportunities, signals and clues that are jumping out at me because #goalorbust.

b) Recognising that you're always creating your reality with the stories you tell yourself about your life and the vibration you emit that instructs life on your behalf. So consciously choose and tell the story that sends better, grander and more rewarding instructions to your life.

B, B, B ! B is where it's at! I believe we should always be checking in with the instructions we're giving to our life through our stories and our vibration.

> The art to setting goals stems from your alignment. Aligned, soulful goals feel really, really good. Fantasy goals that are bullshit or borrowed feel disconnected from your body. They are often made up and random and a detour away from your alignment. We must be aware of the detours that repeat themselves, because repeated detours don't give us much chance of living in our tap. There is a time for aligned goals, but there is also a time for not setting goals and rather choosing a direction. Super meaningful intentions and directions can come from a more open question that the Universe can help you with, What does life want from you?

A little PK aside:

Our stories are everything.

I came back to add this little piece the week before my book went to print. It was just too important to leave out (and I'm pretty certain will be the topic of my next book). Now we know that we can borrow goals without even knowing it, dangerous right? But what's more dangerous is when we borrow *stories*. The stories we tell ourselves about money, relationships, pregnancy, childbirth, success—they make up our identity. These stories and this identity, they give the Universe precise instructions on what we'd like to experience in our lives.

○ Writing a book with a newborn is pretty much impossible.

○ If you're really a conscious 'woke' human who gives a shit, you shouldn't have more money than the average person.

○ I'm meant to crave crappy foods while pregnant.

○ It's going to be harder to get stuff done now that I have a baby.

○ Childbirth can't be enjoyable.

These are just five examples of stories that I've personally decided are NOT my stories this year. I find myself saying out loud multiple times a day 'That's not my story!' These stories below feel better to me.

○ Writing a book with a newborn is so much better because I'm more efficient than I've ever been in my life.

○ Because I'm a conscious human who gives a shit, I love creating income and circulating it in a way that creates the world I want to see.

○ I love nourishing my body with healthy foods while pregnant and I've never felt better

○ I am more productive and effective than ever now I have a baby because every hour spent away from her, I make sure is high performing and worth it.

○ I am so excited to be in labour and to witness how brilliant my body is.

If yourself reading this book thinking 'yeah sounds nice, but what about reality?' Can you see that story in itself? It's just a story that everything has to go for you like it does for others. It's just a story that 'reality' is king. No. Your reality is the stories you're continually telling yourself. The stories you tell yourself, show themselves to you in real life over and over and over again giving you proof.

Be careful not to believe your story, more than you believe in your power to change it.

This is just so important, that's why I had to slot it in right before the book went to print. We have to take more responsibility for our stories and not just lay the big ol' 'easy for some' or 'that must be nice' or 'get real'. What is *real* for you are your stories. Want a different reality? Change your stories.

What stories are you borrowing?

What stories can you choose that are more rewarding?

How can you upgrade your stories so the world knows to respond differently to you?

How do you want life to feel? Do you want some nice surprises to show up? How do you want the trip to Aus next year to go? What kind of mentor do you want to attract? How do you want your relationship to feel? How do you want to feel in your body? How do you want it to feel when you check your bank account? How does it feel when you're pregnant?

Now here's where you change your stories.

There's a bonus section at the end of this book called 'The Script'. It's my ride-or-die, every single day, conscious creation process for setting powerful intentions for my life, no matter where I'm at with 'goals'. It allows you to give life your instruction. It will move you beautifully in the direction you choose and leave room for the details to surprise you. It will also give you a few examples of results from people who use The Script. I use this exercise with everyone I mentor and it's powerful, really powerful. Head there to create your own script once you're done with this book (especially once you're done with the section on money) :)

Celebrate Your Freedom to Fail

Our great privilege (Leading YOU)

Failure is being viewed by our generation of leaders, creatives, and entrepreneurs differently than previous generations. No longer are we bound by the dichotomies of win or lose, do or die, and pass or fail. Failure is not something to be avoided, but is instead something of value. Failure is essential. Failing isn't 'failing' at all. Failing is no different from succeeding, except that it oftentimes comes before success. Failure is the tadpole. Success is the frog. Failure is the caterpillar. Success is the butterfly. Failure is falling. Success is walking. They are both a part of the same process. From here on out, you can see failure and success as one.

We, as a society, give a lot of our attention to success, but stop for a minute and imagine a world without failure. Could you imagine if everything we tried came easy to us the first time or if everything you did you did well—all the time? Could you imagine how absolutely ridiculously boring that would be? Success isn't linear, which is something we've spoken about in previous chapters, and because success isn't linear, neither is failure. This chapter is about changing the way we see failure. It's common to see failure as the end of the road, but what happens when you see failure as just the beginning of the journey—or a step along the way.

> If you don't hit your goal by the time you expected to, did you fail? *No, you made progress toward your goal.*

If your proposal was rejected the first time, did you fail? *No, you now have the opportunity to create something better.*

If you didn't get the deal you were after, did you fail? *No, you are being directed to go after something that is more aligned with your soul.*

If you got negative feedback after giving a keynote, did you fail? *No, you received more information on how to connect deeper with your audience.*

If your company took five years to become profitable, did you fail? *No, you just took a slower journey so that you could learn a lot.*

But what if your company absolutely tanks? Failed, right? *No, You did something bold, risky, and new—all practised qualities that will get your further when you pursue other visions.*

There is so little we would learn if we never failed. For many of us—many of us reading this book—failure is what gives us freedom. The freedom to fail is something to be celebrated. Now, I know that in some countries and cultures, failure is fatal. I am aware that not everyone has the freedom to create a business, a work of art, or pursue their dream. *But you do.* They're in survival mode almost all of the time, and yet many of us have the privilege of being in creative mode, all of the time—never, or hardly ever, having to worry about anything but being in the offensive mode towards our dreams. Your mishaps and mistakes are not the cause of the end of your world. Yes, at times, they may feel like it, but when you begin to treat your freedom to fail as a privilege you will realize the opportunity therein.

> *"When you have your health you have 1000 dreams.*
> *When you don't, you have one."*
> —Proverb

For those of us living in a country where you have the privilege to create every single day and your biggest worry is that you worked a 12-hour day or that you didn't like your pitch deck or that you've got to fire someone tomorrow, then stop, look up, and breathe in. Smell that? That's your freedom to fail. You can fail over and over again, in your creative endeavours, your workouts, your pitches and proposals and how you decorate your bedroom. Everything, all of it, is going toward your lifelong education, which is designed to make you brighter, sharper, stronger, surer, and much more resourceful. Every fail is a gain. Every fail is an experiment.

Yet, so many of us don't begin because of this fear of failure. People can quote all of the cool insty quotes about failure, and can hang out in the most inspiring motivational circles, and talk about how awesome failure is, but they still don't begin because they are terrified to fail. In our privileged part of the world that is the closest thing we can get to failure—not ever beginning.

So, let's see if we can 'fail'.

- ○ Take a moment, and think about that big thing you have been wanting to do, create, build, or try. Now write it down.

- ○ Make a list of all the possible ways you could fail by going for it.

- ○ What are the consequences of you 'failing'?

- ○ Are they really that bad?

- ○ What could you learn if all of these failures happened, but they were really just experiments in disguise?

- ○ Will you die? Probably not, unless you want to free dive off the Grand Canyon.

What if you could be thriving in the thrill of life, feeling closer and closer to success (2.0)? Wouldn't that be better than sitting here and waiting for the possibility of failure to evaporate from planet Earth? News flash: that ain't never gonna happen. Why? Because shit would be wa-ay too boring and success would never taste as sweet.

You will grow and evolve because of your willingness to fail, to suck, to navigate murky waters, and to trust that regardless of what happens, it's all perfect and you are finally, truly, participating in the big game, the most privileged game of all.

What a Privilege

As much as we can rewire ourselves to see failure as freedom, it is equally important to acknowledge the opportunities we have been given, because it's easy to take stuff for granted. We can wake up every day, open our laptops, and create anything we want. Through our laptops we have the ability to connect with billions of people, all the while wearing flannel pajamas and a vintage Mickey Mouse t-shirt. We are always only a few degrees of separation away from anyone we want to connect with. The only thing from stopping us from writing the book—starting the business, making the move, creating the project—is our own resistance.

We have events, books, programs, and self-education that is worth billions at our fingertips. We are surrounded by a world that is more supportive than ever of our creativity, our excellence, our craft, our risks, and our whack-ass ideas. This world has never been more ripe and ready for the big leap you are itching to take for the company you want to create to spark the movement you want to begin that becomes the book you are going to write.

If all we have to do is step up and out to create epic shit, then why do so many of us forget and fall into a little whinge about how hard it all is, how challenging it is to risk it all, how brutal it is to fight for your business and wake up every day and show up for it? And yes, all are valid fears. There are twists and turns and unexpected hurdles, but do you have any idea of how incredibly privileged you are to be here right now?

Louis CK has a standup routine about flying. I fly a lot. Maybe you do, too, and I know that people have forgotten what a freaking miracle it is for us to be able to fly. Louis reminds us of this. What a privilege to fly through the air, in pure comfort, and be able to go—literally—anywhere on Earth. You can just sit up in the sky eating pretzels, scrolling Insty on the WiFi, and look out above the clouds. His whole bit is about how people complain about a 30-minute delay, a $20 bag check, that they have a middle seat, or that there is no more walnut salad.

> "Flying is the worst one because people come back from flights and they tell you their story and it's like a horror story. They act like their flight was like a cattle car in the 40's in Germany. That's how bad they make it sound. They're like "it was the worst day of my life. First of all, we didn't board for 20 minutes and then we get on the plane and they made us sit there on the runway for 40 minutes. *We just had to sit there.*"

> Oh really, what happened next? Did you fly through the air incredibly like a bird? Did you partake in the miracle of human flight? Wow, you're flying! It's amazing! Everybody on every plane should just constantly be going, oh my God, wow (yes) you're flying, you're, you're sitting in a chair in the sky!"

He does the same with people who complain about slow ATMS.

> "What the fuck are you complaining about? You push a button and money comes out of a slot!"

So remember, today is new and exciting and miraculous too. Your opportunity to create absolutely anything is new and exciting and miraculous too. Writing a book, building a company, launching a product, building a brand, starting a not-for-profit, creating a program…. It's all new and exciting and miraculous, too. We're just so damn used to the privilege of the freedom of failure that we've been gifted that we forget we can create anything.

So tomorrow when you suit up (in your mickey mouse tee and ankle socks and whatever underwear you do or don't wear), open your laptop and prepare to unleash your epic-ness onto the world through that keyboard, remember what a privilege. And whatever suckiness enters your day, remember what a privilege. And whenever resistance creeps in and makes you scroll Facebook just as you're heating up and crushing your tasks, remember what a privilege. And when your accountant asks you to look over your statements and you eye roll as if it's as bad as crawling through a barricade of grenades, remember what a privilege. And when your emails pile up and you have a little tanty about yours or someone else's inefficiency, remember what a privilege. And when your program launch is delayed by four weeks and it messes up your entire schedule, remember what a privilege. And when you're lacking motivation and you need to hear those three words that put that fire under your butt, remember this… WHAT A PRIVILEGE.

> *The freedom to fail is liberating, exciting, and powerful. If we can remember that failing is a freedom, we'd begin more things and move forward in the direction of our calling and nudges regardless of anything. In a time where we are spoiled with opportunity, options, choices, and freedom, it's easy to take our focus off the miracle and excitement and newness of each day, but once we can fall in love with the privilege not only to create, but to fail, then everyday becomes the best day ever and we begin to create.*

My little starseed,

You are the most creative expression of the Universe, the most beautiful example and expression of Mother Nature. You are the shiniest of stars and the most wild of souls. You are magic choosing to dance on this Earth in the form of a human body. A beautiful, cute, wonderfully brilliant human in its physical body. This body gives you a mind to work with, thoughts to learn to dance with, emotions to learn to roll with, and oh so many earthly human qualities that make you so divinely messy. Messy is the new perfect. Human and perfect do not fit in the same sentence, baby. In reality, there is no such thing as perfect. There is such a thing as real. You are real.

Never ever cover up a single part of your humanness—not your wildest, scariest thoughts, not your deepest darkest fears, not all the things that seem to contradict each other in your life, nothing. Stuff up. Be confused. Look messy. Love yourself even when you judge others, tell a fib, or do something that isn't 'right'. You are magic in a body, and you don't ever have to pretend to be anything other than that divine fusion. You will never go wrong if you can always remember you are both very human and very magic.

Love Mum. XX

Human AF

Equal parts human and magic (Leading YOU)

Earlier this year, I was replying to the request for an interview for a summit where I was to be a presenter. *Include your title* was on the list things the email was asking of me. Every time I read that, every time I'm asked that, I cringe. "What the hell am I supposed to put?" My face screws up a little and I get all, "Am I a speaker? A self-made millionaire? An entrepreneur? A humanitarian? A mentor? A CEO? Someone who posts deep shit on FB?" I used to joke, "I'm Barefoot Bandit Treehugger with a degree in Badassery." I mean, I was only half-joking, because that has always summed me up more than anything other title I've used, which only seem to highlight what *I do* or what *I've achieved*. Who is going to ask who I am?

So on this day, replying to this email, I did something a little brash. Hey, I was feeling like Cartman, from South Park. *Whateva, whateva, I do what I want. I roll with 12 gangs.* I began my reply with, "My title is Peta Kelly—Human AF. I don't care for titles or long bios where I bang on about my achievements…" A few weeks later, the organization released their schedule of events and next to Jack Canfield, "Multiple New York Times Best Selling Author" and Teal Swan, the well-known figure who writes and teaches about spirituality was Peta Kelly, Human AF. (AF stands for As Fuck for those playing at home).

I was tired of introducing myself publicly—at events and on podcasts—by *what I do* instead of *what I am*, and as it turned out fellow conscious leaders got my intention. Sure, I get titles. People need to know why the heck you're relevant and why on Earth they'd want to listen to you speak for 60 minutes. If you say "I like chocolate ice cream, and me and my Tesla go to bed by 10 p.m. latest," people are going to skip your keynote and go find someone else to listen to—someone who sounds like they have their shit together.

But it felt really good, all the way into my cells good, to introduce myself this time as Human AF. Human AF was what I needed to lead with so that people, even those in the pursuit for all sorts of epic greatness, knew the power of being so beautifully, messily human as fuck. For it is when we can accept and embrace our humanness that we stop trying to be a societal robot or someone who claims to be spiritually superior or that we don't bleed anymore or that we never have a meltdown. I was now here to help people get real.

Human AF isn't just about being authentic. It's not just about posting a photo with messy hair and #therealme. It's not about sharing a teeny bit of struggle on Facebook. "Guys, my creativity is blocked. See, even people like me have tough days." That still has a tone of "I have my shit together." Being Human AF is about being authentic about where we're being inauthentic. Like saying "You know what guys? I've been saying that I'm totally on board this climate change thing. But behind the scenes, I've made zero changes in my life." Cos you're human AF. It's about recognizing the parts of us, thoughts, behaviours, or feelings that are so in opposition of who we think we are, that we barely even admit them to ourselves. Like how you're a spiritually sound lightworker who meditates wearing white in the mornings and practises reiki to heal others, but 10 minutes later pulls the finger at someone who cuts you off on the freeway yelling, "Fuck off dickhead!" Cos you're human AF. And because road rage is real. Human AF is being honest about where we are being hypocritical, where we're saying one thing and practising another, where we're still really struggling ourselves in an area we claim to have nailed. Like being a really powerful health and wellness coach and preaching healthy habits, yet in the evening you still eat 45g of sugar before bed cos you just haven't quite nailed the harmonious relationship with food you're teaching to others. These so called dualities—good vs. bad, positive vs. negative—are not dualities at all. The reiki and the road rage are equal parts magic and human.

So often what I teach is what I most need to learn (always). When I'm teaching and when it's flowing out of me like an effortless water-fall (TAP!), I'm in the magic. And then behind the scenes when I'm putting it all into practice, having little meltdowns and experiencing growing pains just like my students do, I'm the human.

Let's face it, being 'raw and real' is pretty commonplace now. It's 2017 and millennials have the greatest BS detectors of any generation to ever walk this planet—hello divine intolerance.

We must honour all of us and realize the power of our magic is nothing without our messy human-ness.

POP OUT: A Facebook post I did about Human AF

Hi! I'm Peta Kelly and I am Human AF. Can someone please make me up a name tag with that title? I'm not a sage or a guru or a mogul of any kind. Yes, "Human AF," thank you. I'm just your homie, and just like you my super weakness is my super power. I'm human—Human AF.

I teach my tribe about radical productivity, but some days my greatest achievement is keeping less than 13 tabs open at once. Human.

I stand on stage and teach very genuinely about the Voice versus the Noise, but the noise in my own mind is so freaking loud that I'm pretty sure it borrowed some juice from Lance Armstrong. Human.

I'm so particular with what I eat and I ask the waiter 25 questions about the ingredients in food so to stay super duper healthy, but I'll happily eat half a jar of almond butter at around 10pm every night and a whole loaf of banana bread before my period. Human.

I wrote a thesis at 21 and got first class Honours for it, but I've had more than my fair share of benders such as the time I left a nightclub in Berlin at 4pm, without my bra. Human.

I meditate every single day without fail, but I will go from zero to psycho real quick if my camera roll won't scroll at the pace I need it to find that pic from October 2014. Human.

I tell my brother off for being on his phone too much, but I'll spend 45 mins cross-eyed on Instagram filling my head with nothing but 20 screenshots of the most inappropriate memes on the internet. Human.

I've read more personal development books than I've had hot dinners, but I still have absolutely zero patience for dumb questions, slow walkers, and condescending tones. Human.

I earned my first million in entrepreneurship by the age of 26, but I started work at the age of 13 for $5.15 an hour and had more than eight jobs before I graduated high school. I used to hide out the back from my 'cool friends' when they'd come into the Subway where I worked. Human.

I'm excited by my vision and projects and I'm so damn grateful to get to do what I love every day at this age, but some days are so overwhelming and challenging that I mope around the house looking for the naughtiest shit I can find to eat and seriously wonder if running away to the jungle would be easier. Human.

I teach and preach some super deep shit about how to be truly free and how to choose your own thoughts and change your energetic story, but somedays I feel so trapped by some persistent, scary thoughts that I forget everything I teach others to do. Human

I sign every petition I can when it comes to global warming or taking care of our planet, I recycle, compost, eat plant based food, give money to environmental endeavours, buy trees for friends birthday. But I still have plastic wrap in my draw. Human

One day I read my book and think 'omg this is so freaking dope' and the next day I look at in disgust like 'this book is a piece of shit and so boring. I need to start again.' Human

I love my family more than anything, but when they come to stay at my house I feel anxious and turn into a mega nag. Then when they leave, I feel so guilty. Human.

I've studied hypnobirthing, anthropology, I've done a LOT of conscious creation work and scripts around my pregnancy and birth, but some days during pregnancy I still look down at my belly and worry if the baby's heart is still beating. Human.

I love my work so much and I love my tribe SO much. But I'd be lying if I said it was easy for me to stay for 3 hours after an event taking photos. Human.

I take this leadership thing seriously, but also lightly. Our #1 job as we lead in The New Way is to remember, embrace, and talk about our humanness. Our generation is going to make some serious magic together and unite like never before. Fo' realz, homies. One team. We are going to wake up together and see some insane things that will be created by what appear to be Super Humans. I'm looking at you, children under the age of 16.

Yet, regardless of how epic we humans become and how many astronomical things we will create, people will always want to hear about how freaking tough it was to do it, how loud our fears got, how our doubt almost killed us—how we did it despite being a human and because we are a human. Cry. Mess up royally. Fail. Swear. Change your mind a million times. Crap your pants if you have to. It's all just as glorious as if you won a trophy. We are infinite souls connected to an infinite multiverse, and we haven't even scratched the sides of what we're capable. We have been made into humans for a reason.

Perfection is the furthest thing from our purpose. Being human is the most spiritual thing we can do. Because we're in acceptance, we're in the wholeness of who we are. We're not trying to be Buddha. Sure, we can be spiritually inspired and always strive to grow into the most compassionate, loving, light beings we can, but we can't ignore the power of the mess. Owning yourself in totality is more inspiring to the world than the fact you can meditate for 45 minutes without losing focus. How beautiful is it when we can love ourselves despite the fact that sometimes our thoughts and behaviours make us feel like frauds? Are we frauds? Or are we just humans?

Now I'm looking at *you,* homie. Are you trying to relate too much to your tribe through what you do and less of who you are? Are you embarrassed to mess up? Or even to spill your food down your shirt? How have you been trying to be the Dalai Lama or Elon Musk in robot form? Think of who you want to serve, do they want to see you, the human who is infinitely capable of everything and anything, or you the robot who was anointed and appointed with gifts and talents that normal folk just missed out on? What makes you human AF?

We evolve differently to others, but not above them.

Once you've embarked on this personal growth journey, you will begin to hear a lot of things that suggest your own hierarchy. A popular one is "Fuck the haters! They are just blinded by your light!" Sure that can get you riled up, and may even be true, but phrases such as this suggest that some people are better than others. Such as, if you go to a Tony Robbins course and your friends don't go with you, you are the one who is as evolved AF and they are just basic. You probably deserve to borrow the Dalai Llama's robe. *No, you do not.* Notice the ego and judgment laced throughout these sentiments, as if there are "levels" to life.

There are not levels. But, there are fields of alignment and that is what we are going to base our relationships from, because you will find that some people are in yours and some people are not. But now you know that there is not "better" or "less" than in relationship. We are here to shift the paradigm. Everyone is exactly where they are meant to be. Everyone is in their own process, using their own tools to the best of their ability. You have nothing to project, expect, or demand of anyone. But you do have everything to ask of yourself. Choose for you, and you will be living in alignment.

Quick note: Remember when being Human AF to share your wins, your joys and your breakthroughs too. Sometimes we over-obsess with sharing our struggles because they feel more relatable. Humans have so much to celebrate, and our wins are relatable too (and they're inspiring).

> *People connect more with who you are, how you mess up, your hypocritical thoughts, your fears, your struggles, your breakthroughs and your pain. We are humans, and are not meant to be perfect in this life. Our goal here isn't to master everything, but to accept ourselves and love ourselves regardless. That does not mean, don't do the work to become better. Of course not. But realize that even if you spend 45 years with Pema Chodron, and feel like you can levitate out of your shoes, you're still human until you leave, and the world needs people who are Human AF.*

Get Real

Neutrality kills authenticity (Leading US)

Before we even begin this chapter, I want you to reveal yourself? Try it. Just answer these five questions with radical honesty.

1) What keeps you up at night in fear?
2) Who do you compare yourself to?
3) What do you preach about that you have not nailed yet?
4) What's stopping you from creating what you want to create?
5) What gives you the biggest goosebumps?

Reveal Yourself to Me

Because if you want to build a **ride or die tribe** in The New Way, the only way you will be able to do it is to reveal yourself. You might be able to build up to a million social media followers by sharing content and nailing the algorithm, but building a ride or die tribe is friendship, not fanship. It's rich and deep and raw and real. It's Human AF, and there is only one way to build it—reveal yourself.

When you post online, do you post as if you are talking to your friends? If you are the kinda girl that drops the F-bomb at lunch with your best bud, then why are you writing online as if you are the next Shakespeare? You, my friend, are sending a mixed message. You will be attracting the highbrow literary folk when all you want to reach out to is people who are rough and raw, like you. You know, Human AF.

Social media is full of motivators, influencers, inspirers and teachers who have miles of great content to share, but do you want to know how your tribe is going find you? You must go beyond the truth when you speak and write and share with others. Truth is essential, but truth will only take you as far as accuracy can go. To reveal yourself is a new depth. Think about what goes through your head for 90% of your day. So why do you post a run-of-the-mill motivational quote? Why not share with people—in your own words—what tough shit you are really working through today. Or maybe what effortless flow of life you are experiencing throughout your day?

To find your people, you must learn to stop holding back what you really feel. You know, those fiery rants you go on to your husband when you're getting ready for bed, but you're just so lit up you can't hold back a single thing, because he's your man and he's not going to judge you. Well, guess what? The people in your tribe are not going to judge you either. You must make the shift to stop telling others what they need to hear and start showing them who you are. There are no amount of 'likes' in the whole world that matter more than one soul seeing themselves in another soul.

You don't have to "reach out to your tribe," instead let them come to you as you open up who you are.

Move them, don't just impress them.

Have you ever been in the audience and been so impressed by someone's speech, the way the sentences tie together, the words they choose to use, the flow of their narrative, the ease of their stage presence? I sure have. I just love watching these masterful speakers nail the art of presenting. How many times have you left a presentation, be it online or in person, and felt so moved that you had to make a change? I mean, you look back and remember the exact part of the presentation where you felt the shift in your cells and you began to understand something differently. Maybe that even felt invasive or uncomfortable, like that person just reached into your body and changed something, woke something up. Good, they did. It was your truth.

I'm guessing a few of you have experienced this, but the majority of us simply remain impressed by people's work, rather than deeply, soulfully moved. There is absolutely nothing wrong with impressive work, but we are here to move people. You want people to hear you and feel as though they've never felt so understood in their entire life. Impressing people is fun, but there is nothing like moving someone to take action. "For the first time I feel understood" feels deeper than "She is so epic."

Courageous leadership is that it goes beyond where most people are willing to go, whether on stage, on social media, in person, or in a book. Perhaps it's the brother or sister at the wedding, giving a speech right from the ticker, that has everyone feel the depth of their relationship to the point of goosebumps and not just a recited version of "that time the groom got so drunk and pissed his pants." (I went to a wedding like this recently. The brothers speech was a highlight of my year let alone the wedding!)

Or the yoga teacher who begins class by sharing an intense conflict she had over the weekend that upset her and shook her and reminded her that this week she needed to be extra kind to herself and prioritize her practice. She connected with her students more powerfully than even the most powerful OM. Or the Dad who looks their teenager in the eye and shares with them that he felt so bullied and abandoned by his parents growing up, and that sometimes that's why he appears controlling to his kids. Because he just wants to over-do the love so they never feel like he felt. Or the best friend who sent her girlfriend a handwritten letter right before she gives birth, telling her everything she loves about her, how strong and brave she is, and how much her feminine grace inspires all of the females around her.

I'm not here to tell you how to speak, but to show you the difference between 'impressive' and 'moving.' You can move people with any style, and we are moved by people who go deeper, and get more real.

Lisa Nichols has a well-rehearsed keynote she presents called, "I'm just here to stir your soul." Yes, she's nailed it now. It's a rehearsed keynote, but when she does it, she drops in, looks into people's eyes, feels every word and doesn't finish until people are visibly moved. I remember seeing her present it in Vegas before we started working together, and she moved me. So many people in the audience had tears, including her. She cares about mastery when it comes to speaking, but she cares more about moving people.

Then there is someone like Gary Vee, who, to me, is equally as moving. I don't think he's ever rehearsed a keynote in his life. He gets on stage, arms often folded, and sometimes dives right into QandA. His style is very much 'let it rip on what's on my heart and let me show you the passion I have for my work, without covering up a single detail (or a single fuck).' He is seen by some as obnoxious, over the top, and potty-mouthed. But he moves the shit out of me (and I'm sure you can imagine, our styles are a little bit similar). His ability to tell people exactly what is true, without any sugar coating it and without giving any fucks as to whether or not they approve pierces through my body and into my cells like a laser beam. That's why he does it. He wants people to change, he doesn't just want people to say "Gary Vee is the best speaker ever, OMG."

Two very different people with two very different styles, but two people that move people.

Stop Trying to Sound Good

One way I help my students craft presentations and get ready to speak on video or on stage is with these simple words, Stop trying to sound good. Anytime you are trying to sound good or articulate, be smart, look perfect, and speak in a way that the 60-year-old from Seattle will think you're exactly eloquent, you are speaking from your head. I want you to speak from your heart. People did not travel across the world or hit play on YouTube or read your blog post or come to your yoga class that morning to hear from your head. Speak from the heart, connecting heart-to-heart with other souls is what will move people. And it will move you, too.

I've sat in audiences and watched people, very reputable people, read slide after slide, 60-minutes straight from the auto prompter. I zone out. Don't you? Sure, I can listen and hear your words, but there is not a whole lot I feel from you. We do need our heads to speak. Our minds are the guide, keeping us on time, allowing us to access words and memories from our brains to share, but never to filter our heart out to the point where everything we say is a watered down version of what we really mean. Words that 'sound soooo good,' but lack the charge of a truly moving share. And I'm not just speaking of speakers, but anyone who lets it rip on video or hosts their message on Facebook Live.

Your purpose is to move people and help them see things differently, and your teleprompter ain't gonna do it for you. Speak as if the slides got lost, your notebook burned, or the program just crashed. Keep your message directly linked between you and your people. Oh my, what will I say? you're thinking... You're going to say what you know. What you know is in your heart—the exact place you want to be speaking from, because speaking from the heart is the language of The New Way.

Trust me, it's easier to trust yourself over your slides. It's easier to speak about what is true than what you've taken two weeks to prepare. I'm so blessed to have so many people come to me after my presentations to tell me how moved they were, and I can say with all truth and humility that I know why. When I stand on a stage to speak, I'm not trying to sound good. I'm trusting the people in the audience with my heart, and allowing them to feel the depth of what it shares. This connection you can create with someone—especially within a big group—when you stand there and as if to say "Here, see me. All of me," is not just delivering to the audience, but receiving what they are delivering to you. I look at them—not my teleprompter. I stand on stage as a human, who is trusting in her ability to share with them what is real, what is true, and what has never been scripted. They can feel that my main work on stage is not in remembering what I have to say but in connecting with each of them.

Here we can see—nay, feel—how your energy speaks way louder than your words. You say so much with your energy alone. It's just not about the words as much as it's about what you're saying on there with your energy. Have you ever forced a Facebook post? Tried so hard to make it sound epic even when you didn't feel anything at all? But you hit post anyway, only to find that nobody out there is connecting with it. On the flip side, have you ever written a Facebook post that you sat and hammered out, barely any sentence structure but a whole lotta heart and fire, only have to have people comment and say "Wow. How did you know what I was feeling today? I needed this."

When you're standing on stage, writing a post, writing a book, or even just chatting in person, your energy is being received by others' Bullshit Detectors. Each detector out there, being dialed up and up, to determine if the words and phrases you are transmuting are your real message, what your soul wants to share.

A little PK aside:

The Bullshit Detector.

People frequently ask me how I speak so candidly and openly. "I love how raw you are," someone will say. "How do you do that?" I speak the truth that's in my heart—all of the time. Any time I speak from another place, my body reminds me, like an alarm going off that makes me stop and think: Wow, it's hard to get these words out...STOP"

We have a little device, which was gifted to us at birth, that allows us to navigate our consciousness more easily, with less distraction and more clarity. This little device has a knob on the side that controls its effectiveness. This device is called your bullshit detector. Yeah, it's a real thing, and it really works. It's for detecting the degree of authenticity in our words and in our energies. This special device allows us to feel beyond what anyone says, what anyone writes, or what anyone posts on social media by stripping information down to the true and real intention behind what we are reading or seeing. You can think of this bullshit detector as our tool for receiving truth and the Universe, is constantly turning the knob to dial it up every day, every week, and every year as the need for detecting bullshit grows. Some people frequently use theirs, while others, I feel, have tried hard to find that knob and turn it off—because it's easier that way, taking things at face value. Others, like you and me, prefer to be able to read energy beyond that. That's probably why you're reading this book, because you are ready to dial it up, to level up, to go deep, and to get even more real. So why not use that clairsentient gift we've all been given? We all have one, but it's up to each of us if we choose to use it.

I love my bullshit detector. I let the Universe turn it up, and I turn it up myself whenever I can. I use it to help me seek out the intentions behind communication and to determine those words and messages that don't match the intention and truth. However, I do not use this device to bust others on their bullshit. No, I use it on myself. I dial it up and allow it to guide me to communicate as truthfully as I can with others. I dial it up before I speak and write and share—even on social!

Before we continue, let's clarify one thing. This is not a "lie detector," which you can find at your local police station. This is a Bullshit Detector and lies are far less complex than bullshit. When I ask, "Are you BSing me?" I'm really asking "Are you sharing all of your truth?" If you're holding back, that's BS. That's what this device is can detect.

◇◇◇

In this new era of evolution and awakened consciousness, more and more people can tell what we truly mean. Why? Cos we need to be able to. It's an evolutionary requirement. We're exposed to so much more information than any generation ever before us. Think about it.. all the podcasts, TV shows, documentaries, live events, FB lives, social media feeds. In any one minute we can scroll through hundreds of people's daily messages, and unless we can choose what we accept and what we don't, we drown in it. Information is everywhere and we need some sort of new equipment that allows us to sift through it and decide what we pay attention to. This information overload signals a requirement that we go deeper in order to engage and understand each other, and we must go deeper to speak beyond superficial conversations. Time to get real.

There are no variances in real-ness. It's real or it's not. It's true or it's false. It's black or it's white, and I have learned that I prefer not to dabble in the grey. A few years ago, when I began to understand what the power of speaking was all about—and I'm not talking just on stage but in print, in person, and online—I took the lid off. I began to let it all out. Because that is what The New Way commands us to do. Get the megaphone out, and yell "Get Real!" with me. We are the generation who is here to share it all authentically, because authenticity is the only language of the generation whose Bullshit Detectors are tuned up every day.

POP OUT: 5 Keys to speaking on stage powerfully.

1. Practise letting rip. If you need to practise on your own just pressing record on a video and going for it, do it. Practise letting the channel open and speaking from your heart and not your head. You want to be able to speak whenever, wherever, at any time of day with no notes, and guess what? You can if you don't try to over curate what your heart already has nailed. Sure, we want to master keynotes and be a responsible speaker who stays on task. TED talks have a specific time limit and so do most speaking gigs, I get that. But you want to approach every 'speech' with 100% trust that you're fine even if your mind blanks. This is why practising just 'letting rip' on FB live is so good. Cos you can't edit it.

2. Trust. This is the most important element of any form of public speaking ever. Trust that what you're called to share is what people need to hear. Trust that what you know in your heart is legit. Trust that you can't fuck it up if you simply share what is real for you. Trust that when you open up and realise you're the messenger and not the message, you will have words flow through you perhaps you've never heard before. Trust also that your heart won't ever say anything that is not exactly what the people watching need to see/hear.

3. Speak only on what is true and hot for you. The hack for powerful speaking is speaking on what you KNOW. You're an expert on your own life and what is real for you. Even if the slides turn off, and your mind blanks, you know everything you need to know to share powerfully. Remind yourself of that.

4. Craft 5 key points that structure your presentation and leave room for letting your heart speak. This is how I structure keynotes. I create the 'heart beats' of my presentations, and write down some relevant stories and points I need to hit within each. But the rest of it, is what I know for real in my heart. And I wouldn't speak on anything that isn't real in my heart.

5. It's more about the transmission than the photo of you on stage. Your #1 job whenever you're speaking on stage is to transmit something beneficial to the people who are trusting you. Remember this is the #1 job, before getting the photo of it for Insty ;)

Specific is Terrific

So how are you going hit your people? Get raw. Go three layers deeper than you'd planned. Get personal, maybe so specific that only a few people will relate, but those who do are like, "Holy shit, is she in my head?" How about the stuff that makes your stomach bottom out when you hit *post*, but your soul is grinning ear-to-ear, saying "That's the only way, baby!" When you reveal yourself you jump off your high horse and onto the ground, yelling "I am Human AF!"

Once you reveal yourself, you will realize that a tribe is not a triangle with someone sitting up the top preaching down to the masses. It's a circle of people who are all contributing to each other's journey as equal humans, regardless of who teaches. Revealing yourself isn't about the people who are not going to vibe with you. It's about the people who will. When I started speaking in the language of what I really felt about business—as in referring to my business as my chief entity, my boss a spiritual being—I attracted a soul sister who felt more like home, more than most anyone had in my life. She feels like my twin. We can talk for hours about anything and everything, and that talk is going on at the depths of our cells. Now, we're collaborating on big, magic projects that were only able to be born by us together, not by us apart.

I used to think speaking of my business as an entity was too out there for most on social media, but it was just too out there for most people, and I wasn't trying to connect with most people. In fact, I was speaking and posting in the exact language of the people I wanted to attract. And thank God I stopped watering it down, because I was finally starting to reach them.

Courageous and conscious leadership demands we speak and share from the deepest parts, the parts that make us shake when we hit post, the parts that make us feel like we need to take a nap after our share—however vast or intimate our audience—because we just lifted so much energy in the form of truth from our cells that we'd been carrying and keeping to ourselves.

It's the time of radical authenticity. All hail the realest realist.

So, who is it that you want to reach/attract/impact? What would make them stop scrolling and say, "OMG, I know her!" It's time to make the soul connection. What details, specifics, and realness could you share that would land on your person but perhaps not the other 6.9 billion?

What gives you goosebumps? What do you care most about? What are you growing through right now? What are you reading and which parts tug on your soul? What scares you? What are your guilty pleasures? What is the dialogue in your head that makes you human AF?

Last Wednesday I went to a new spin class. The lovely, very polite, instructor started the class with, "Okay, let's do this shit!! Are explicit lyrics ok?"

I smirked. One of those smirks that says "Ma girl! Yes, ma'am! Biggie for the hill climb please!!!"

That whole spin class I was thinking about what made me smirk. Was it the fact that she swore? Was it her energy? Was it just that she didn't give a fuck? I smirked because that one thing she said at the beginning of the spin class made me feel at home. From that one question I recognized her insides, because some part of them were like mine. I feel home when classy, smart, genuinely kind people swear. You know when people have a big vocabulary but they choose the f*bomb anyway? I just get those people. They're my people. My language is one of not holding back at all. It's one of truth and love and fire. When others talk like that too, I feel… home.

Your *home*-ies are everywhere. They'll find you when you make them feel it, but your homies can't find you if you're curating everything you say to please Betty, your Mum's friend who thinks posting photos in your bathers is skanky. Your homies won't find you if you edit your beautiful, transparent Facebook post 456 times to make sure you're not going to offend Jeffrey in Alabama, who literally gets offended by everything anyway—all the time.

Ready to dial in and dial it up and lose some followers? Good! Now you can finally speak in a way that allows your homies to feel at home.

Shed the layers of superficial shares, stop trying to impress, to "be kosher" and "copasetic," and scrap the crazy, constant pursuit of sounding like Tony Robbins or Deepak Chopra. Drop from your noggin down into your heart and speak from that place. Reveal yourself, and you become a magnet for your tribe. Our bullshit detectors are working at an all-time efficiency right now, so tell me something that is going to hit every nerve in my body that general motivational lingo doesn't hit anymore.

POP OUT: Love Letter to my Home-ies. An example from my facebook.

My homie,

I call you homie, not cos we grew up in the same street and used to egg houses in our hoodies together back in the 90's, cos we didn't (I did). I've probably never even seen you in the flesh. You're my homie cos we find home in the same thoughts, cares, struggles, excitements and things that give us big fat goosies. People used to tell me that writing, speaking and creating specifically for a specific person meant that I was excluding people. But I knew that if I tried to please, serve and impress every man and their dog, I'd exclude the person who I'm actually here to serve—You.

When I film a video or write a big heart felt FB/ insty post, or when I sit down to write my book every morning, I'm not thinking of the masses. Oh what an energetic shit storm that would be. I'm thinking specifically about YOU (I know, creepy).

I just so get you.

You're watching Abraham Hicks one minute and then screenshotting the most inappropriate memes in the world the next. You're not offended by swear words and actually feel quite at home around a good ol' F bomb cos freedom and radical authenticity are two of your highest values. You know that being a good freaking human is more important than sounding like a rose petal. You get goosebumps when you see jeaniius in someone—that 'divine thing' flowing through like when MJ moves his feet or when someone lets rip on their vision, or when you see rad conscious enterprises being created by your homies.

You're energetically sensitive, have a solid BS detector and feel really awkward around fakeness, inauthenticity and sucking up. You feel before you see and hear. You don't wanna earn a lot of money so you can wear a huge gold chain with a $ sign on the bottom. But you DO know you're not wrong or greedy for wanting to create the money you need to do what you're called to do. You get frustrated by the size of the gap between your BIG ASS vision as it appears in your head, and where it is in the physical world right now. You get so caught up in step 5 rather than just beginning at step 1 and overthinking almost always stops you from starting in the first place.

You're not into religious separation. You love and respect ALL for their beliefs and don't wrong those who don't justify Source/God/the Universe differently than you do. You know that there are a million ways to Rome, but it doesn't change Rome (Rome is love).

You love investing in yourself and froth on the feeling of a solid event, a cell changing book, or a juicy FB live. But you've become desensitized by the same ol' motivational material and aren't moved by anything but DEPTH and REALNESS and 'omg I can't believe they shared that.'

You're equal parts Deepak and Tupac. You'll read some Marianne or Eckhart in the morn then drive to a cafe to work playing 'Bump bump bump' by B2K. You love your baddassery, you love play. You don't want life, business and personal development to be so serious all the time. You love the fun feelz and you totally get me when I use Z on the end of my words sometimes cos it reminds you of the glory dayzzz ;)

You're a massive introvert but not in the way the dictionary describes. You refuel on your own and need your own space, but you THRIVE on being part of a tribe of togetherness, collaboration and TEAM and would always rather combine magical powers than hoard and go alone. You're conscious and aware, but not on a high horse about it. You're Human AF and love being Human AF cos you're messy, weird and sometimes contradictory—but finding out that is totally OK was one of the biggest breaths out you ever took. You feel a deep responsibility for your work in this world and that is your greatest strength and weakness at the same time. You're rough around the edges and have a divinely intolerant attitude built into your cells with a bonus 'b-rules' (BS rules) repellant. You question what doesn't make sense, always.

So when I use the word 'my homie', now you know. I'm writing from the place in me that's 'home' to the place in you that's 'home'.

I'm not here to change the world, I'm just here to change my world. I'm not here to serve everyone, I'm just here to serve some. I don't wanna impress the masses, I'd rather really move a few.

I get up everyday to make stuff, write stuff, and serve my homie and I know there's at least a million of my homies out there. That's how I change 'my world'.

Love you, my freaking stud of a homie. X

X

I want to share some of comments—just to give you an idea of what you're capable of when you get specific.

—Girl !! Yes ! This is why flying to Sydney for your event after only following you on fb for like a month did not feel all that crazy to me. So fucking happy to have found you and the tribe.

—Sheeetzzzz. Just took one BIG OI' breath out. For the FIRST time I feel a depth of a total understood in the big heart felt words without me explaining a single WORD. How in the world is that even possible!?! You just so freakin' get it. It feels like home when someone is also feeling it too and recognized all that.. Love you loooooong time homie. you knew.

—Absolutely made my day, and goosebumps all over.

—OH MY GOSH—when you speak I feel ageless and relate to every single word I just drink this so thank you so much!!!

—How do you always know?!

—You get me! ❤ Thanks for speaking my language!

—Peta my homie! We are so connected that I shiver when I read your posts! Keep creating for you, for us and don't do it for the masses.

—YASSSSS! Home slice all day every day. The home in me honors the home in you!

—Holy Shit soul sista...you are really are writing to me! Keep doing what you are doing ... thank you for shining your light

—WTF????? Was that written to me, for me? I felt every word. Peta Kelly you are amazing, these words will not go to waste... I get it! Thank you very much!!! I have tears in my eyes!!!

Notice their language. Notice how free they feel to speak in their language to me.

Notice how much they appreciate me getting to know them and speaking to them. Notice how much they use the word "home." Home. That's what you want to create for people and your tribe—the feeling of home.

POP OUT: Some tips for when people are nasty online.

There's a difference between speaking your truth, and just being a dickhead and disguising it as 'speaking my truth'. In this new era where we're all spilling our guts out online, it's important to know the difference.

The truth is, people are being dickheads online. Let's just say it how it is. Just yesterday a friend texted me to ask for advice after seeing over 20,000 hateful comments on a really beautiful post he made. I looked at it and wanted to vomit. My heart sank for him. I won't share examples of the comments because I don't want them or their energies in this book. I've had several occasions where I've woken up to threads of nasty comments, mostly by people who don't have a real profile photo. Of course, right? It's easy to be awful when you're hiding behind a lego character profile photo and a fake name.

The saddest part is online bullying is a real issue, and it's happening to children and adults all over the world, sometimes to a fatal degree. We all have different truths, and our truths are true to us, and the truth is, when people comment mean shit online when you're sharing your truth, it hurts. TRUTH. Words project such powerful energies even through a screen. And when we're showing up courageously online in order to reveal ourselves and impact others, chances are the feedback isn't always going to be 'you go girl!'.

I doubt if you're reading this book, I need to tell you not to be a dickhead online. But just in case, Hey, don't be a dickhead online. Debate all you want, disagree all you want, but don't be mean. Disagreeing and productive debate, that's one story. Hurtful, hateful comments, that's another.

Now, for those of you who are leading online, sharing parts of yourself, truths and beliefs that leave you open to criticism and debates that can get out of hand. Here are eight tips that I've found to be helpful. Just put them in your tool box.

<u>1. Take a minute to just get rational for a minute.</u>

Is it likely that everyone will agree with you?

Is it ok that everyone does not?

How boring would it be if everyone did?

Have all of the most courageous leaders on Earth been ridiculed at some point ? (YES!)

How freeing does it feel to be in your truth no matter what?

Who are you really here to serve? How can you focus on them more?

What is this contrast teaching you?

What are the gifts of this?

<u>2. Don't feel you need to reply to everyone.</u>

If you created a debate, it's one thing. But if a feeding frenzy started on your post, that's another. Just because you're invited into crazy energies online, it doesn't mean you need to go.

Remember just because others have the time and energy to sit at their computer tapping away at strangers, it doesn't mean you do.

Is this the most rewarding place for your energy to go?

Would you rather be dancing? Reading? Surfing?

If you do feel genuinely called to reply (i.e., it's an open conversation and discussion and not a nasty feeding frenzy), then do so. But trust your gut and don't ever feel obliged.

If it's an important conversation that you opened, remember sometimes it's most in alignment for you to stay in it and move through it. Just check in with yourself.

3. Send love, for reals. If someone is being a flat out nasty prick, don't stoop, send genuine love.

I feel it sounds condescending sometimes when you see a spiritual type person write online 'sending you love cos obviously you need it'. I cringe, cos it seems sometimes like a back-handed 'well get on my conscious high vibing level you unconscious loser'. That's anything but conscious leadership. So when I say 'send love', what I mean is quietly, in your own way, with genuine intention, send them some love. Don't just write it, send it. I often sit with my hand on my heart and say "May (Insert name of people or peoples) experience happiness and the root of happiness" about 10 times. I got that from Pema Chodron. It opens my heart and helps me be in the compassion for the other person/s and not in the judgement or rage. 10 deep breaths helps too.

4. Shut the laptop and phone off—in a few days it will clear up.

Sometimes we feel so indebted to our phones and laptops and forget that real life is not out there, but in here (*taps chest*). Feel ok with taking a little 'holiday' from the web if you have a little experience that takes up too much of your energy and has you feeling like you need to sit and monitor your FB all day long.

5. Tell someone you know how their comment/s make you feel.

A lot of the time I wouldn't do this, I'd just lash out at how ignorant and mean they were. Now, if ever I am feeling bothered by anything on social media, I just tell my husband or my mum or a friend how it makes me feel. This way I can get the debris off my cells and not carry it around. Cos when I do this, I'm at risk of writing a passively aggressive post. I'll say "It hurt. How could they be so fucking mean to another woman? I feel totally misunderstood. I feel like sometimes it's easier not to speak up. I just wanna live in a jungle in Bali off the grid." Just get it off your cells in a way where you're not trying to figure them out and make a psycho analysis on why you felt they were so nasty.

6. Remember that a lot of the time, you are talking German to someone talking Spanish.

Metaphorically. Or you are talking Lithuanian to someone talking Egyptian. A lot of the time, you aren't on the same wave length at all and your words and energy will sound like gibberish to them. You don't have to defend or justify anything and sometimes, that's actually impossible.

7. Keep standing in your light and your truth.

This doesn't mean you need to get all crazy bold that you scream your truth in people's face. It just means, choose your alignment, rather than choosing to wish others would 'get it'. Regardless of who says what, your truth and your light are unarguable.

8. Accept that everyone is living from their own experience and frequency, instead of wanting to agree.

Accepting that everyone is at their own place of evolution is so much more freeing than wishing everyone was on your page. Use these little stings as more motivation to stand even more in your light and attract more of the people you REALLY want to serve. Contrast can make us so much bolder in our vision, and shed so much clarity on what we're really for in this world.

Your JEANIIUS

Your Soul's genius, your Soul's purpose (Leading US).

What you get if you put your passion, purpose, gifts, and genius into a smoothie?

Jeaniius: your secret spiritual sig-nature); your soul's genius; your unique gifts that aren't necessarily intellectual

Have you ever watched Michael Jackson dance and felt like you were going to cry? If you're anything like me, the answer is yes. When I watch his feet move and his body glide, I can hear the lyrics of his art. My whole body, all of my cells and my soul are moved by something far greater than his sparkly sequined jacket. How about watching Elon Musk unveil a new Tesla model? I'm covered in goosebumps when I watch him speak about the environment and his vision for sustainable transport. I am so in awe of his—what seems like effortless connection—to huge, groundbreaking work. Sure, I'm obsessed with the planet and Teslas, but my whole body is moved by something else. How about those X-Factor videos on Facebook, where the 12 year-old girl belts out Andrea Bocelli at the top of her lungs, and your whole body shakes from head to toe? I'm mesmerized by her voice and her talent, but it's something else that makes my soul smile so big that I feel like I need a new body to fit it. There's even the everyday person—the accountant, the teacher, the mother, the barista—who is so freaking good at what they do and is so lit up by the service they provide that it's infectious. These are the people that inspire something in you that goes far beyond

146

the work they do for the world. What is that thing, that invisible thing that moves and inspires you when you see it in someone else?

That, my friend, is their jeaniius, and they've realized what it is, learned how to live in it, and are now gifting the world with something remarkably magic. Be it dance, technology, or just the way they live. You too have a jeaniius. It's your secret spiritual signature. It's a specific, intelligent, 'limited edition' gift that was placed into your DNA as part of your primary equipment for your time here. It's a present that is intended for the entire world, but it's placed inside of *you*. You're the only person who can unwrap it. You're the only person who can make sure the world gets your gift. Nobody else has this special code, but you.

Unknowingly, for the last few years, I've been studying the concept of spiritual signature or as I call it, 'jeaniius'—the soul's genius or the soul's purpose. I never vibed with the word *passion*. I liked fire better. *Purpose* felt too heavy, like it was something we needed to dig up and find or we were just huge failures. *Gifted?* That didn't feel right. How could some people be gifted and others not? Everyone is. *Genius* was loaded with expectations—nerdy glasses, Guinness World Records, and successful Rubix Cube completions. To me, all humans are nakedly brilliant, capable beyond measure—whether on a big scale or small scale, whether quietly behind the scenes or up on stage.

So I was on the hunt to redefine passion, purpose, gifts, and genius, and this one word found me. When someone can speak on stage effortlessly and pierce souls with their energy, jeaniius. When someone can create music as easily brushing their teeth, jeaniius. When someone can pour words out on a page as easily as water into a glass, jeaniius. But just as much as jeaniius can be a specific 'what' like dancing, writing, counselling or soccer, it doesn't have to be. Your jeaniius is all your very own. You cannot compare jeaniius. It's theirs. Find yours.

Are you gifted?

It has always has bothered me when people say things like, "Oh, well, John is just gifted." Or "Sarah is soooo lucky." Or "Janna is just born that way." I don't believe any of it! There are no gifted and un-gifted people in this world, because everyone on Earth is gifted. The trouble is that most people have been looking under the wrong Christmas tree to find their gifts. Everyone on Earth is gifted with their jeaniius. *Including you!* And if we can acknowledge that everyone has a jeaniius, then we'd be living in a world full of real superheroes, people who are plugged into their cosmic destiny and divine purpose. All people would be living in a high vibration of alignment, and that is what this planet needs more than anything.

> *"We have reached the point where our role as spiritual tourists here on Earth is history. We have now shifted into the fulfillment of our cosmic destiny."*
> —Unknown

The simple act of discovering your jeaniius makes you a superhero. You will drop the chase, drop the comparison, and learn to go inward to listen to what is calling you to a higher vibration, and it's your higher vibration that Earth most wants.

The Elements of Your Jeaniius

The Elements of Jeaniius

Grab your journal for this part.

Understand: The Source and The Force

> "There's an external broadcast always happening and we're here to tune in, to listen to it, and then be its expression"
> —Michael Bernard Beckwith

The first element, of the anatomy of your **jeaniius** is *understanding* where it comes from and what it is. It's a force that comes from Source. (You can say it as a rap, OG style if you're feeling spicy.) Jeaniius comes from the same infinite library of goodness that your tap pours from, and before you were born your jeaniius was placed into your DNA, right alongside divine intolerance, in the form of a secret spiritual signature where it lives, nudging you, hinting at you, and throwing you subtle and not so subtle clues until you can recognize it as the gift that it is for both you and the world. Every person is born with a jeaniius, so don't go thinking there was a cosmic mishap and Source just missed you. You may not recognize yours yet, but it's there. Chances are you've spent a lot of time admiring others' jeaniius and not ever once thinking to look inside to find your own.

It is easy for us to recognize jeaniius in others, so let's start with that. Once you learn how to recognize it in others, your own jeaniius will become more familiar to you.

Answer the following questions to help you get a taste for jeaniius. Smell it, feel it, see it, notice it. There is nothing more beautiful than walking around with jeaniius goggles on, looking for divine brilliance and creative sparkle in everyone (including you, homie).

1. Who do you watch 'do their thing' and think to yourself, 'wow they are so in their element' or 'that's exactly what they're here to do.'

2. Think about people in your life who are so naturally good at things and you've always noticed it. Maybe you've said

things to them like, "You love it so much, you should make a business out of it."

3.   What do you notice in people who are doing *their thing*? Are they calm? Is their energy high? Does it feel like they're channeling something? Does it give you goosebumps?

4.   How does it make you feel when you see someone like MJ gliding around the floor as if his sequin slippers are made of God? Who are some other people (famous or not) who move you like MJ moves me when he moves?

When you can notice Jeaniius in others (whether they're famous for their art, your sister, the accountant at work or the guy next door), you can start to notice it in yourself.

Listen: for Clues and Communication

> *"Let yourself be silently drawn by the strange pull of what you really love. It will not lead you astray "*
> —Rumi

Listening is the next element. Listening is when you start to notice the subtle, and not so subtle, clues that are flowing through your tap, which reveal your secret spiritual signature. One thing I want you to listen for is your ideas and your nudges so you can begin to form a ride-or-die relationship with your intuition, your downloads and insights. What is your relationship with your ideas like? Do you look at each one like it's crazy and brush it off? Do you embrace each one and spend some time imagining? Do you listen for new ones? Sometimes the most powerful and accurate guidance for you is the most subtle. That rush of excitement that goes through your body every time you think about starting this new not-for profit or quitting your job or moving to France might seem subtle and fleeting. "Excited, so what?" we say and get back to the grind. But, *NO!* Excitement is never "so what." Little butterflies of excitement are text messages from the cosmos suggesting to you, "go there, do that, start this…"

I encourage you to spend more time listening. You can get quiet in nature, sit in meditation, flow with some yoga, or anything that allows you to get into your body and out of your head. Then you can listen. I want you to imagine yourself as a jeaniius detective, noticing and appreciating the big and small notes from the Universe sent especially for you to help you expand into your divine, expansive, brilliance.

1.   What are some of the consistent and persistent ideas that visit you that perhaps you've been ignoring?

2.   What are some thoughts that consistently excite you? Perhaps the thought of starting a project, signing up for a class, or leaving to move to a more high vibe, creative city.

3.   Where and when do your ideas and moments of clarity and 'uh huh!' most visit you? Is it the shower, when you're hiking, in a spin class, yoga?

4.   What do you do with your ideas and 'clues' when they come? Do they feel safe to keep coming or do they feel often ignored?

Recognize: the Clarity

"One of the oldest and most generous tricks the Universe plays on human beings is to bury strange jewels within us all, then stand back to see if we can ever find them. To hunt to uncover those jewels, that's creative living."

—Elizabeth Gilbert

Recognizing is the element where we move from 'listening' to more specific awareness, where we start to pinpoint more specific things we do and parts of our lives that could be getting us closer to our jeaniius. First begin with the clues. Seek out the things that come naturally, that increase your energy, that create a buzz in your cells, that you wouldn't care if you got paid to do or not. Recognise also that these invisible nudges are all the evidence you need. Often nudges and clues are so clear to us, but we don't let them be clear.

We know the answers, but we shun them because we think 'oh it couldn't be that easy to discover'. Let the clues become clarity.

1. What do you do that makes your energy go up? After you do it, you just feel so lit up and on another plane, like you are *alive*.

2. What do you do that feels most natural to you? Perhaps people have said to you 'It's just your gift'. Or perhaps you've simply felt it.

3. What do you do that makes time stand still? You get so lost in it that time doesn't matter at all?

4. What could you stand up and talk about on stage with no notes and no preparation? Just you and your pure fire for it.

Choose: Courage

> *"Always leave enough time in your life to do something that makes you happy, satisfied, even joyous. That has more of an effect on economic well-being than any other single factor."*
>
> —Paul Hawken

This is when you *choose* to move in the direction of your jeaniius. Whether it's on a small scale or a big scale and comes with a giant leap. Whether it's rearranging your calendar to include more of the things that get you excited—like an art class on Saturdays or a Spanish tapas class on Tuesdays—or whether it's beginning the startup that's been on your mind for a decade. Making the choice to live in a vibration that is better and higher, is the goal here. When we choose our jeaniius, we are choosing courage over feeling like a fraud, getting it wrong, appearing irresponsible, or relying on logistics.

Ready to choose?

1. If you had just 5% more courage, what would you choose to do? Go nuts here.

2. What are the most common fears you have around doing things you feel excited to do, but don't do?

3. What are your first thoughts or feelings when you think about pursuing what *could be your jeaniius?* Perhaps starting the company, writing the book, tutoring, starting a band, travelling to volunteer as a nurse. Get specific.

4. What would you choose if you could choose differently?

Live: In Your Zone

"You don't need more hours, you just need to decide."
—Seth Godin

What you do each day matters, because what you do each day turns into what you do each week, which turns into what you do each month, which turns into what you do each year, which turns into your *life.* How you spend your days is how you spend your life. This element is about rearranging your life so you have more time to be in your tap, and your zone of jeaniius. The people who inspire you the most in the world probably have solid boundaries around their time and energy. What we do each day adds up to what we do each week, adds up to what we do each month, adds up to what we do each year, what we do each year soon adds up to reveal our whole, freaking life.

Think of your schedule like a cake. Some ingredients make you feel energised, healthy and alive. Some ingredients make you feel nauseous, heavy and tired. Some ingredients don't allow you to live in your zone of jeaniius. You want to bake a cake (schedule) that feels amazing, tastes delicious and allows you to operate at your optimum.

1) What ingredients (activities and commitments) in your cake (schedule):
    ○ Make you feel tired or heavy?
    ○ Are made purely out of obligation or guilt?
    ○ Will you be relieved to remove from your calendar?

2) Can you remove them? Will you remove them? When?

3) What ingredients (activities and commitments) would you like to add that:
   - ○ Excite you the most right now?
   - ○ Make your energy go up and feel most alive?
   - ○ You love to do but don't have time for?

4) Can you add them? Will you add them? When?

5) What are the possibilities for me if I remove what's not rewarding for me and add what is?

Start small. If you want one or two evenings a week free to go Salsa Dancing, or to do a sewing course, or to learn a language, remove something. Remember, living in alignment takes courage and it's not always easy to say no, to cancel or to quit things that aren't rewarding for you anymore. But to live in your thriving, juicy, expansive zone of jeaniius, you have to. Remind yourself of question #5 above.

Master: Commitment to Practice

"No one can arrive from being talented alone, work transforms talent into genius."

—Anna Pavlova

Michael Jackson spent more time in rehearsals than most people would ever be prepared to. Steve Jobs worked on computers day in and day out until he was basically a computer. Tony Hawk didn't just wake up one day the best skateboarder in the world—he recognized his gifts and went to work to master them. Your jeaniius requires masterful attention to be fully unlocked, and *mastery* is about committing to practice. You must learn to spend more time on your jeaniius than you do on irrelevant stuff that has no real reward.

We've all heard the importance of delegating. Masters do this because they want to channel more of their energy into their jeaniius. So, does your jeaniius require you get some extra lessons? Read some extra books? Take a class? Study some people in the same field? Practise it more?

Now, the questions:

1. Who do you consider to be masterful at their craft?

2. What skills, talents or natural abilities of yours do you want to master?

3. What resources are available to you? Courses, events, mentors and don't forget, your own invested time.

4. People underestimate what they can do in ten years, and overestimate what they can do in one. What's possible for you in the next ten years if you focus more on your jeaniius and less on obligations and commitments that have no real reward?

The Gift: of Beginning

Think of all of the people you admire most in the world. Is it Pierce Brosnan (that may be my slightly biased silver fox crush speaking)? The Beatles? A sporting star of some kind? Mother Teresa? Martin Luther King? Michael Phelps? How about Rosa Parks? John Lennon? Tupac? Your Third Grade teacher? Your dad?

Whoever it is, take a moment with me. *Pause,* and imagine the journey that they had to take to get to the point where they have made such a profound impact on *your life.* The persistence, the courage, the application of talents, the radical boundaries they had to set around their time and energy. Each one of them has gone as far as they could with their jeaniius so they could gift it to you. They had to listen, recognize, choose courageously, create their life around it, master it, and then gift it to you. You have your own. Your jeaniius may just extend to gifting it in some way to your local community. It may extend to gifting it in a book or a play or anything at all a bit beyond that. It may extend to your family. It may extend as far as Earl Nightingale's or Arnold Palmer's. How far you take it is 100% up to you, and there is no right or wrong.

When you can recognize the pure gift that other people's jeaniius is to you, then you have a little more ammo to follow the steps in this chapter and focus your energy on gifting yours to the world too.

1. If you were told you had a year to live, what would you 100% have to leave with the world before you left? There is nothing like mortality to remind us of the preciousness of our time and energy.

2. How can you immediately go to work to begin, regardless of whether or not all of the steps are clear?

3. Who would miss your gifts if you didn't gift them?

4. What is possible for you if you do choose to unwrap your jeaniius? Please do. This isn't a question, just a request from one superhero to another.

Our generation is the generation high on the word 'purpose'. We are sometimes so desperado to find 'that thing' we're meant to be doing. We strive to find our specific purpose, without realising that we're living it everyday. Your jeaniius doesn't have to be a thing. It can be a *way*. You lace your soul purpose, your jeaniius through everything you do—like how you dress, what you post, all the different things you create, who you collaborate with, what you attend, how you eat. You can have several 'purpose babies' that shoot out as a result of you knowing how you want to live to make your soul feel alive.

Jeaniius isn't like genius, in being purely intellectual. Jeaniius isn't simply your passion or your purpose. Your jeaniius is your secret spiritual signature, placed in your DNA very specifically so that you could go on the thrilling journey of finding it, unwrapping it, and sharing it with this planet. It isn't a chore, or a job, or a heavy responsibility. It's a gift from Source that recognizes you as a unique, badass superhero with gifts hidden inside of you to gift to yourself, your family, your community and in some cases the whole world. Your jeaniius is a key to your lightness, your play, your enjoyment and to your higher vibration. It's just as much a gift for you as it is for others.

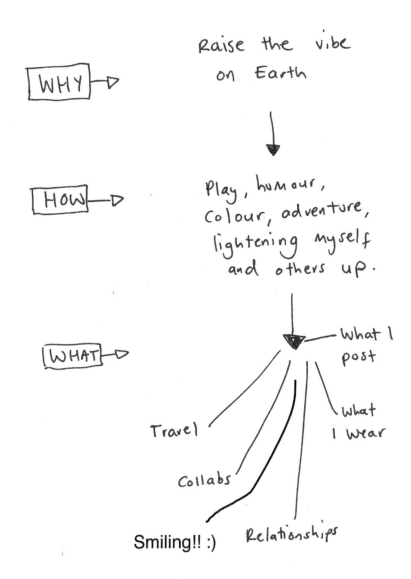

Working With Your Vision

How to work with the ideas, projects, movements and companies that want to be born through you. (Leading the WORLD)

I want you to know something straight up. These visions you see so clearly—the possibilities you see for our planet and for the people around you, the business of the future that's already complete in your head—are visions that chose you. The vision came to you the human and said, "Here I am. I am the future. I know that *you* are the human to bring me to life here on Earth." Just imagine getting naked for your beloved for the first time. *That* is what your vision did for you and what it does every day. It doesn't go around just getting naked for anyone. It finds a human it trusts, and shows itself to them. It doesn't just do it for fun, like on snapchat, where you can send a nude and then 10 seconds later it disappears. Visions show themselves to humans because they need to be made real, built, and shared with the world in a way only a human can.

And about you? You are absolutely more than capable of sharing this vision—the one that came to you—with the world. The vision knows. If you weren't, then it would have chosen to get naked in front of someone else instead. What you see is not a mistake, it's what you are guided to do and to build. It's a divine connection between you and an entity. It's you and a being you are going to bring to life, so the world needs you to nod *Yes*, and accept the divinity of this new partnership and gift it to all. Because let's get another thing straight.

This vision is not yours, it's the world's, but it chose you to bring it forth.

"Shall we change our little piece of the world together?" That's all your vision wants from you— love, support, and action.

Bringing Your Vision To Life

All you can do is stare at that giant gap, that metaphorical chasm, between what you can see in your vision—be it your business, your brand, your band, your project, your family, your community, your book, your world—and what you are living now. Yet, every time you see your vision, your tummy drops. You get so excited about it as if it's already a reality, because to you it is. It's *sooooo* good you want to jump on Facebook and launch a business FB page for it immediately. You fire up Wix and start building your website. You text your husband, your BF, your girls, your mum, and to say, "I'm writing a book!" "I'm building a company!" "I'm starting a non-profit!" "I'm moving to Hawaii!" "I have the best idea ever!!!" This raging excitement takes over your entire body, and all you can think and feel is *OMG This. Is. It.* You get moving on it fueled by all the enthusiasm in the entire world. As a human, you get to work to make it *real*. You start mapping, planning, organizing, sketching, researching, and writing down all your thoughts on the subject. Days go by, weeks go by, months… you've now jumped over more hurdles than you can count. You've been struck by more entrepreneurial challenges than you think is normal, and you begin to wonder… *Was that vision even real? Is this even realistic?* You can no longer see it so clearly, the building of the studio, the website, the brand, the enterprise, the book. Frustration creeps in and your life just can't keep up with your vision. *What was I thinking anyway? I was tricked by a dumb idea.* So you go back to what you know, because that was *never gonna work anyway.*

Ammaright?

You Are Playing Crash Bandicoot

Now, you know from the previous chapter that Jeaniius is a what? *It's your spiritual signature.* But Jeaniius is also the name of my company, or Chief Entity as I call her. I remember when Jeaniius first started speaking to me. First it was her blog posts, then website, followed by a few of her events, and before long she got bigger and bigger until all I could see was jeaniius—everywhere. I even saw her 50 years into the future. It was hard to keep up with what she was showing me. I was constantly, feverishly drawing sketches of what I was seeing. I'd create sitemaps and make lists of her functions and missions. I'd show my husband as excitedly as if jeaniius was already around, because that is how I saw her. Full, complete, and carrying along half a century from now. It was my mission to create her and get her out there into the world, and fast. She had chosen *me* to bring her to life! I was going to create her in a year, all of her. I had a million things to plan. Her buildings, her book, all of her events, her website, and everywhere she existed online and in real life. Do you know that feeling? The vision is so clear so you feel like it all has to be done *right now*? I was so overwhelmed and always feeling like I wasn't doing enough. Unless it was complete by tomorrow, I was failing. Now I have to laugh, because jeaniius is 10-year plan, and I tried to squeeze her all into a year.

It's not a bad thing, to be quick to act, but I learned something even more valuable at a quarterly leadership mastermind with a small group of entrepreneurs in Carlsbad, California. We were asked to create "The 10 year plan." I cringed. *A 10 year plan? Really? I have no idea what I'm gonna be doing in 10 years! What a waste of time!* I thought. But if there were mega successful entrepreneurs around me swearing by it, then how bad could it be? I started with 10 years from now, where I'd be with Jeaniius, what it would look like, how it would function and it suddenly hit me. I felt like I could breathe. I felt like Jeaniius could breathe. I'd been trying to cram everything into the next 12 months, and it just wasn't a 12 month plan. When I drew it out over 10 years, I could feel my vision for jeaniius breathe as if to say, "Thank you. Now can we focus on the next 12 months with a little more space."

When driving a car a long distance in the dark with its headlights on, you can't see more than a few meters in front of it at a time. But you can get the whole distance, that way. The same goes with our big, beautiful visions.

"People underestimate what they can do in 10 years and overestimate what they can do in a year." Bill Gates

I started with a social media—a Facebook page and Instagram. Next, it was two global events (The New Way Live), a Jeaniius grant and The Supercharged. *What a breath out...* Just because a vision shows its entire self to you (and me) does not mean that there's a timer clock on how long we have to bring it to life.

Our visions trust us, we the humans who tune in and ask for guidance in the process. What next? What now? You can think of your vision as your chief entity—your boss—which is why I speak of Jeaniius as a 'her,' because I respect her as her own entity. That's the relationship we've formed and how I can now respect her and her timeline and not put my own human pace and expectations on her. This is important for you to know and it will help you work *with* your vision rather than *as* it. The vision and the human are partners, but they aren't the same thing. Your vision chooses you as the human to bring it to life. It chooses you to put one foot in front of the other, to talk for her, make decisions for him, collaborate on its behalf. Your vision has its own timeline, and that's the greatest job you have as the steward of your vision—not rushing it or not slowing it. But learning it's pace, even if it's different to your own (ya hear me speed demons?)

Employed by an invisible boss, yes you're crazy. We all are. But this is a great boss, because you can always ask this boss for guidance. Journal, listen, sketch, and envision your vision in the world and how she acts and plays and what she accomplishes. You'll be surprised at how much guidance you'll receive once you open up to working for it, and with it, and not as it.

Your vision is like a video game, like Crash Bandicoot. The whole point of the game is the journey, the levels, the hopping from stage to stage, as you earn your capabilities and the knowledge of your next level. Could you imagine logging on to play Crash Bandicoot and being fast tracked from Level 1 to Level 9 without completing levels 2-8? You wouldn't have collected all of the tools, you wouldn't have learned all the moves, and the jumps. It just doesn't work that way. You wouldn't survive Level 9. The same goes with our visions. We need to be fully present at level 1 and to learn all of the skills, tricks and tools we can here. Then, fully equipped we move to level 2. Then we do the same at level 2 to get to 3. We have to honour each level and gather all of the equipment we 'win' at each level, before we can move onto the next.

Your only job right now is to nail where you're at. Then, take your new equipment, skills and prizes and move onto the next level. One level at a time.

Your vision isn't yours and it's not you. You're the human it chose to bring it to life, and sometimes it feels like you need to complete your entire vision in one year, because you can see it so clearly. But it didn't show you its fullness to rush you, but so you could understand it fully and form a relationship with it. Stop trying to cram all of its parts into this year and you can tune in and ask, what do I need to do now? Start playing Crash Bandicoot.

POP OUT: The 10 Year Plan

This is for the visionaries whose vision is <u>so big</u>...If you've got a big, larger-than-life vision right now, I feel you. You probably feel overwhelmed by how huge it is and confused about what you should do <u>right now.</u>

Hire Someone? Start a FB page? Research? Lease a space?

The purpose of the 10 year plan is to help us get our vision out onto paper over a spacious 10 year period. This lets us focus on what we need to do <u>right now</u>, without trying to do everything, right now. (Insert breath out here).

Ready? Let's go. Grab a piece of paper—A4 or larger. Then fold it into 5 parts, long-ways, so that you have 5 columns on each side. On one side write "Personal" and on the other side write "Creative / Professional / Organizations / Company. Next, label each of the four columns, from left to right: 90 DAYS, 1 YEAR, 3 YEARS, 5 YEARS, 10 YEARS.

It looks like this:

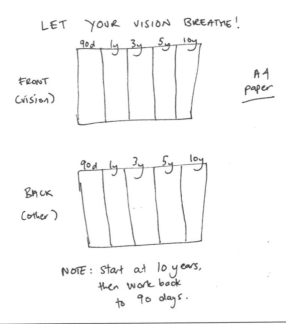

LET YOUR VISION BREATHE!

90d 1y 3y 5y 10y

FRONT (vision)

A4 paper

90d 1y 3y 5y 10y

BACK (other)

NOTE: Start at 10 years, then work back to 90 days.

You can start on whichever side you wish, and write dot points, or get a bigger piece of paper and go nuts. You know what to do. As long as you have five columns and two sides.

Start this exercise at 10 years on each side. You will begin at 10 years and work your way back to 90 days. The reason you start at 10 years is because when you write your vision 10 years from now, you are starting off big and expansive, and then working your way into smaller, practical steps. This is KEY!!

1) Start with 10 years: a) how do you want it to feel? b) how do you want it to look?

Write how it feels and what you can see around you.

2) 5 years. Do the same

3) 3 years. Do the same

4) 12 months. Do the same

Your 12 months should feel a LOT more spacious than it did before—Having a lot more clarity on what needs to be done now, and what is for further along the timeline. So you don't have to recreate Mars all in one year.

5) 90 days. Do the same

Here's what I'm hoping you're feeling. Your next 90 days should feel VERY simple and straight forward like a plan. Just a super simple plan. Your vision has been written out in its entirety in a timeline that makes SENSE to you. And now you're simply moving forward in a way that lets you BREATHE!!

Are you breathing out hugely right now? Just know, you don't have to stick to the entire 10 years like glue. Stuff changes, things open up. What matters is that you give your vision room to breathe and give yourself time to sleep. Yes, some visions require hard core action right now. But you can be in hardcore action intentionally and purposefully and not all over the shop.

Change Your World, Not the World

Some of it's your job, but not all of it. (Leading the WORLD).

"Miss Williamson, I'm going to be the Prime Minister of Australia." I was five years old, swinging on a swing next to my friend.

"Are you now?" I nodded. "Well, you definitely can be if you want to," she said with a look that read, Really, kid? You're thinking about the state of the world? "Someone has to take care of the country," I said as I kept on swinging.

I was a pipsqueak, with ears too big for my head, on a teeny tiny frame, filled up with a heart that cared about everything and everyone all throughout my childhood. It was my responsibility. I cared about the kids that were bullied, knowing I had to tell off the other kids or at least tell the teacher. I cared about everyone's grades. If we had a group assignment, it was all "Don't worry, guys, I'll get it done. Just put your names on it." In sports, I was the team captain. I'd stay late and pack up the equipment and on game days I'd bring streamers and balloons for the kids watching us. At home, I was the chores police. I had to help out my single mum working full time and raising the four of us and our one millions sports activities and my beloved Nanna taking care of us all. "Nag of all nags," teased my siblings. But it was my responsibility to get shit done. In high school my Nanna died. "Don't worry, I'll take care of Mum." That was the note I left in her casket. It was my job.

Welcome to my greatest asset and my greatest weakness. Responsibility. I've got to check myself and make sure that my sense of 'it's my job' doesn't land me a job at the ol' consciousness police station.

Beware The Consciousness Police

I have tried and tried to write the siren sound, but between my editor Janna and I, we couldn't for the life of us agree on the onomatopoeia of getting pulled over.

eeeee orrrrrr eeeee orrrrrr

That just sounds like a donkey. Okay, imagine this: You're driving in your car along the highway, cruising, minding your own business, listening to the radio (pop music with lyrics purely about dat booty), slurping your coffee, and all of a sudden you see red and blue lights flashing in your rearview mirror. *Gah! Forget the donkey, we all know this feeling.*

"Pull over! It's the consciousness police, and you're under arrest for committing more than a dozen class A felonies in the County of the Cosmos. Not recycling. Being on your phone all damn day. Eating too much meat. Not wearing an orgonite pendant. Going to work without meditating. Listening to the radio. Watching more TV than you read books. Driving a gas-guzzler. Preaching your religion. Being blind to conspiracies. Unconscious spending. And, lastly, whinging about saying stuck and not knowing the infinite power of your creativity."

Whoa… does that sound familiar? I'm talking to all you conscious, 'woke' and aware homies who sometimes feel your nipples are made of crystals. And, hey, I'm not worried about *you* getting pulled over. I'm here to ask if you are the consciousness police. Do you roll your eyes when your read political posts on Facebook? Do you feel it's your job to make sure every single person knows the facts about climate change and agrees with you that it's at a very concerning state of progress? Do you rage when people you're around are always on their phones, in a trance to their newsfeed, and think *Omg wake up, look up!* Do you right and wrong people in your head and lump them into conscious or unconscious? Woke or not woke. Aware or not aware. Thinker or sheep. Maybe you do it to yourself—silently beat yourself up when you miss a day of meditating, *as if the Universe ain't gonna speak to you for a week*. Have you ever bought a brand which doesn't align with your beliefs cos you REALLY wanted that sweater and muttered to yourself, "OMG, you are such a hypocrite."

If you're anything like me, then you are nodding so hard right now, because as *woke* and *conscious* and *aware* and *awake* and *tuned in* and *tapped in* and *with it* you, me, and many millennials are, it does not mean that pursuit of consciousness is without judgment—judgment toward others and toward ourselves. We're all human AF, so in this chapter we're going to talk about that judgment.

I know how seriously you take your consciousness journey, but it's time to take it a little lighter. You have seen new amazing things and received new rad insights that you can't un-see, and yes, you have come *a long* way in becoming beautifully aware, heart-centered and awake, but it doesn't mean your purpose here is to be the consciousness boss. There are no levels here. We're all working in unity. We're all doing our bit for the contrast of our planet. We're all equally as relevant. Because, while we are human AF, we are not clean of these mental discrepancies, but we are next level conscious leaders who must notice them and choose something much more rewarding than judgement. Homie, we must begin to work with our contrasts rather than against them.

Think about why you do your work. What is the contrast in the world that inspires it? Is it the hectic and terrifying state of our health, the misinformation and misdirected education of the government that is leading so many people astray? Is it that you cannot stand that so many are ignorant to climate change and feel red in the face when people joke about it? Is it that you feel sad and frustrated by people who live in the poverty mindset while you know that everyone is a conscious creator and can choose anything? Is it that you are sick of watching people feel stuck in the nine-to-five grind, ignoring their soul nudges, their dreams, and the possibilities that are real for them? The contrast is our fire. It's our fuel. It's what gave us the clarity and shed the light on our work for us. That contrast is probably why you do what you do.

But as we move forward to create, teach, and do all the things that our clarity and vision is asking us to do, are we in the lightness or the heaviness of it? Are we in the offense or defense of it?

A few weeks ago, I was at a dinner when someone said to me, "When your baby cries, just leave it. That's the only way I teach him not to cry." My blood was boiling. *How inhumane is that to ignore your baby's one and only signal to you! You are so wrong.* This went against everything I'd learned and knew to be true about parenting and babies and the natural continuum. I wronged that guy so hard in my head that I felt my heart close off immediately. I'm pretty sure my face crinkled up. I judged him. *How can you be so ignorant? How come you haven't read what I've read? You just left your baby? Uncompassionate turd!*

But this is just another day in the life of a human. A fiery, Human AF human. That's me—for sure—and I don't write this chapter from the place of someone who has nailed it. No way! This chapter is for you, me, and many a millennial, because it is important for us all to rise up above judgment and the wronging of others who are 'not up to our spiritual par'. We are courageous conscious leaders. Let us collectively turn off our sirens, throw away the keys to our cuffs, and put away our megaphones. No one needs more policing, and you and me and we need to be spending our energy and time leading in the light—in your light.

In the words of Abraham, 'Don't freak out when people choose a lower flying disk than you. It's all good.' But more accurately....

Don't freak out and judge when people choose a different story, vibration, or action than you.

Live In The Light

Go do your thing, Homie. Go speak, teach, and live in complete alignment with what is true for you, but drop the wrongness of everyone else.

It's so easy to bang on about what we're so *against*, but few live in the boldness of what they're *for*. Imagine all of the wild and free energies you could put towards your work if you didn't spend so much on trying to figure out why others don't see what you see. Imagine all of the possibilities that your energy could generate if you didn't try to get every single person on your page. You could be in the YES of your work, and the YES of everything you teach and share. You can live in the YES of a big, global awakening with as many people as possible who want to share you light. But you cannot live like that if you are wronging those who are not living on your latitude right now.

Your light is your work. Do your work. It is the work of your soul, not the work of the entire Universe. We must acknowledge that conscious leadership is not about changing the world. It is about changing yourself and changing *your* world, which consists of you and those who are being impacted by your work and all of the beautiful ripples that flow from the things that you do. So as passionately concerned as you are about climate change, your most powerful work isn't in wronging those who are not yet energetically available to the information that you know about the state of the environment and the impact of humans. Nor is it in judging the corrupt governments and companies that make you furious beyond comprehension. Homie, let me tell you, you are not even here to defend anyone, not even yourself.

> *"Everything is perfect, and so is your desire to heal the planet."*
> —Prince EA.

That one statement changed my game. It helped me lighten up, loosen up and realize that as serious as I can get about these big world issues, my job is not to fix anything. Instead, my job is to be in the joy, the privilege, and the alignment of what I believe. I am here to pursue what is true for me and my courageous, conscious work.

Channel your desire to un-wrong those who are wrong into a game of light tag. Do your work, speak your truths, create your programs, serve your people, write your Facebook posts all in effort to shine a light on what you care about. You don't need to justify, defend or explain this light, but you also don't need to make others justify, defend, or explain their light—what is true for them—either. Your vibration is your greatest gift to the planet, so what if you could be in the privilege, the play, and the lightness of your work all the time? Even when it's deep and you're feeling human AF, can you put more energy toward your light than your fight?

That energy of right versus wrong is so heavy, homie. And so is that megaphone. It *is* a privilege to know what you know, so let your contrast feed your fire. The reason I get up every morning and work with as much fire as I do, is because of the contrast. It puts a fire in my belly when I see the huge opportunities to help others, and what gets me hotter than ever is the opportunity to unify people and experience more harmony with our planet. And all I have to do shine my light, find my vibe, and live in my tap. However there will be days, days when I catch myself rolling my eyes, days full of wronging people like crazy in my head, and that is when I just pause, take some deep breaths and ask myself some powerful, perspective shifting questions.

What am I choosing right now?

What could I choose that feels better?

What's easier, spending all of my energy on wishing other people would change and trying to control that, or taking responsibility just for my own vibe?

How much more fun could it be?

What could I do with all this extra energy if I didn't spend it on trying to fix others?

What am I choosing now, tiring control or peaceful acceptance?

Acceptance

"Out beyond ideas of wrongdoing and rightdoing there is a field. I'll meet you there. When the soul lies down in that grass the world is too full to talk about." Rumi.

We have all the energy in the world to work for what we believe in when we're not spending our energy on fighting those who don't believe the same. We are not here to be the grand jury of the Universe, to decide who is right or wrong, yet we take that job on voluntarily. Why? Do we need more jobs? Do we get paid for it? Unless you're a prosecutor or a district attorney or, a self-appointed member of the consciousness police, then no. Choose something better and lighter—*acceptance*. Acceptance acknowledges that it's not our job to wrong or right people, and that job is such a heavy one. When we choose acceptance, we choose to get our energy back. So that we can actually go to work for what we believe in, whether it be climate change, the refugee situation, saving the whales, sustainable eating.

An elemental part of your consciousness journey is the harmony between the ethereal, conscious, 'high up there' stuff and the grounded, physical, emotional, mental 'Human AF' stuff. Give yourself credit for the amount of personal, spiritual growth you've already allowed yourself to experience. (Stop. Put your hand on your heart, give it a little rub and say 'kudos, me'). Acknowledge how far you've come and how much more clearly you see the world now. *Isn't that so rad? Isn't your new viewpoint so epic?* Just appreciate that for a minute. Be in the gratitude *of your* journey, because not everyone is experiencing your amount of clarity. What a gift that you get to see how you see, right? Let yourself off the hook, let others off the hook. Care, but care without policing.

Lightly, homie, lightly.

It's not your job to be the Consciousness police. The Universe has that job covered and doesn't even take it as serious as we do. Conscious leadership is calling us to rise above right or wrong. It's easy when we're so sure of what is right that we focus energy on who and what is wrong. Instead, live in your light. Use the fuel and fire from the acknowledgement of the contrast that inspires your work and let it make your work even more of a light and a magnet to those you are meant to serve.

POP OUT: Everyone cares about different things.

The vegan who refuses to use plastic bags at the checkout, but doesn't know a thing about sex trafficking issues.

The bricklayer who doesn't give a shit about meditating but fosters sick, stray dogs.

The school teacher who spends his days pouring love into our next generation of humans, but drives a gas guzzling car on the way home.

The couple who gives a large percentage of their income to organizations helping children access their basic needs in Kenya, but doesn't know so much about factory farming.

The Mum who circulates old toys and clothes to less fortunate mums, but isn't up to date about issues of race and gender equality.

The young entrepreneur who works her ass off to earn great money so she can reinvest back into her community and build things that matter, but doesn't really give a shit about being vegan.

I could go on and on. Just because something becomes our truth, it doesn't mean it's time for it to become the world's truth. Everyone cares about what they care about and we don't all have to be as fiery about the same things.

I wrote this FB post recently, a few months after writing this chapter. I felt it was relevant to back it all up. And, my facebook posts tend to be a bit more spicy and to the point than my chapters. I'm human AF, bare with me.

There's a chapter in my upcoming book called 'The consciousness police'. It's a loving ass kicking to all who are 'woke', 'conscious', 'aware AF', 'nipples made of crystals' or whatever other labels we throw on ourselves and others when we start to know new truths.

Lately I've been feeling like I don't wanna use the word 'conscious' anymore. I've seen more online bullying and hurtful language from people who 'really care about the world' than from anyone else on my feed.

Our fight for unity and togetherness sometimes feels more like a display of BS spiritual hierarchy. It can turn quickly from a rewarding 'this is the world I wanna see' to a non-rewarding 'you're wrong and asleep if you don't get it.'

There are 8 billion people on this planet, the chance of everyone evolving at the same rate and arriving at your truth when you do, is pretty damn slim.

Everyone is doing their best, guys.

Everyone is seeing through different eyes.

Everyone has different stories.

Everyone is here with a different soul's purpose.

The person who doesn't give a shit about meditating or composting but today is taking care of a stray dog—Thank you.

The sex trafficking activist—thank you.

The school teacher—thank you.

The foster parents—thank you.

The doctors on mercy ships—thank you.

The filmmaker—thank you.

The artist—thank you.

The volunteer at the homeless shelter—thank you.

The yoga teacher—thank you.

Those protecting the indigenous—thank you.

The Mum and Dad—thank you.

Those for equality—thank you.

Those smiling today—thank you.

The planet protestor—thank you.

The farmer—thank you.

The entrepreneur—thank you.

The author—thank you.

The mad recycler and composter—thank you

The bricklayer—thank you.

To YOU—thank you.

My chakras are probably blocked all the way up to Jupiter and there's a lot I don't know about so many global issues. But f***, I'd be adrenal gland-less if it was my job to change the whole damn world while I'm here. The same goes for you.

We're evolving as a TEAM so freaking rapidly, guys. So how about we honour that for a wee minute? Regardless of what it is you care about, and whether or not you and I agree, I honor the shit out of you for doing your best.

Thank you for caring.

Unconditionally Compassionate Leadership

When the world goes low, go high (Leading the WORLD).

First, a little PK aside:

In 2015 I moved from Perth, Western Australia to Scottsdale, Arizona. These two places couldn't possibly be any more opposite. My husband (then fiance') Erik is American and with my work being more flexible than his, it just made sense for me to go. The decision was easy, and I moved over there with not much thought other than excitement and faith that it was the right decision. Little did I know that my soul was leading me into some of the greatest lessons and challenges of my life. I'd travelled to the USA before several times and loved so many things about it, especially how you could jump on a plane and in 90 minutes be in a new state that felt like a new country. Living there was a whole different ball game, and that's exactly why my soul included it on my journey.

In my new home, I felt like this free spirited Aussie was being put through an emotional, personal and spiritual tough mudder course. I knew the USA was more religious than Australia, but never did I expect I'd be called 'Satan' for using the word 'Universe'. I was publicly shamed for using swear words in my posts. I was personally phoned to be told that, "I've had several complaints" and can you "tone it down" after I wrote a simple post about how crazy I thought it was that we celebrated Thanksgiving on Thursday and then less than 12 hours later Black Friday flips us to incessant consumerism. And "Go back to Australia, bitch!" wasn't uncommon.

Not only did I feel wronged, I felt confused by the dynamics of this country, and super challenged by how big it all felt. What didn't help, was the fact I moved over just as Donald Trump was beginning his campaign to be the President. My husband would remind me, "It's not usually this much of a circus," but whenever I was in a waiting room, there was Donald Trump talking about "grabbing pussy," staring back at me on the TV. Or there was a story of a shooting. "Shooting? Why are there even guns here? There are no shootings in Aus cos there are no guns in Aus," is something I thought of daily. Conversations with people about how they went hunting, 'killing 5 deer' had me in tears. I felt super defensive of Muslims who were being targeted because of what was happening in the Middle East and was constantly telling my husband how one-sided the news on the middle east was.

As an empath, I picked it all up as if everything going on in the USA was a job for me. I felt tired, I felt sad, I felt misplaced. It just felt so separate. It just felt so intense. I hated it. It felt like I moved from relaxed paradise to a circus of crazy energies and insane separation. I cried most weeks, telling Erik that I wanted to go home.

"This isn't where I'm meant to be." I'd tell my soul.

"It is." She'd say back.

"Why?" I'd beg back.

I felt like there were so many separate teams in the USA and I wasn't on any of them, but the truth was, I had picked a separate team.

> 'How can these crazy religious people seriously think their way is the only way?'

> 'I can't look at Donald Trump.'

> 'How can people actually say they're compassionate and then go and kill deer and put it on their instagram. Fucking gross.'

> 'How can people glorify war and be so naive as to what's actually happening in the middle east.'

I was Team Consciousness, and I identified with someone who wanted peace, unity, togetherness and love. I saw myself as being pretty 'awake', and aware of the bigger picture, what was most right for the world. Sounds pretty positive, feels pretty good, right? But here's the issue—it was still a team, separate from the others. I continued to do my work, create big events about The New Way, mentor millennials, give to charities, speak messages of light at big corporate events. But that stuff came easy to me. Leading in that way, came easy to me. I was being challenged to step into a new realm of leadership that was bigger than just my work, more impactful than my events, and more important than anything I said online.

I was being invited higher, to drop any unrewarding and bullshit thoughts of spiritual superiority or 'classes of consciousness,' and to lead in a way that really challenged me. To lead in a way that most of the world's leaders *were not*, to lead in a way I previously had not been.

Unconditionally Compassionate Leadership

It's called Unconditionally Compassionate Leadership. So, I tried it. I tried unconditional compassion on. It *really* fucking challenged me. When I witnessed people comment in a way that would previously have me thinking, "how can you be so ignorant," I'd try on compassion. Soon, I got a little better at it. It started to feel good. I practised phrases and thoughts that went a little like this:

(Insert name) was raised totally different to me.

(Insert name) is doing what they feel is right.

I know what it's like to do what I feel is right. Can I understand others doing the same?

We're all doing our best with the tools we're given.

Imagine all the experiences (insert name) has had that are different to me.

(Insert name) is doing their very best.

Isn't it beautiful that all humans are doing their best?

I loved how it felt when I tried compassion on like a coat. Compassion felt good to me, even when it was hard. I started asking questions when previously I would have silently judged.

"Tell me how you feel about the war."

"Explain to me what it was like growing up."

"What do you care about more than anything?"

"What did your parents teach you?"

And my favourite: "What sort of world would you like to see?"

Almost everyone wants peace. We just all have our own ways of believing we're going to get there. My friend recently got really mad at an NFL football player who knelt during the national anthem. He knelt to stand in solidarity and show respect for African Americans who had been victims of police crimes and just awful ongoing racism. My natural response to this is "Fuck yeah, what courage!" I think it's beautiful and important that people with a big reach, make statements like this to bring awareness and love to chronic issues like racism. My friend though, was disgusted. Before I started practising Unconditionally Compassionate Leadership, I would've just argued with him and felt bothered that he didn't get it like I did. Instead, I asked him, "Tell me what It means for you when someone kneels during the national anthem."

"I saw people go to war and fight for our country, come back in their early twenties shitting in a nappy and needing full time care from their parents again," he said.

"I understand," I said. He went on to explain.

"I just think that you can make a stand for what you believe in, but it doesn't have to be during the national anthem which honors the people who died for our country," he said.

While I agreed with the guy who knelt, I understood my friends view and am so glad I asked. That's what Unconditionally Compassionate Leadership is about. It's about understanding, *not* agreeing.

Everyone Is Doing Their Best

Think about the people in the world who piss you off, bother or challenge you the most. The ones who can take you out of a good mood in 0.4 seconds. Whether it's something so small like the old lady driving in the car in front of you at snail's pace when you're already late or a politician with orange hair signing an order to dig into sacred land. Remember this… *Everyone is doing their very best.*

My husband and I always remind each other of this when we're on the verge of a big ol' rant about Mr Rude or Mrs Nasty, it instantly helps us feel better. *Every human being is doing their best.* Doesn't that feel better? Unconditional compassion is so much easier than trying to calculate whether or not someone deserves it. So, put your excel spreadsheet and karma calculations away. "Do they deserve it?" is not your job. Love is. Compassion is.

Imagine the lightness of our planet if we all put our karmic calculators away, if we stopped trying to play the role of Consciousness Police, if we quit trying to take the management position away from the Universe. Imagine if we started doing what was in our soul and began to practise what came through our free-flowing tap. Radical compassion is our next big, generational job. We are not all going to be Mother Teresa tomorrow, and this work will not come easy, but we are ready and able to move in that direction. Many of us conscious and courageous leaders are already moving in that direction.

We can either be Karma Physicists or we can Next Level Conscious Leaders in The New Way. It's tough when you care so much, when you're a fiery human who wants people to see what you see. It's tough when we've been taught in so many ways that some people are deserving of it and some aren't, but that mentality halts the growth of our generation. You don't have to be best friends with people you hold compassion for. You don't have to see them, invite them for over for dinner, or go rollerblading with them. But the compassion you feel in your heart for them will be what changes the world. You will be shifting the energy, sending out your high vibes and being a courageous and conscious leader.

Everyone is doing their best.

Even Donald Trump.

When The World Goes Low, Go High.

3 Steps To Unconditionally Compassionate Leadership

1) *Try compassion on.* Ask whatever questions or state whatever reminders you need to so that you can soften and humble your heart and be understanding (not agreeing).

2) *Speak up, but with your compassion coat on.* Once we have our compassion coats on, we can continue to do our work. But we're speaking, writing and creating with a stance of 'this is what I'm for' and not 'this is who and what I'm against.' Our tone changes, our intention changes, and we've got the benefit of being a lot more spiritually mature.

   Sometimes it's time to speak up and voice your opinion, other times it's not. Which brings me to the third step to Unconditionally Compassionate Leadership.

3) *Hold Space.* What do you do when you don't have anything to say? Just be the vibration you wish the entire world would be on. Sometimes it's your job to invite the world up with your vibration, not your words, FB posts or protests.

POP OUT: What do we do when it feels like shit is hitting the fan globally?

Terrorist attacks what feels like weekly, news that makes antidepressant drugs the new black, abuse of our Earth? What do we do? How can we make it better? What do we do when we're so mad and frustrated at our political leaders and lack of love and compassion we see destroying innocent lives? Do you ever just have moments like that? When your blood is a mixture of anger, helplessness, and confusion?

I wrote this FB post after a moment like that after asking myself 'What can I do?'

Leadership isn't always about speaking out and having bold opinions when others do. Sometimes the most courageous and necessary thing a leader can do is to shut up, go in and ask 'what's really required of me now?'

Last night I went to bed in tears after reading about the 30+ beautiful people killed in Baghdad. I was just so f***ng over this merry-go-round of blame, separation, brutality and ignorance and so frustrated by the feeling of not knowing what I could do. My husband (while trying to cuddle a pregnant lady curled up in a rock hard ball having a sook), reminded me of something I shared in my opening of TNWL Sydney last year .... "If you really wanna change the world, don't let anything you see rob you of your smile." I said to him during my sook "easier said than done."

But it was my own advice and I needed to chew it up and eat it. There is no one country to blame, not even a sleepy president we can all point the finger at. The world will know peace when the collective vibration demands it—period. While these attacks are still going on in our home whether it's Manchester, Syria, Baghdad, it's a clue. It's showing us the direct result of our collective vibration—including yours and mine.

We are not separate. What goes on in 'your country' is not separate to what goes on in 'that country'. If you really wanna be a leader during this time, pay attention to your frequency.

Pay attention to your attitude towards the people around you and in other countries, religions and political parties. Pay attention to how and who and what you routinely judge. Pay attention to the thoughts you think and the feelings in which you spend the most time. What the world needs right now are people who can rise up and hold a frequency that many are unable to reach for.

We don't need more opinions, judgement and 'well my country is safe soooo....'. We need people who can take radical responsibility for their own frequency even when it's 10x harder than posting that tempting low vibe rant on FB. When the world goes low.... WE need to go HIGH.

I'll say it again, the world will know peace when our collective vibration demands it. While there are still things going on in the world that upset, horrify, confuse and anger us.... it's not our cue to rant. It's our cue to go higher.

Remember when pointing the finger, there are 3 fingers pointing back at you.

Q) Where is your focus?
Where is your vibe?
What can you tidy up?

Be a renegade for Team Earth.

That's the answer. You're equipped to lead. And by lead I'm not talking about standing on stage and preaching to millions or becoming the next President or Prime Minister (unless you want to, you go Glen Coco). I'm talking about you living in the new way and leading by inviting the world into new standards through the space you hold, the things you do, and the vibration you emit.

So how do we go high when the world seems to go low?

We take responsibility.

If my vibe was an energetic text message to the world, what would I be sending?

How am I responding to the atrocities of the world? The things I disagree with?

Where am I still judging people who don't agree with me?

We remember.

That everyone is doing their best. That we are so privileged to be here now.

We trust.

That all is well.

> *When we give a shit about our world, we can get pretty firey. But the Earth isn't hiring us to agree, She's hiring us to soften. Unconditionally Compassionate Leadership is about understanding others, without needing to agree with them. When we 'try compassion on' first, we lead the world to a new relationship with each other.*

All Is Well

Even amongst all the craziness, all is well. (Leading the WORLD)

Do you not watch the news? How can you say all is well when people are starving, chemical weapons were just dropped in Syria, and have you heard who's President of the United States?

All is well.

How can you say that? Aren't you paying attention to the vaccine arguments and reading the new research that's coming out about it? Haven't you looked into the sky recently and seen the chem trails? Have you seen the size of GMO avocados in the supermarket?

All is well.

Are you serious? Did you see the shark attack on the news last weekend? Didn't you know there was an outbreak of Ebola? Didn't you hear about North Korea's threat to bomb Australia?

All is well.

Can we be aware of everything going wrong with the world right now while reminding people, of what's going right?

This brings me to Peter Diamandis. He's an international pioneer in the world of innovation, including space travel and human longevity. He has more companies than I can count on one hand, and they all blow my mind for how progressive they are—taking people to Space, extending the healthy human lifespan, transforming entire industries to solve humanity's biggest challenges. He is to me, a legend.

I ran into him at the Montage in Laguna Beach recently and ran over to him like the unabashed fan girl that I am. He remembered my name! Maybe cos it's the same as his only with an A on the end, or because he's a genuine badass who understands people and loves to connect with them. Regardless, he's rad and even though he is well-read, super educated, and completely in touch with the state of the world, he reminds us all that all is well. Here's the reason.

It's easy to borrow the story of fear and 'the world is so fucked up'. It doesn't take any particular strength to do that. Just watch the news, gossip with your friends, and share status' on facebook about all things grim and atrocious. But if you were to ask Peter Diamandis, who has two young sons, whether or not he's worried about the future, I'm quite sure he'd say "No."

I'm on Peter's email list and even though his emails go to the 'updates' section of my Gmail amongst many others, I always pull his out and read them top to bottom. Often his subject line is something like : The world is (still) better than you think. *And the body of his email?* Reminders of everything that is progressing in the world. His focus is clear, forward, fresh and incredibly inspiring to me. I'll share some direct stats from his emails and website with you.

Did you know:

- ○ In September 2017, the government of Finland announced a partnership with MONI to create a digital money system for refugees. This allows people to participate in the economy and rebuild their lives.

- ○ Life Expectancy. Just 100 years ago, a child born in India or South Korea was only expected to live to 23. Today in 2017, India's life expectancy has tripled.

- ○ In Bengaluru, researchers at the Indian Institute of Science are fighting deforestation with camera-equipped drones that drop seeds in areas they otherwise wouldn't be able to explore. Their goal is to seed 10,000 acres in the region.

○ More people around the world have access to electricity than ever, and the absolute number of those without access to electricity is dropping (despite population growth).

○ Globally, 18.6 percent of the population was undernourished in 1991; by 2015, it dropped to 10.8 percent.

○ Over the last 30 years, the share of the global population living in absolute poverty has declined from 53% to under 17%.

○ In the last 16 years, the number of children working in child labour has been reduced by more than 50%. As we head to a world of low-cost robotics, where such machines can operate far faster, far cheaper and around the clock, the basic rationale for child labour will completely disappear, and it will drop to zero.

○ In the last 25 years, under-five mortality rates have dropped by 50%. Infant mortality rates and neonatal mortality rates have also dropped significantly.

○ In the U.S. in 1820, the average person received less than 2 years of education. These days, it's closer to 21 years of education, a 10X improvement.

○ Within the next 20 years, the best possible education on Earth will be delivered by Artificial Intelligence for free— and the quality will be the same for the son or daughter of a billionaire as it is for the son or daughter of the poorest parents on the planet.

○ Global literacy. Rates have increased from around 10% to close to 100% in the last 500 years.

Data taken and quoted from http://www.diamandis.com/blog/data-world-getting-better and Abundance Insider: October 6 edition.

I just want to remind you of the progress we are in fact making as a whole and the direction in which we're moving. How different does it feel to focus on what's going right? This is our work, and just because we have work to do, it doesn't mean that everything is going to shit. And it especially doesn't mean we should forget three of the most important words of a courageous leader, a new superhero.... *All is well.*

When you remind yourself, and others that all is well, you are standing on the side of the Universe, and not against it. Think about it. If you truly believe that all *isn't* well, are you sided with Source? Are you trusting of Source? Are we putting our faith in each other and in the Earth? *All is well* is our way of siding with Earth, siding with Source, and siding with each other.

When you hold the perspective of all is well *no matter what,* you're choosing a vibration more similar to Mother Natures and the world responds to that. It shifts. People smile. You smile. People lighten. You being in *all is well* invites all people and beings, to stop focussing on the constantly negative news, pretending that our life here isn't as magnificent as always and be in the acknowledgement of the privilege it is to be here at this game changing time.

All is well is not an ignorant stance. It's the most rewarding, magnetic approach we can take as people on a mission to raise the vibration. It may seem a little crazy right now on Earth, but that's what happens as new consciousness emerges. We're equipped for this. You're equipped for this.

Yes climate change is so damn real, but we know what to do and our world is full of people who care and are willing to change. Consciousness is tilting in our favour, so all is well. Yes, homelessness and starvation are real, but we are brilliant humans who give a shit and it's a priority for so many and we have what it takes to completely eradicate it, so all is well. Yes, crazy people are being elected as presidents that has us all wondering when Ashton Kutcher is gonna yell out and scream PUNK'd but craziness shakes people up, snaps them out of inaction and brings them together, so all is well.

> *All is well because you are here, I am here, we are here. We are living on the most nourishing, supportive, patient planet and our time isn't up. There is nothing dished up to us by the Universe that we're not equipped to handle. This is our work.*

Pause & Play

Another handmade crossword, brought to you by my inner 5-year-old.

1. BEWARE THE _____ POLICE

2. UNCONDITIONALLY _____ LEADERSHIP

3. GET THIS FROM YOUR SOUL BEFORE BED

4. RIPE OR DIE _____ .

5. MAKE SURE YOUR GOALS ARENT _____

6. EQUAL PARTS MAGIC + HUMAN = _____

7. YOUR SPIRITUAL SIGNATURE /SOUL'S GENIUS.

EARNING

Money is our teammate and business is our portal, for creating conscious change for our Earth and all people.

"Money is like water. It can be a conduit for commitment, a currency of love. Money moving in the direction of our highest commitments nourishes our world and ourselves."

—Lynne Twist

Creatively Earning is the element of The New Way that is all about redefining money and business by: recognising the spiritual bosses of our companies; rewriting your money story so we can upgrade the collective money story; lacing consciousness and soul through the DNA of everything we create.

Conscious Enterprise

Money is our team mate, business is our portal.

"Business is the only mechanism on the planet today
powerful enough to produce the changes necessary to
reverse global environments and social degradation."
—Paul Hawken

Business and money are two of our greatest team mates when it comes to our pursuit for a more conscious, unified, awake, and love-filled world. Fact. Doesn't shit just sound so much more compelling when you tack "Fact" onto it? *Yeah, I thought so.* But yes—even for the hippies, the hyper-conscious, and those who tend to shy away from these more masculine-appearing (keyword: appearing) aspects of evolution—business and money are two of the greatest opportunities we have to better our world. We are being asked right now to not ignore enterprise and money, but, instead, to rewrite the current collective stories and methods of business in order to invite them into a more conscious game that rewards our planet and more of our people. We call it The New Way.

This is why "spiritual" people get into business, because business holds the power that catalyzes the change they want to create in the world. Don't be fooled. Money *is* power. We can shy away from it, judge it from our spiritual high horse, or we can step into this arena with our big hearts, our bountiful intentions, and our fierce protectiveness for our Mother Earth and change the game. Money *is* power and it's calling upon the superheroes of our generation, the team members of The New Way, to use money to create and collaborate for a reason. Look around, and you will see the millions of hungry entrepreneurs who are creating epic shit in alignment with the vision of The New Way, because it is our time to rewrite the story, recreate our impact, and reclaim our planet. The rise of entrepreneur is not egocentric, but soul-centric. We are here to be divinely inspired, creative, loving, and revolutionary.

Creatively Earning is an element of The New Way that shines a light on how our generation is doing business differently and treating money differently, how we can create epic shit through conscious enterprise and art, how we replace old systems and companies that no longer serve our planet, and how we invite the collective into a higher, fresher way, that does reward our planet. The spotlight is on money, and not just money as we know it, but what we of The New Way call "conscious money." For that is what all of the light workers, aware beings, lovers of love, and conscious leaders want—for money and business to nurture and nourish our planet and our people.

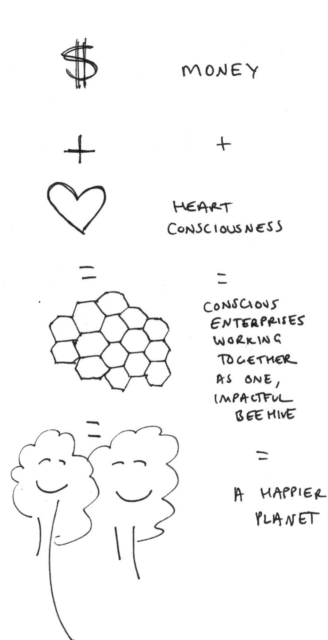

$

MONEY

+

+

♡

HEART
CONSCIOUSNESS

=

=

CONSCIOUS
ENTERPRISES
WORKING
TOGETHER
AS ONE,
IMPACTFUL
BEEHIVE

=

A HAPPIER
PLANET

As we begin this journey into the business of The New Way, let's first focus on conscious enterprise. (We'll get to money a little later.) Now, I am going to use the word *entrepreneur* a lot, but business terms aside, know that this section is for *all of you*—all of you creatives, artists, business owners, Mums, Dads, authors, yoga teachers, poets, painters, fashion designers, speakers, employees, food gurus, rock stars, bricklayers, and number-crunchers. This is for any of you who are interacting with any sort of community each day—online or offline. You are all creating something, which is equally as relevant to the world, regardless of whether or not you consider yourself an entrepreneur with a *Shark Tank* worthy product. You're creative. You're here. You're playing the game. This is for you. All of it. All of you.

And now, a little **sacred geometry** to help you understand Conscious Enterprise.

Whatever it is that you are creating right now, whether it's a company, a brand, a blog, a product, or any form of art, you are creating a hexagon. Doesn't matter if you are an entrepreneur, the founder, a contractor, one of the employees, or even one of the customers, you are contributing to one or more Hexagons. Conscious Enterprise is a hexagon.

But why a *hexagon* you ask?

Picture a hive. Bees work together as a collective, one by one forming their large bee hive. Each bee and team of bees goes to work on one hexagon at a time. They fit each of the hexagons together like perfect puzzle pieces. They do this with laser focus, until they've created something beautiful together—their home, their hive. One hexagon won't do. One hexagon alone doesn't create a beehive. All bees with all their hexagons must be working together and on the same page. All hexagons are part of the whole hive, which illustrates how we approach Conscious Enterprise in The New Way.

The Hexagon represents every conscious enterprise on Earth.

Each one is badass and unique, and they're all on the same page, fitting together to create something even more beautiful than one hexagon on its own. Your hexagon is part of our new, thriving home. You are the bee. Your team and your tribe are your fellow bees. You're all building hexagons and you're cheering on all other bees as they do the same. Each Hexagon represents the company, movement, or organization that is the vessel for the future we want to create. Every enterprise is contributing in some way—big or small—to build a better world. This hexagon is the model that can help *you,* the entrepreneur navigate the world around you and create a solid foundation for your business.

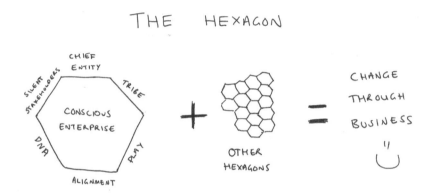

THE   HEXAGON

"If you have built castles in the air, your work need not be lost; that is where they should be. Now put the foundations under them."
—Henry David Thoreau

Every conscious enterprise begins as a vision, a castle in the air, because it is touching Source. Then, when it's ready to come into being, to find a foundation, the vision will choose a human to start the building of it here on Earth, as we now know. In ten years, we won't have to put the word 'conscious' in front of enterprise or say 'conscious business' or 'conscious entrepreneurs,' because in ten years almost all enterprises will be conscious enterprises and all business will be conscious and all entrepreneurs will be conscious ones. It's just evolution.

We will be light years from where we stand now. So many of the big companies, corporate giants, and global brands that we've known of our whole entire life were built on principles and processes that were well-suited for life as it was a few decades ago. The collective strain and pressure we were putting on our environment back then didn't seem as harsh. The demand for sustainable practices didn't seem as urgent. According to findings on ourworldindata.org, in 1960 we had 3 billion people on Earth and in 2015 we had 7.4 billion. Worldwide population growth has naturally led to the establishment of more companies responding to the demands of more people, which has relied on us taking more from the Earth's natural resources to make the cycle go round. Unsustainable consumption patterns have been the common and accepted standard.

Until now. The Earth is roaring back. We are now roaring back. Times they are a changin' and we, as the next generation, have more evolved standards. Millennials are soon to be in spending and voting power, and as a result, the world is going to see a massive shift in the way organizations are formed, businesses are run and are built, and what companies affect. We millennials are creating conscious enterprises, made by entrepreneurs and organizations who create and innovate in a way that is not only badass, brilliant, and rewarding, but also beneficial for our planet and all of our people.

> *Business is the only mechanism on the planet today*
> *powerful enough to produce the changes necessary to*
> *reverse global environments and social degradation.*
> —Paul Hawken

A few months ago I was at a wedding in Palm Springs and I spotted a Solemate! Right there, underneath a woman's high heel was that clever, clear plastic attachment that kept her heel from sinking into the grass. *Shark Tank!* I thought with a pang of excitement. I mean I'm obsessed with the show, like, seen-every-episode obsessed. I love nothing more than seeing entrepreneurs in their creative brilliance, in their innovation, and in their pure ballsiness. With a show like *Shark Tank* we are able to witness the evolution of the values and standards of entrepreneurs and see people push the edges of human potential. Watching these people work from their tap gets me red hot and inspires the shit out of me.

Sure, not every product on the show is the ideal product, but the direction the products and the people are moving in are incredibly insightful. There are the clues everywhere that reveal The New Way and the glorious rise of conscious enterprise. I see and hear more people pitching their products and business with a "profit sharing plan" and a "people planet, profit model," or "100% recyclable compostable materials". I see more entrepreneurs than ever stand by their company and their vision regardless of any deal they're about to strike if it doesn't align with the soul and spirit of their work, or what I like to call the chief entity, which we'll talk about very soon. And I just love how the entrepreneurs strut into the tank wearing jeans, Chucks, with their natural hair, and little to no makeup. I have yet to see one baggy suit from five years ago, because we are in The New Way, which has nothing to do with your outfit, your hair, your shoes, or anything about your outward appearance. Though I would not encourage walking into a meeting with Forbes in nipple tassels and hot pants.

The New Way Is About Radical Alignment

The world of enterprise is all changing. It has to change. Not because millennials are throwing a tantrum and demanding that things be "cooler" and more "hip", but the way we do things has to change because business either takes more from our planet than it's giving or it gives more to our planet than it's taking. Business either moves us more towards radical alignment, collaboration, unity, equality, play, and a higher collective vibration—or it doesn't. That is why the ways we do business have to change. We have no choice but to move toward alignment. Sustainability, freedom lifestyle, and high-vibe work environment are not just nice words that make millennials froth at the mouth, they are the practices, regulations, and standards that were built into our DNA when we were born. Our desire for new standards isn't a selfish one. It's not a disrespectful one. It's not entitled or naïve or privileged. Our desire for new standards is our divine intolerance to what no longer serves our world.

We came into this world with refreshed expectations and a drive to ensure that the world holds true to them because that's how we can ensure our children a thriving planet, a community, and a team (which we call humanity, or Team Earth as I'll refer to it later) of which we can be proud to be a part.

We're seeing this divine intolerance displayed as we see sustainable and responsible companies built with spirit and love, two such assets which had previously not been objective enough to be considered assets when it comes to building businesses. Not anymore. Not only are we displaying our divine intolerance by building companies, movements, products, brands, and organizations that are driven by The New Way, but we are seeing the world respond. We're seeing existing companies change their packaging to make it recyclable. We're seeing them change their vision and mission statement to include more awareness about global issues and people outside of their customer base. We're seeing collaborations and abundance become more fulfilling than competition and scarcity. We're seeing work from home policies, extended maternity leave, free dress days, and permission for employees to work in funky cafes, because that's where they're in their tap.

Big corporations can no longer get away with destroying our planet, because our generation won't let them. This is not a matter of "We are millennials, hear us ROAR." It's pure survival. We want our children to have a planet to live on and we know that businesses as a collective force need to step up and modify practices and policies so that we are all moving in the direction of a thriving planet and team.

We vote with our dollar. We know that our dollar is working for us twenty-four-seven. We know that where we spend our money matters. We know that's how companies thrive or are replaced—by the support they do or do not have from their consumers—so we are demanding more by spending our money where our hearts are. Listening to the hearts of millennials isn't just going to help big organizations thrive, it's going to ensure that they survive. Because us kids, and our kids, are made of different stuff. We're made of what we need to be made of in order to move our planet in the direction we need to move in, towards that sweet, sweet h-word harmony, where we're vibing at a frequency that is closer to Mother Nature than it is separate from her, a world where *all* people thrive, and a world where our work is bringing us closer together and not driving a wedge between countries or classes. Because we get to choose, why on Earth would we move towards anything else? Conscious Enterprise is our bestie as we pursue our mission.

Conscious will be the way of business. Our generation was born with a divine intolerance, unable to tolerate standards and systems that don't support the quality of world we're here to create. Business is one of our greatest opportunities to gift the world a new operating system that moves us closer to harmony between each other and the Earth. Times are changing, our generation is roaring on behalf of Mother Nature, and she is weaving her magic through us and the companies and creations we're building. The New Way is here and conscious enterprise is our jam.

POP OUT: HEY!!!

These next few chapters are all about entrepreneurship and business. If this doesn't interest or apply to you, just skip through to money on page 229 and meet us there. You won't wanna miss that conversation. X

Invisible Boss

You don't work for yourself.

"I work for myself."

Have you ever said, or heard anyone else say that? Have you ever posted or seen a post on Facebook or Instagram with a photo (any photo) and a caption that reads, *Today's office. Or Life is good when you don't have a boss.*

I have said those words. I have posted that caption. Because for the first 6-12 months of my early entrepreneur days, which were in network marketing, 'I work for myself' was my attitude. I thought I worked for myself. I said I worked for myself. And I posted on social media that I worked for myself. That's what entrepreneurship is about, right? Working for yourself. Having no boss? That was the life, right? I would wake up before the sunrise (even when I didn't feel like it) and work until nearly midnight (which is so unbelievably past my bedtime). I'd get on planes when I didn't want to get on planes. I'd keep my computer open when my eyes were burning. This was my job and I was working for me—to replace my income and to free myself from any other obligations so I could be working full time. I was my own boss. I couldn't live under the constraints of the "typical" working life and financial stresses that plagued my generation.

With my intense drive and insane work ethic, it sure didn't take me long to reach that point. I was free and never had to answer to a "boss" again, yet I kept working with an increasingly insane drive, long after I was taken care of myself. Just because I didn't have a physical boss—looking over me telling me what to do—I didn't quite feel like I was unemployed. I didn't feel like I was on my own when I sat down at my desk to work. Some days when I felt like stopping, it was like I couldn't, because I was being pulled by something so much bigger than anything I could imagine. I would hear random Gee-Ups (like, inspiring pep talks) and wonder where they came from. Sometimes they were motivational like "How many more people can you support today?". Sometimes they were instructional like "Fly 27 hours to Chicago and do a one day event on conscious leadership!" I could not understand how other people building an organization anything similar to mine had so much time off. It felt physically impossible for me to take time off. Forget physically, it felt spiritually impossible to take time off. There was a mission taking place, and I was being used as an instrument.

It was just me, so I created my schedule. I got on the phone calls. I stood on stage. I planned events. I worked long hours. I sent all the emails. I set my own goals. Yet deep down in my cells I was beginning to feel that I was not my own boss. I had an invisible boss, who was not a mean boss like my old boss who told me to do my hair better (eye roll), but an important boss who was pure and loving and certain, a boss who knew my vision better than I. This boss wasn't even someone I could call God or the Universe or Source. This boss may have been sent by Source, directly to me, but it was not the same being.

I didn't know it then, but I had been working for a vision. Remember those from a few pages back, the visions that pick humans? Well, this vision had specifically chosen me to bring it to life, and thus had anointed me with what we humans call "a mission." I wasn't working for myself at all, and this realization made my entrepreneurial life suddenly click. I understood business. I understood business and spirituality and how they were one. I understood the nature of ideas and the specificity and accuracy of the downloads and messages I had received, and that OMG!! They were really meant for me! But, most importantly, I understood two very crucial differentiations. Human and entrepreneur are not one in the same, and business and vision are not one in the same.

You Are Not Your Business Or Your Vision

There is a grand vision out there, a **divine entity** that is has chosen you to bring it to life in the form of a business, a product, some magical art form, or a rad organization. You have been chosen specifically, because you are most equipped. But let's get one thing crystal clear. You are not the boss. You can be the painter, the CEO, the founder and creator, the author or the baker, but you are not the boss. You have a boss, and you are never, ever working for yourself. That feels kinda good, right? You're not alone. It sure felt like a big breath out to me.

"You're not working for yourself," can take on a whole new meaning.

Back in the early stages of building Jeaniius, my ride or die conscious enterprise, I had to let someone go, and I was struggling with it. Peta, the human, was ferociously loyal and felt terrible about letting go of someone who was a nice person and was doing their best. However, my business needed me to act. She simply didn't have the right competencies for the role and we were paying her more than we were receiving in value. Still, I'm human, so I delayed having the really hard conversation, which would turn out to be the beginning of my hiring and firing journey.

"Peta, you are the ambassador for your business," my mentor said when we were discussing this "firing" conundrum on a call. "Who else is going to do what your business needs if you don't?"

That was the question that changed it all. Thinking of myself the ambassador for my business synced up everything I was putting together about entrepreneurs, creatives, artists, and anyone whose work is driven by a calling or a vision. Where else was I making decisions on behalf of me and not my business, I wondered. A week later a test came. Both my personal and business credit cards were skimmed—stolen. Even though the bank caught it and alerted me almost immediately, and I shut them down, a small amount was charged on each. When I thought about the time and energy it would take to chase a few hundred dollars down, I couldn't imagine spending my hours sitting on the phone with the bank and with detectives searching store videos. I had chased money from skimmed cards before and it hadn't been worth my while. When it came to my personal card, I decided this was not worth it. But what about my business card (the test!)? It wasn't a game changing amount of money taken from this business account, but If I didn't get every single cent back on behalf of my business, then who would? My business can't grow legs and walk into the bank and demand the money. I am those legs. I am the legs the business grew to walk into the bank, and if it's not me, then who else can do this for my vision. I am selected carefully by my vision because I am equipped, and it was time to take that very seriously. I am not just the one bringing this vision to life through my business, but I am the one who is speaking up, acting on behalf of, making decisions for, and being the voice for my vision, because that is exactly what it needs.

"I am going back into the bank to fight for my lost money!" I wanted to put on a cape! "I am my vision's human! I am the chosen ambassador!"

This was not a mistake. I went into the bank and went through the entire card fraud process. Looking back I suppose I could have had my finance team do it for me, but I wanted to do it myself. It all of a sudden didn't feel as pain staking a task as it used to feel. It felt good to respect every single dollar on behalf of my company because, that's what my company would ask me to do if it could talk.

Is it always worth spending time and energy to retrieve money if it's going to suck even more resources from you? I don't think it is. But we've gotta make sure that when our company/entity/vision needs something, we're checking in and asking "Am I making this decision on behalf of me or on behalf of my vision?"

Homie, whatever you're creating right now, remember this. You are the ambassador, the protector, and the decision maker that speaks on behalf of your vision. No one else is.

Your vision is already full and whole all on its own, but after scouring through the 7 billion humans on the planet, this vision chose you specifically, because you are the most equipped for its needs. Only then, once you respect and admit that your vision (business, art, organizations, book...) is its own entity. It's your boss, and you will be guided by it, speak for it, and work with it. But never as it.

This is not always easy. The decisions you (as the emotional human) want to make and the decisions your business needs you to make are not always going to be the same. The moves you want to make (as a logical human) and the moves your business needs you to make are not always going to be the same. But you will always be guided by the essence and that is where consciousness and business are one. Your vision is not something your imagination conjured up while sipping cacao barefoot at Bondi Beach. Your vision, your business, your art, is its own entity. We can now see business is spiritual and conscious because your business is consciousness itself and has its own consciousness.

Humans are divinely and carefully selected by these entities to be the people who make them real on Earth. The vision we see when we 'see it' is real and already complete. It just needs to become complete on Earth. The New Way of business is the relationship with an open entrepreneur and their divine entity that has chosen them. The New Way of business is consciousness in the most rad form ever. We must acknowledge that businesses are their own divine entity complete with their own consciousness.

> *"I work for myself." Is not something that comes out of the mouth of a true entrepreneur. Entrepreneurship is not about sitting on a beach with your laptop, working 'only when you feel like it' so you can hashtag #todaysoffice. It's fun most days, but true entrepreneurship requires more. Entrepreneurs do have a boss. You just have to learn how it speaks, what it says, and what it wants you to do. It's a partnership that is more thrilling than any journey I've been on in my life. And it's the privilege of all privileges.*

The Chief Entity

The spiritual boss of your business.

This is where shit gets real. We talked about business when we talked about conscious enterprise. We talked about bosses when we talked about your Invisible Boss. In this chapter, we are going to bring conscious business up to the next level as we come to understand and connect to our Chief Entity.

To begin, from the most logical place, we start with a proper 'org chart.' A business' organizational chart shows the roll each individual fulfills to keep the company functioning, efficient, and turning profit. In the last chapter, we debunked the myth that you are an independent entrepreneur working for yourself, because you have an invisible boss—your vision—that has handed picked you based on your abilities to bring it to life here on Earth. So now, you may be thinking, "Peta, WTF do we need an org chart for?" Like, what are the reasons we need to know how big or small a business is, its common responsibilities, and all the positions such as, CEO (Chief Executive Officer), CFO (Chief Financial Officer), CMO (Chief Marketing Officer), and COO (Chief Operations Officer)?

The truth is, the typical 'org chart' doesn't apply to businesses in The New Way as commonly as previously. Today you have to change the names around a bit. Take for example, my friend Makenzie, who has positions in her 7 figure company like 'Chief Breath Taker' whose role (along with important day to day tasks) is to ensure the organisation as a whole is breathing, not rushing, and operating in integrity with its purpose. Then there's the 'Soul Frequency Officer', whose role is to ensure the organisation is functioning from and making decisions from the soul of the vision and at the most rewarding vibration for all. Regardless of whether you have a big company with a typical org chart, or if it's just you and your invisible boss right now, or you, your invisible boss, your intern, and a tech nerd, or you and your editor, you still need to understand the power of organization. Be it two people or twenty-two-hundred, create a position at the tip top of your org chart, above you, anyone else and any title with C-something-O. This is for your Chief Entity, the CE.

Your Chief Entity (CE) is your vision. Only, now it has a definite role in your organization. You can think of your CE as your spiritual boss, the essence of your business, the vision that picked you, the control center, the flagship, the cloud, the prover, the guider, and the Mamma and Papa bear.

Your CE is always tapping you on the shoulder, reminding you that spirituality and consciousness make businesses better.

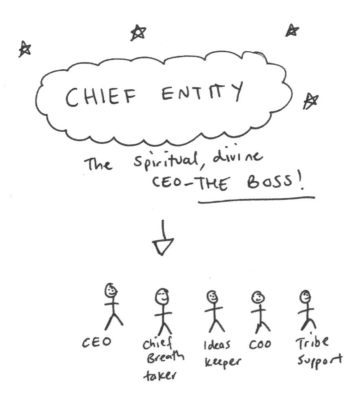

You may be reading this with a very clear idea of what your CE is or you may have no idea what I am talking about. Perhaps, instead of trying to identify your CE as a person, you can find its presence in moments. Your CE is trying to communicate with you when you're about to go to sleep, and then, "Oh shit, I need my notebook! Gotta scribble these notes down!" Your CE is that clear picture of the completed project, the building, the company, the movement, the product that may not have a name yet but is so real for you because you can see it in your mind clear as day. It's the consistent and persistent ideas and impulses that feel so big and important and exciting—and they just keep coming. It's that 'thing' that wants to be built through you, created through you, and made real on Earth by you.

"Okay so… it's, like, think about Netflix… Well, really, mix Netflix with Amazon Prime, and … Yeah, I'm not explaining it well, am I? Just trust me, it's going to revolutionize *everything*. I just need to find an investor, and explain this better, and Oh-My-God, I make no sense."

You've just gotten so excited about your next big idea, and you try to explain it to your best friend, your barista, or your Uber driver… and your friend, your barista, or your Uber driver say not a whole lot more than….

"Yeah, okay…and?"

Does this scenario sound familiar?

So you hang your head, feeling like the 'typical entrepreneur,' who is just getting those crazy ideas and getting all excited about something they can't even understand. *These* are the moments when your CE is talking to you, the moments where you must *listen*, because that excitement is real and that clarity (even if only in your own brain) is real. Your CE is channeling through you; however, it's so easy to fall victim to what happens to most entrepreneurs when they get those crazy hits. Your CE shows you your vision in its entirety—so *you* can see the completed picture, but that does not mean you must immediately show the world the completion. When I showed Jeaniius to the world at my first TNWL event, it was more than a year after she first revealed herself to me. So many entrepreneurs open up enough to get to this space of seeing their CE fully, but then they go off and try to create the website, build the company, or write the book all in the following month. No one has to build a building overnight, just because your CE gave you the blueprints and all the tools.

This is the reason I've become so big on teaching about the CE and also the process of working with your CE and the relationship you can build. I am here to show you how you and your Chief Entity will move together—step by step—on the work you are to reveal to the world.

The Process

Before you read on below, where I share how the process of getting to know, beginning your relationship with, and working beside your CE starts, let me first say that this is a guide. The steps of this process may not apply to you in this order, and some of the steps may not resonate with you at any point. I ask that you think of these next few pages as "open to interpretation." After all, as each CE works with each human individually and uniquely, how could we ever capture what works for all involved? We can't, so enjoy this sketch, and then know that you can enjoy the unraveling and revealing that precedes that which will be one day be brought into the world by you and your CE.

STEP 1 is where you'll want to yell YIPPPEEE!!! all the time.

Excited Curiosity

Excitement is the first clue that something is tapping you on the shoulder. This feeling of expansive enthusiasm has arrived when you cannot stop talking about *how cafes should have raw cacao, and how everyone would be so much more creative if they could drink raw cacao.* It's such an exciting idea that you must tell everyone—so much more exciting than anything else you've been working on. You see this vision and feel it in your cells. *People sipping this ancient Mayan drink and making magic.* Yeah, this has to happen, so the question is how? Once you get that kind of excitement that comes with curiosity, you've got a match made in heaven.

The Repetitive Idea

No not just any old idea, but that one idea that keeps coming back to you—over and over and over again. It's like it has its heart set on you. You are its human it is not letting go until you listen. Its persistent and consistent, and every time it visits you and you listen, it evolves and expands and has more to reveal to you. *A book about…* At first visit, it was vague, with no idea of what the final result would be, but its existence was clear as day. *How people felt when they were reading it.* The more you nurture the idea, the more it keeps revealing itself to you. This book you're reading revealed new parts of itself like "add The Script wins," "write letters to your starseed," and "self publish me," and the more I trusted that these ideas and visions were for me, the more I paid attention to them, the more was revealed to me. You know, sort of like a strip tease. Can you think of some ideas that feel like this to you?

Synchronistic Signs

If your CE feels that you're not receiving it or hearing it, then it will try different avenues to ensure that you listen. There are excitement and ideas, but it will also use signs to get your attention. Those 'chance' meetings or that 'venue that became free at the last minute,' for the one weekend you'd imagined holding your event, or when your eyes randomly dart to find the one article that details the reasons there is a big need for your CE. What about when you see someone else moving in the direction of your idea—there ain't nothing that gets you to pay attention like someone else fulfilling your dream! Sounds competitive, but it's true! Even though there is no competition from the viewpoint of a CE—because there is no ego involved at all—the CE knows just how to get its human to pay attention. You'll put on an episode of *Shark Tank* and the second pitch is creepily similar to what you've been called to and you feel so damn bothered by the fact it's not *you* up there. Everywhere you go, your chief entity is plotting little signs.

Step 2 is I want to tell the whole world!

The Click

The moment that you realize—ah-ha—that this very specific instruction, this request that's come right to you, is not fleeting. It is not a dumb idea or a crazy thought you had in the shower. It is real, and you know that because you haven't felt this much excitement and certainty about something in a very long time. Soon you become one with your CE. You merge together and begin to plan, because this is your job, and it's not going anywhere. Evidence of that is everywhere and that feels very good, very right. You stop feeling like it's a maybe, you stop spending energy going back and forth deciding whether or not it's real and worth pursuing, you stop questioning whether or not these ideas are different or just like 'all the others'. Your approach to these new ideas matures and it settles into you like a real commitment.

Tell Everyone

Now you are so excited that you can't possibly hold it in any longer. You want to tell everyone and anyone. I call this the Entrepreneurial Dribble phase, where you have such an urge to make sense of this. It's as though you want to triple check that you are not 'crazy,' so you tell others, ask for advice, draw site maps, brainstorm with friends, research, and even seek out funding. You feel like you need to do it all overnight. Smooch this excitement period. And request that this excitement is trickled into your blood like an IV drip over the next 5-10 years. Cos this early phase excitement is fuel like no other. Relish in it and drink it up, but don't let it burn you. You feel there is urgency, but remember that when you are working with a chief entity, or anything as close to Source as that, their energy inspires you and you feel that your human pace is always too slow. It's not. Your CE chose you, the human, for a reason, and will always let you know if you're moving too slow.

STEP 3 is giving birth.

You're Pregnant!

You need a pen and notepad around at all times. The Notes app is on the home screen of your iPhone, because one minute you'll be driving just singing along to *Savage Garden* (Don't mind me, I've taking a trip back to the 90's while cruising on Tesla radio), and the next you'll feel the need to stop and write it all down. You'll be hiking and you feel you need to sit by a rock and take some voice notes, because you just got *the next step* revealed to you. Like an unborn baby, you must nourish your CE. You start to feel like its nutrition is your responsibility. You are pregnant with it. You don't go a day without feeding it, drawing it out, adding something to the grand plan, or paying it a lot of attention.

It's here!

Some days you feel like it's growing bigger than anything you've ever carried in your body before, and there is natural worry about whether it's going to be as healthy as you hope when it arrives. There is also natural fear and doubt. You question yourself. "Am I really up for this?" It's so big, so scary, and everything is going to change when it's here. You may have a long, beautiful natural labour. Or you may have a short swift one. But it's all good, because once you birth what you've been growing, your CE is in the world now.

STEP 4 is you have an invisible partner.

Ask

The key here is to know how you communicate with your CE. In other words, how do you turn your tap on? Maybe you sit and journal and that's how your guidance comes. Or you take a walk in the woods. Meditate, run, or knit—anything goes. You might even ask specific questions and listen for signs in your body. This relationship is something to nurture and develop over time so you can understand how you and your CE communicate. Maybe it's just through excitement, downloads and ideas. In time you will find that your CE will show you things by putting people, opportunities, and reminders right there for you. This is the step that takes things from "Oh, I have a vision," to "Oh, I'm partnered with an entity."

Execute

This is where you do something. Nothing changes without an action, right? This is where something must move. Sure, it's important to map out a 10-year plan so you can see the spaciousness of the vision, but you don't have to trip over how accurate it is, and let that keep you from making the first move. There is always a first step, an action. And humans with their logic and their emotions, more often than we'd like to admit, often don't make it to this step. Your CE will guide you more when you're a train moving along the tracks. It's hard to steer a train that's not moving, but it's easy to steer one that's in motion. Here you trust your guidance—that flowing tap you're in and move by making the first step that "feels right." That step might be big and external—renting a building, hiring a tech guru, taking out a loan, booking a trip. That step might feel small and internal, like committing something to yourself, beginning a Facebook page, scribbling it all out on paper. Just begin.

STEP 5 is the wild journey

Now it's time to buckle up for the most rewarding, beautiful, meaningful ride ever, because the long term journey with your CE has begun. You will build a team, you will hire and fire, you will make moves that surprise you, delight you, and scare you. You will be mentored every day by what is a $1 billion strategy coach, who works directly with the Universe itself. You will grow more as a person than you could ever imagine because you become humble, you become connected, you become involved in something so much greater than any other endeavour. When you're working with a CE, it's easier. You realize you're not the business, the project, the company, the organization, the album. You're the instrument. And the instrument is always being used by a hand that knows how to use it. Your CE does know how to use you. And you are the most equipped human on planet Earth to commence the process.

So smirk, really smirk, do star jumps or rolly-pollies or put on some *Destiny's Child* and crump for a minute, because this is exciting, *super exciting.* You have all resources available to you! You are infinitely supported! You are at the beginning of a grand adventure! What you're building will live on forever, and no one is more equipped than you are. No one—or else your CE would have visited someone else.

PS: It won't be easy.

Let's not pretend this is all glitter and woo-hoo, just because an idea came to us and we're guided by a conscious entity all of our own. With the most rewarding times will come the most challenging. Your CE will stretch you and test you more than any other person can—more than any mentor, coach, book, or family member can. Growing pains will come in all forms.

There are the entrepreneurial business type of growing pains. It's like being forced to put your CEO 'big girl pants' on and get to it. You will write budgets and create plans, even if you loathe doing such activities. There will be people you must let go of, because that will bring your company, work, vision to the higher standard, but that does not mean that you will be able to articulate these needs gracefully or objectively. However, your CE has a low limit for "one more chance" decisions. This will be especially challenging as you reach the point—only in some cases—of moving beyond your mentors, because their guidance no longer fits and your gut is yelling something loud and clear. You must listen, because you CE is on the other end of that megaphone. Sometimes you'll just learn lessons the tough way. Sometimes that's exactly what your CE (and your soul too) wants you to do.

I've made investments and decisions from fear, instead of faith, and the entire time while making them, I've known. I remember investing in someone last year and the entire process leading up to it my gut and my CE were both saying "This isn't right!" followed by "But you're gonna learn that." I've learned so much more from my disappointments and 'stings' than I have from my easy wins. Our CE will lead us into situations that make us a better human, molding us into the person we need to be to lead and create more powerfully in the world.

There are the creative expansion and personal development growing pains. They are you being called to create something that is newer, fresher, and beyond what has been conjured up yet. Scary, right? But you go on faith and you go forth anyway, because you are listening to something higher and that is only going to take you somewhere higher. Or you sit with your notebook and sketching out a program for six months, only to be clock-blocked and redirected again and again. "What a complete waste of time!" you say. "All part of the process, baby," says your CE. "No creative time is ever wasted."

I've had days where I'd be so overwhelmed, I'd find myself crying in the corner of a cafe, texting my husband things like, "I just don't know if it's worth it." Boy oh boy. A partnership with an entity as pure, certain and powerful as a CE, is naturally going to invite you to go higher. And that's not gonna be a walk in the park (duh!). Talk about being stretched! It's just like when you're in an intimate relationship with someone who feels like your constant mirror. It's rewarding. You grow and thrive, but it's challenging. This is the kind of person who helps you sees what sometimes you can't see and grow beyond it.

In working with my CE (Jeaniius), I've had to consistently face off with my responsibility pattern. You know, the one where I take on more energetic and emotional responsibility than one nervous system possibly can handle. My over-responsibility makes others under-responsible. That's a key finding of my personal growing pains. I've had to grow ballsy AF in regards to my alignment, despite it being the toughest thing in the world some days to say no to people I care about because I simply, cannot do everything (and have finally learned this. Through growing pains). I've grown through the stings of receiving blunt, but honest and constructive, feedback and had to learn how to receive it meaningfully and powerfully—not put on my ninja turtle costume and respond back in heated defense as if it's personal. I've had days where it felt like the Universe accidentally emptied it's bag of 'challenges' onto my front door all at once. Like an avalanche day. Not a creative avalanche kinda day but a 'omg you're fucking kidding me. Is this really happening?' avalanche day.

Even when the avalanche days come, and the work feels bigger than the fuel, just stop and remind yourself of the word *privilege* and take a step back and realize what you're doing. There is no perfection needed in this work. It's not a one man show, but a dance between you, your team, and a divine entity who is guiding you and able to resolve anything and everything and will always show up in the purity of the visions it sends you, as long as you keep participating in the process.

And once you do, you can thank yourself for your big, beautiful divine work and for working with a CE to bring forth a vision that is profound and world-shifting. So, *thank you*, from me to you. We are now living in The New Way and are able to understand and to operate business at a higher level. Businesses—or should we say all creative and entrepreneurial forms and collectives—are here on Earth to evolve human consciousness, and they come wearing the disguises of projects, budgets, numbers, computers, bank accounts, and staff meetings. Look under every coat and you will see divinity. Your chief entity is your personal development and soul evolution wrapped up into one. You will be shown. You will be challenged. And things will be requested of you that you might never have requested of yourself. You have a CE, which has been employed by Source, so that you can change your world.

It's not your job to know it all. That's the job of your Chief Entity. Your relationship with your CE is one of the most profound you will have. CEs guide us, as the humans that were chosen to bring them to life. You will be humbled as an entrepreneur as you are subtly guided to realizations of it's not about you. You will be stretched and supported, and through this relationship you will bridge the gap between consciousness and business. You are the human, hand-picked by your CE. It's here to serve you, just as you're here to serve it.

POP OUT : Some Chief Entities

The CE: KAKAO Ceremonial Drinking Chocolate

The human: Makenzie Marzluff

I came across Guatemalan Drinking Cacao on the internet, and being in the food industry, I was curious as to why I had never been educated about this before. After learning that native, whole-bean Cacao is the original strain from Mother Earth, I immediately ordered some. Who knew that Mayans had been drinking this for centuries for health and spiritual purposes? This sacred drinking chocolate, or should I say the plant goddess Cacao herself, begin fueling my days with energy, creativity, connection, heart-expansion, and bliss. I fell in love with pure cacao as nature intended, and KAKAO the entity was born. She started tapping me on the shoulder, and finally I heard a voice "go to Guatemala." To the rest of the world it looked irresponsible, because I was knee deep in credit card debt. I was scared shitless, but there was no way I could deny the divine guidance.

My first trip to Guatemala flowed perfectly, and I have been guided every step of the way. My 'ride or die' tribe came with KAKAO's birth very quickly (thank you PK for sharing the love), which is an example of the beautiful flow that happens with Chief Entities when you fully trust and allow them to come through, despite all fear or outside forces.

The CE: The Collab Nation

The Human: Amie Berghan Paulet

I work for and with my Chief Entity, Collab, aka the Collab Nation. Our meeting was a long time coming but there was so much work that I had to do before I was ready for him. You know those really deep, soulful friendships you have, where if you had met during your rave days the friendship would have probably crashed and burned and it took years of lessons, self-discovery and growth before you were ready for that friendship?

We're like that. When he came into my life it wasn't like he suddenly showed up out of nowhere. It was as if we'd been bumping into each other for years, off and on, but he finally tapped me on the shoulder and was like "So, are you going to sit down with me and listen to what I've got for you, or are you going to keep ignoring me? If so I'm off. I'll find someone else who can bring me to life."

The tap came in the form of an idea, a vision of a big bad ass company and this overwhelming emotion that washed over me all in one moment. When I said yes to sitting down and listening to him—this idea that was forming, this business that was coming to life, this entity that was so separate from me that he couldn't just be called a business or idea, he flowed so clearly and so audibly through me onto the pages I was writing on that I knew if I had said no, or if I came back later, I would have regretted it for the rest of my life.

The essence of Collab is that of an innovator and problem solver. The conversation around sustainable and ethical fashion is by no means new, but he's making it fresh by really throwing the old rule book out the window. He really couldn't give two fucks about how things are 'supposed' to be done and is much more interested in how things can be done. Papatūānuku (Mother Earth), those whose hands make the clothes we wear, and the future generations are the number one stake holders in all business he touches. He gets that there is no one solution in the fashion industry and that there will always be trade-offs, but the labels and brands that get him so hot are those with transparency and a constant commitment to evolving and gifting Papatūānuku our utmost respect while making threads that are fresh AF.

The Silent Stakeholders

Keep a seat at the boardroom for the kids and the Earth.

Stakeholder: a person or a party who has an interest in a company or organization and what it does. They can either *affect* the business or be *affected* by the business. Typically, the internal stakeholders are the investors, employees, and the customers and the wider, external stakeholders are people like the suppliers.

As The New Way becomes the new normal, many companies are now also considering their community to be a primary stakeholder. Altered Seasons is a company founded by Kelly Reddington at age 14 (legend). It's a one-for-one model, so for every candle sold, Altered Seasons provides a meal to an American in need through Feeding America. Wholefoods created a Local Producer Loan Program, which gives up to $10m loans to small local producers to help grow their businesses. We, the millennials, are redefining the terms that we use to do business, and that is often one of the topics I'm asked to address. Take for example, a podcast interview I did for my friend, Jeff Slayter.

Jeff's work is in coaching high-performing entrepreneurs who lead big organizations and helping them to lace consciousness throughout. The topic was Billionaire Business Owners, and Jeff was asking me to shed some light on how these behemoth corporations can prepare for the next 10 years of evolution now that we are in the world of The New Way. *Pretty rad, right? The New Way is making waves.* So he and I got to discussing how stakeholders put the pressure on companies. Stakeholders demand impressive ROI, and companies aim to please. Therefore when making many decisions (definitely big decisions) corporations must take into consideration how decisions and changes affect their stakeholders. And now that we are in the world of The New Way, these corporations are being called to make a lot of changes. Change to be more sustainable. Change to be more conscious. Change to be more evolved. Changes to The New Way.

Now it's all well and good for the CEO and founders and presidents—and all the forward thinking millennial employees—to understand the ways of The New Way, but what about company stakeholders? If they can't support the small increase in costs to fund the installation of solar panels or the new rule that employees are permitted to work in funky cafes (to open up their tap) or the eco-friendly packaging, then will they be on board? Hmm… How often is it the stakeholders that are the ones holding back the evolution of conscious business? *Scratch that.* I want to ask an even more important question.

Who Are The Stakeholders?

The investors or the owners or anyone that has a 'stake in the business?' The stakeholders, are they customers or are they employees? Are they the people who sit on the board of directors? Most of those answers are spot on, but in The New Way we are adding two new seats to the board of the directors, which invites two more stakeholders to the table. These two seats are the most important stakeholders. Bold claim. I know, but it's true. These two seats are for the silent stakeholders.

Planet Earth is a silent stakeholder. Sure, you won't see the Amazon Rainforest waltz into your board meeting with her brief case and some snazzy specs to sit down to discuss your next big move and how she would be affected. You won't see the Arctic Ocean plop down in a rolly chair, silence her phone, and take a sip from a fresh cup of coffee. Oh how differently companies would do business if they had a big ol' oak tree sitting at the conference room table while they scaled their inventory, changed their packaging, and increased their profit margins. Would we be pleasing these board members? Would representatives of Planet Earth invest in moves that affect her future?

Our Children is a silent stakeholder. Just picture a 3-year-old waddling into your board meeting, sporting a tiny suit, carrying a cell phone, and sitting down to discuss the company's financials and proposing ways to cut back on carbon emissions. Or a 9-year-old who crawls up onto a leather chair, flips her pony tail, and pulls out a sparkling wand to point out her suggestions for becoming LEED certified and allowing a flex schedule for employees on the Power Point. Would these kids be pleased? Are we taking care of their future and creating a world where they are able to thrive? What would our kids say if they could pull up a seat at the table.

> *Imagine if at every board meeting, there was someone speaking on behalf of the planet, and then someone speaking on behalf of the children, and these two people were considered the most valuable stakeholders of them all.*

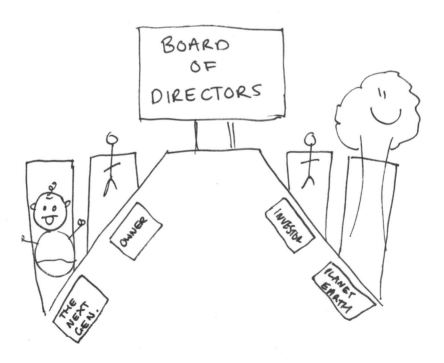

It's survival. These voices will be heard whether you have open ears or not, and the needs and wants of these voices are very wise, fundamental guides for anyone looking to make a business decision over the next 10 years. Millennials play an important role in business. For it is their ideas and proposals that represent these two silent stakeholders. Our generation is the voice for Planet Earth and Our Children until they have their own. Yes, Mother Nature will have a voice, she already does, but she's not roaring like she will soon roar. And children will have a voice, just you wait. Their divine intolerance is on levels that we can't even imagine. Everything will change when they come into their voice. Just like so many things are changing now as we, the millennials, are coming into ours.

But What About The Real Investors?

Peta, it *is* real business we are talking about, so those real investors do matter. I'm sure some of you are thinking just that, to which I say, "Yes! Absolutely! 100%!" We cannot ignore the traditional elements of business that help it grow, because we know that conscious enterprise needs growth in order to thrive. Acknowledging that there are silent stakeholders will not take away the drive and ambition of a company to crush it, but if you are crushing it *and* letting down the two core stakeholders, is that really crushing it? Congrats on your EBTA (earnings before tax and appreciation), your slot on the Forbes 500, and that you're going public, but is that the real and whole success of The New Way if our planet's and children's needs are not being met? Is that sustainable success if our planet's and children's needs are not being met? No, it's not.

Is it too hard or unrealistic to build a company like this? No. It's easy, and more importantly, it's necessary. With infinite resources, imagination, and guidance, we have no excuse not to expand into more consciousness, awareness and to allow the The New Way to teach us how to do to do business, conscious business.

We are asking that companies adapt to The New Way, not because it's 'hip and trendy' but because it will become the only way to thrive into new consciousness. It will be for survival. Going forward, I encourage all companies to have two seats at their board table—one for The planet, and two for Our children. Their voice matters and their voice is very useful for helping companies move in the direction of evolution and consciousness over the next 10 years.

POP OUT: Psssttt, money wants to tell you something

Oh my beautiful, conscious human,

I love that you picked up this book. You're called to being hired by Earth in a lighter, more fun, more playful, and more impactful way, and I know you love exploring consciousness and I know how deeply you care for the planet. Guess what, so do I. I'm an energy, here on Earth, to serve our evolution just like you are. Only I don't have legs to walk, so I can't throw on a pair of Nike Frees and run to the hippies and beg them to take me like you can. I am pure energy, and the only way I can move is to flow to my exact energetic match. And I'd love if the most conscious, heart-centered people on Earth were the people who called me in the most—like you.

And it's tilting that way. Oh boy is it ever, finally, tilting that way. Those who have money that you wrong—the people who pollute the environment and lead with greed—are not meant to make you hate money. But they do. And I know this. And it's heart-breaking, because that hatred makes your magnificent work suffer. I want to help you, but I cannot discriminate between energies. I go where I am invited. I am available to all who can get into energetic alignment with their desire for me and their callings that require more of me. I, too, can be a valuable member of your team. I want to be there for you in amounts that have no bounds. I want to flow to you in ways that have your jaw drop. I am so much more than the number you see in your bank account. I want to surprise you.. I am the alignment you feel between you and me. I already show up in your life. Didn't I help you buy this book? I want to show up for you in greater ways.

I just can't stay if you keep talking crap about me, resisting me, judging me, and wronging me. It's energetically impossible for me to, and I want you to know that. My divinity doesn't change. My desire to serve you doesn't change. My employment by Source doesn't change. Your invitation of me does change. This isn't a game of me, it's a game of you. I want to serve you. So stop running from me. Stop hiding from me. Stop wronging me. Stop borrowing the money story of presidents, family members, people who have used money in ways that don't vibe with you. I want to play a role in your life that allows you to be free of worry and fully in the creative pleasures and privilege of your life. Your ideas, I love them. I'm over here putting my invisible shin guards on ready to come in a play, but I just can't, until you truly, invite me. You love the planet, and you want to contribute to some big planetary shifts.

You and me, we have a relationship of our own.I want your intentions to be the ones that circulate me around the world. I want you to give me instructions of how to generate, what to generate, and I want you to kiss me with consciousness every time you do. I want your heart to be one that touches me. You have a role to play. We all do. Even me. That's why I'm here. I want the global money story to change and not just be rewarding for a few. The people who love money the most aren't the ones with the heart like yours. Imagine if the people who loved money the most were the ones who cared about the planet the most, people the most. That's why we need you to change your story around money, so that the next generation doesn't inherit a money story that stops them from rewriting it for the entire collective. It's up to you to shift, so our relationship can thrive. We can have a rewarding relationship, or a non-rewarding one. It's up to you. You don't need to get rich. You already are. I'm here for you in boundless amounts, but you don't need it all. You don't want it all. All of the resources you need to do what you're called to do, and thrive in your creative bliss—that's what you deserve.

There, I have laid it all out flat. My stance hasn't changed. I am eternally and boundlessly here to serve you—your joys, your desires, your callings, your endeavours and all of the epic shit you want to create. I am here for you. I will meet you exactly where you are energetically. I am a valuable member of team light, team conscious, team create epic shit, and team love. I am all yours.

Open up and let me in. That's what superheroes do.

I care about climate change. I care about making sure the Amazon is here for your children and their children and their children. I care about eradicating homelessness completely in the next 20 years. I care about supporting companies with a social cause and ensuring all companies rise up into this new consciousness you already embody.

I don't care if you need a lot of me or just a little. I'm don't get my joys on making people filthy rich. I just care that you know that I am doing everything I can do, and it's now up to you to now get into alignment with me. I want to create the epic shit you want to create, too. But you're the one with the hands, the feet, the computer, the reach, and the influence. All I do is flow. We've gotta be on the same page in order to work together.

So, tell me. How can I help you do, create and give to the world like you so badly want to?

Xx

Money

Your Money Story

You don't have to choose between consciousness and money.

We can't talk about business without talking about money. We can't enjoy the fruits of our conscious enterprise without talking about money. We can't even slap #consciousentrepreneur on our Instagram bio without a nod to money. Money is one of my favourite topics to discuss because it is one of the most taboo and triggering topics out there. People spend so much energy trying to avoid the energies of money.

Money is one of the most mistaken energies on our Earth. It's often viewed as something we have to struggle to get, something that defines our place in this false hierarchy of success (which you know is false after reading this book). Call it what you will—a resource, an exchange, an energy—everyone has a natural response, a formed relationship, and story around how money is or isn't a rewarding part of their life. More often than not the story is the latter. And sure, there are those who have a beautiful, rewarding relationship with money regardless of the amount they have. *Hallelujah!* But I think you'd agree that right now on Earth, many believe money just to be something we must earn in order to live. There is collectively a lot of unease and general *ugh* around money.

There is also another story being told, a story spread around by the spiritual and conscious folk, who say that every single person should have the same amount of money and that anyone who has more than they need is "greedy," and in order to be a respected member of the conscious collective, we must never go after more than we "need." In other words, the *nice things are nice, but are not for me* mentality. I'm sure you've heard a version of this before, and, in some part, I can understand its origins. Historically, money has become a collective story that where people see a lot of money, they also see a lot of greed. It is easy to see where there is a parallel drawn—money = anti-conscious. It's also incredibly tough for heart-centered, conscious people to see such huge inequality in the world—both locally and in other countries. I know it doesn't sit well in my belly to walk past homeless people who have slept a night in the freezing cold, starving, and watching people one by one walk past them in $1,500 shoes and a snakeskin belt that cost more than some people's cars. I understand people feeling like, "If I truly care about all brothers and sisters, then I am not going to pursue any more resources than I need, because if I have more, then they have less."

Is that story true? *It's up to you.* Is it rewarding? *No.* We are only seeing the contrast, the difference between the experience of people on both ends of the spectrum. It is that contrast that creates the emotional tug. *Why do we feel that way? What is this contrast telling us? Is it asking us to hate money? To feel bad about earning and creating it?* That's one story you can create.

But think about it. Every feeling is a clue, it's an invitation. Why else do we see this contrast and feel this contrast? It doesn't present itself in our lives and orbits just to piss us off. This contrast is inviting us into something bigger. It's inviting us into a solution. It's inviting us to create a new story that doesn't make us feel guilty, shitty, and sad whenever we see it, but inspired, grateful and fully equipped to participate in creating some sort of change. It's inviting us to participate and to rewrite the story. Beginning with us, and then flowing onto the rest of the world.

Money is not evil. Money is not the culprit here. Money is used for a lot of good in this world, and I think we can all agree that when money is used to create life-saving technologies, it's a divine energy. I think we can all agree that when money is handed from a stranger to a homeless person with love, it's a divine energy. I think we can all agree that when money is used to fund scholarships for under-privileged children, it's a divine energy. I think we can all agree that when money is given to women who are finding their feet again after domestic abuse, it's a divine energy. I think we can all agree that when money is used to grow organic fruits and vegetables to feed communities, it's a divine energy.

So when is it *not* a divine energy? *When you choose for it not to be.*

You Don't Have To Choose Between Money And Consciousness

Money and consciousness are not separate. *Your story* about money and consciousness says they're separate. Just like we want to see the entire Forbes 500 run by conscious leaders, we want to see money in the hands of heart-centered, conscious people like you. How else do we expect the collective story of greed, struggle and inequality to change if the people with the big hearts don't participate? If you don't like where money is being spent, create some, and let your heart spend it instead.

Money is not something to shy away from as we expand in The New Way, but something to love, to celebrate, and to redefine. We can do big, beautiful things with money.

We can completely eradicate homelessness in the next 20 years. We can ensure nobody goes hungry in the next 20 years. We can do anything in the next 20 years, but it's going to require people like you stand up and participate. Not just by meditating, reading and protesting, but by noticing that the contrast and inequality in this world is what tugs on you emotionally. Money, however, is inviting you to participate and not to avoid. Our generation has a huge opportunity to not only rewrite the money story for ourselves, but to rewrite it for our children and for all children to come.

You don't need a flashy car or a fancy watch, but if you do want nice things, have them. There is no lack of abundance in this world because you want something sparkly. It doesn't take away from your generosity and heart-centeredness. Money wants to bring joy as much as it wants to bring change, and the key here is to eradicate judgement around what brings people joy. So we can be in a conscious, beautiful, rewarding and choice based relationship with it. We are a free-willed Universe and we all have the energetic capabilities to create whatever we want to create. Just because someone's vision requires one billion dollars, it doesn't make them any less of a beautiful, conscious human than someone else who needs $40K a year to live and paint. Judgment has to stop. And this desire for everyone to have the same amount of money, regardless of what they do, has to stop. It's never going to work that way.

Every single person is not capable of energetically holding the same amount of money. Every person does not require the same amount of money. Every person is not equipped to have the same amount of money. And not every person chooses the same amount of money. Money is energy. Could we get the exact amount of sleep, run the same number of miles, drink the same amount of coffee? *No*.

But here's the thing… everyone deserves to have *enough*.

The Goal Of An Abundant World

Everyone deserves to have enough. The fact that there are people hungry, while some are bathing in a $45,000 tub of goats milk is an interesting contrast that pains and inspires so many of us. Our generation will help to bridge the gap of inequality. We will eradicate homelessness and poverty by the time we leave, I'm sure of it. We will give it our best bloody shot to gift our children a world where we all take responsibility for those who are suffering. But first, the story around money has to change. Our understanding of true abundance has to change. We have the power to distribute resources in ways that appreciate that *all lives have equal value*. But we have to also appreciate money's role and we have to include it as a member of our team.

We can appreciate the divinity of money and its purpose on Earth to create happy, fulfilled lives and make change wherever we see change necessary. It can be an exciting resource that we always have available to us, as long as we energetically align with it. Consciousness and money are partners. Just like consciousness and business are. But they're only partners if conscious people play.

Change the story. Let your relationship with money turn a light on for the collective.

If you want money to work differently in the world, you've got to play. Too many people are borrowing stories about it that suck. Money is begging to be circulated in a way that changes the game for the greater good. So, we need those who give a shit about our Earth and our people, to participate in upgrading our story. It begins with your money story.

Your Money Story

When asked, *What is money?* what would you say?

> *Money is a—currency, resource, energy, something we use to trade goods and services.*

> *It's the biggest stress in life, a vehicle for greed. Money creates inequality.*

> *Money is a loving, divine entity that wants to serve the collective, a great instrument for change.*

> *It's a tool that allows people to live rich and fulfilled lives to whatever degree they choose.*

> *Money accelerates humanity and connects us more than ever.*

Yeah, okay. Money is all of those things. I can agree with that, but do you know what all of those things are? They are stories, and that's what money is. Money is a story. We all have a money story. It's a relationship, a viewpoint, a set of beliefs. Your money story is no different from your spirituality story, your food story, your marriage story, your climate change story, your race story. And the thing about stories is that it's impossible to give the whole world the same story and have it apply to all. You couldn't pay me a million dollars to eat a raw T-bone steak, just like you probably couldn't pay a truck driver in Alabama a million dollars to eat nothing but raw veggie patties with hummus and sprouts for the rest of his life. Everyone sees the world through different eyes, has different beliefs, and therefore tells a different story. In fact, we are constantly constructing our story, which is playing out in our lives as fast as we are writing it.

Do people who love money have more money because they love it? Or do they love it because they have more of it? What about those that hate money? Is it because they don't have it? Or do they not have it because they hate it?

There is just so much "stuff" around money, and most people's stuff is not rewarding or positive. For example, I posted a video inviting people to come to TNWL Sydney that showed people laughing, crying, and declaring that this was the most transformative experience of their lives. I've had people say things like "My cells are completely different now." and "I've been to Tony Robbins five times and I've never been moved this much." The event is really effective, and the value is far greater than a $3,000 ticket; however this 2-day event costs less than $500. I don't yet make a profit on these ticket sales. TNWL is a big festival, and no corners are cut on fulfilling the mighty, glorious, colourful badass vision—because I want the whole vision to come to life for everyone.

> "I bought one for me and my sister! I just know how valuable this is!"

> "I'm doing whatever I can to fly from Denmark!"

> "This price is a steal"

> "This is priceless!"

> "Why the fuck do you charge so much for this shit?"

> "You're ripping people off!"

Just in one video post, you get so many different money stories and different perspectives. Needless to say, each one of those commenters will experience a different outcome. No judgment on anyone. Not even a good, bad, positive, or negative vibe from me. All there is, is rewarding and unrewarding, which leads me to what I want to yell from the rooftops....

"Money Is Not The Problem. Your Story About Money Is!!!!!"

Stop talking shit about it. Stop being so mean and nasty. Stop talking behind its back and acting as if it's the most needy, annoying, and careless relationship only to complain about why it's not showing up in your energy field (your life). Money isn't judgmental towards humans, humans are judgmental towards money.

Would you not agree that the money story that many people are playing out in their lives is one that makes them cringe at the thought of it, makes them want to run and hide when they have to check their bank account, or scoff at other people who have more than they do? From this perspective, can't you see that most people focus on the "wrongness" of money more than the opportunity to create a new story. We've all been raised with a different money story, and most of us were not raised with one that was positive or rewarding—and positive or rewarding has nothing to do with amounts. Let's look at some examples.

○ Some children were raised seeing one parent threaten another—with money.

○ Some children were bribed—with money.

○ Some children were raised in a family with money understood as the root of all evil.

○ Some children were raised in a home with plenty of money but little abundance.

○ Some children were raised to believe that money didn't matter, because community love and collaboration were so strong.

○ Some children were told not to give money away.

○ Some children were told the rich get richer and the poor get poorer.

○ Some children were raised in a conscious community where people chose between being spiritual and being wealthy.

You must rise above the collective money story and create one that is rewarding for you, your family, your tribe and the planet, and I'm here, with this chapter, to tell you that you can.

A little PK aside:

Peta's Money Story

I was not 'born into money', nor was I born into a rewarding money story. I was raised by a single mum who lived on a full-time teacher's wage and raised four kids, none of which ever went without a single thing growing up. I believed in Santa Claus into my late teens (not embarrassed about that one bit), because I had no idea how our mum could manage a trampoline, table tennis table, soccer boots, bathers, and those special pencil cases made out of wetsuit material all in one Christmas. She never missed a beat, always surrounding us with love and care, and I have no idea how she did it, money-wise. But we knew—things were tight and mum was stressed. Every week was a balancing act, and there was always something. Lose the house, hot water tank broken, our taped-up van windows, borrowed cars, the time when she didn't even have a bedroom of her own to sleep in and had to sleep on the couch because we were five in a three-bedroom house. It's not like we were cheap kids either, with our lives filled with sports, all of us excelling and needing the newest equipment and gear and having to travel.

I wasn't raised with money, but instead raised to see how the lack of money could cause so much stress to someone so generous. My mum not only gave to us kids, but she gave to her community, to the parents of her students, to other teachers. Her operating mode was straight up give. Go above and beyond. I believed that my mum deserved more money. She deserved a break. She deserved a breath out. My nanna died when I was 15, and I wrote her a letter stating that I would look after my mum. I would retire her as a school teacher. I had no clue how, just knew that I would. It was time for my mum to travel, to explore, to stop worrying. That is what she deserved. I would do it through my science career, I originally thought. I worked hard in school, and I learned how to manage my money well. Once I went to the bank as a teenager, and the bank teller who saw the $12K in my bank account, said "Wow! Go you!" But that was me, working odd jobs since the age of 13—bakeries, supermarkets, door-to-door gigs, leading horses around fairs, the waterboy (well, girl) at football games, sandwich artist. I always worked, because I had a plan.

I'd retire Mum through my science career. Yes, I'd get an Honours degree, publish a thesis, get a PhD scholarship, and be a doctor in my field at age 25. So I left high school with high marks and was accepted into the one of the most prestigious exercise and health programs in the world at UWA, and as you know I ticked off my goals all the way up to getting that PhD. Leaving my PhD I had no clue how I was going to keep up with my plan to retire my mum, but I knew I loved health and that money was a part of health. "If you had your health, but were loaded with chronic stress about money, then did you really have your health?" These were questions I began asking.

So many people I knew saw working as a means to an end, earning just enough money to get by, never having enough, and if you did have more than enough, then you were taking from others. I thought that was all BS, and I didn't want that to be how I saw money. I knew how to work, had been doing that my whole life, but I wanted my efforts to translate into more than just an hourly wage. I had examples of this around me in my early twenties. I had wealthy friends who were incredibly successful in their entrepreneurial endeavours. They were older friends in their 30's and 40's who'd 'come from nothing' and created a new money story for themselves and their families. They all had one thing in common, they were super generous and all were involved in philanthropic endeavors, as if it was part of the package—acquiring more money meant acquiring more social responsibility.

I went to money mindset seminars, and I plugged into anything and everything I could learn about true abundance. I listened to Earl Nightingale's *The Strangest Secret* over 200 times, and soaked up anything that taught or talked of the spiritual and energetic aspects of money and abundance. I rewired myself, because it was my job. When my income hit six figures for the first time, I felt so rich, and it was not because of the money, but because I could feel the effects of upgrading my money story. As my income grew and grew, I gave more and more. I became the example of what life in your twenties could be like with hard work and a different money story.

I knew the power of what I could do as an individual if I upgraded my money story, but so many of my friends, peers, colleagues, and people in circles around me didn't.

I had friends who did not like my money story. "All you care about is money," I had one friend say to me. "Who do you think you are wanting more money than most have?", I heard others say through the grapevine. They didn't know my drive. They didn't know how it felt to watch the person I loved more than anything come home stressed after a 14-hour day wondering if we were going to have a house to live in. They didn't know the responsibility I felt to change the money story, not just for my family, but for some of my generation. They didn't know how much I gave, how generous and creative it allowed me to be, and that every day I felt I was helping to bridge the gap between consciousness and spirituality and money. They had their own money stories.

My money story was different:

> *I love money and money loves me. I am trusted with abundant resources from the Universe because I know to circulate money in a way that supports a more conscious world. I want money to do more good in the world—to better support the people who need the basics, to support people who are creating epic shit for our planet to support conscious companies so that we can replace those that are no longer operating at the standard we require. As I create more money, I can circulate more money in the direction of the conscious world I want to see. I appreciate the way money works in my life, and how it allows me to have fast WiFi, organic food, airplane tickets, and memorable experiences with my family. I love the way it can be used as an exchange and a way for us to let others know what we value. I know money is here for a reason and regardless of what the world thinks about money, I*

am grateful for it. I choose to team up with it, not worship it. I choose to honour it, not berate it. Money trusts me and loves working with my heart.

In April 2015, my brother and I retired my mum. She loves routine, she loves family, and she doesn't want a lot. She now travels the world more than she ever has, but mostly she just lives a simple life in our childhood home. I know that we've added at least 20 years on to her life, and I have a good feeling that my starseed will have her nanna for much longer than if I hadn't have rewritten my money story—for my mum and for my generation.

Change Your Own Money Story, Change The Collective's

The other day, I was sitting in a café on Bondi Beach, and a young girl came over to me. She was the waitress at the restaurant and had the sweetest energy. She came right over to my table without any hesitancy at all. I could tell she was so excited to share something with me, by the big grin on her face.

"Are you Peta Kelly?" she asked.

"Yesh," I said, with my hand over my mouth, mid mouthful of food.

"My name is Mikhaela. You have completely changed my money story. For the first time in my life I'm no longer afraid to earn more of it so that I can do more of what I love for me and for others. I can't thank you enough."

It made my day. Not because I wanted Mikhaela to go off and buy four islands next to Richard Branson's, but because she was choosing her own story with money, and not borrowing it from the world. I want to help us write a new money story together. One that isn't always about blaming the rich, but rather equipping more people to be in the abundance that is available to them. I want my generation to stop borrowing money stories from each other that don't serve them. Because when you stop, then you really can enjoy organic food, give to your fav not-for-profit, travel more, buy sustainable clothes labels even if they cost more, live on the ocean, give to those in need without batting an eyelid, build conscious enterprises that support your communities, or take care of the people you love, or buy a Tesla.

Homie, your money story is 150% up to you to change. So it's time to change it. You can re-write your money story at the end of this book in the Bonus section called—THE SCRIPT. But first there is a super important step.

Love Letter To Money

To change your money story once and for all, your relationship with money has to change. In order to unlock resistance around your new story, you must soften to money. There is one very powerful money exercise that has changed the game for so many of my tribe. We have all written a Love Letter to Money, so that is what I'm asking you to do. Grab a pen and paper and write a love letter to money. You don't have to show a soul this letter, you just have to drop into your heart and let out whatever you've always wanted to say. There is no right or wrong way to do this. Just let it out as if it's an old high school boyfriend or girlfriend you never forgave and it eats away at you every day. Just let rip.

○ Write down everything. Money already knows everything, so let it all out. Write how you've treated it in the past, and why. What you're sorry for. What you thought was true. And how you want your relationship to change. Tell money want you want to do with it. Why you want more (if you do). How you want it to show up in your life. Let it all out. And let money listen. Let the charge you have around money dissolve, by remembering that money didn't define your relationship with it, you did.

○ Address how you feel about it. Write how you used to think and feel about it, your new intentions for your relationship, and your deepest feelings around why you want more (if you do) and what you want to do with it. Speak to money as if it's a member of your team and an energy that wants to listen. Speak to money as if it's your friend, because money is your friend. There is no right or wrong, bad structure or good structure. Write no differently than if you were to write a love letter to someone in your life. The key is, to drop into your grace and remember, *money is going to read your letter.*

○ Be honest. If you're angry, write about it, share why. Don't leave anything unsaid. If you're afraid of it, share that. Tell it you don't trust it, don't like it, or wish it would like you—whatever you're really feeling. You won't offend money. If you feel like it's leading to such-and-such, let money know.

○ End with love. Finish your letter with love. Share your new intention and describe the relationship you would like to have and believe that you can.

○ Add appreciation. What does money allow you to do right now? Do you have hot water? Wifi? The ability to fly to see friends and family? Go out for nice meals? Stop and thank money for the way it's already showing up in your life.

Essentially, we are clearing any old residue in your cells that affects your relationship with money. And then we are creating and initiating your new relationship with money. You're going to need your journal, a blank page, and an open mind and open heart.

Questions:

Answer these questions without thinking. Just write down whatever is true for you.

○ What does money do?

○ Where do you find it?

○ What are your first thoughts about it?

○ Who has influenced how you feel about it?

○ How do your parents and family feel about money?

○ How do you feel when you check your bank balance?

○ What typically comes out of your mouth when talking about money?

○ What are some common phrases and terms you've grown up hearing about money?

Now let's have some fun.

○ How is money already showing up in your life?

○ What does money already allow you to do, experience or have?

○ How do you want to feel when you check your bank balance?

○ Who and what do you most love to give to?

○ How would you like money to show up in your life?

Note: Another reminder because it's important ;) At the end of this book there is a bonus section called 'The Script' where you can re-write your money story and start to embody a totally new one—a better more rewarding one. We start with the love letter to money to dissolve the charge around it and create a new story from a place of gratitude and love.

While it's important to understand money in its essence, and all the tips and tricks around attracting and maintaining it, we must first take a look at our own story. Our individual money stories have been defined not just from our childhood, but from lifetimes ago. It's no wonder most people have a non-rewarding money story, but once you know that you can change everything by changing your money story, your choice becomes all the power you need to allow all the abundance you choose. You can start by writing money a love letter.

POP OUT: Love Letters To Money

Love Letter to money—Peta Kelly.

Dear money,

First up, thank you for allowing me to live the life I live. The fact I can sit and write this book on a laptop that I can carry anywhere with me, is such a freaking privilege.

Just yesterday Erik and I were talking about grateful we feel that we can eat the healthy food we most want to eat, without worrying. I just want you to know how grateful I am for this. Thank you for always being there for me to make the food choices that make me feel vital, happy and strong.

Sometimes I crack the shits when my Wifi goes really slow, but then I lol to myself and think of the old plug in internet that barely allowed us to play solitaire. Thank you for allowing us to evolve so that everything can become more convenient for us. We are spoilt little shits sometimes, and I want you to know how damn grateful I am to be able to pay for the internet every month.

Thank you for giving me the choice to spend my time creating for my generation. Not a day goes by I'm not so damn grateful that I get to spend each day doing what my soul most wants me to do. I can do this, because I don't have to go out and chase you, trading my precious time for more of you. You're so there for me. Thank you.

Thank you for that feeling I get when I can circulate you in the direction of those who need some hope. I feel sometimes that's what you are, you're hope. When I give money to people who are homeless or hungry, it's not the money they smile at, it's the fact that a human cared enough to give it to them. Some people are just so without hope, money. And you're the one blamed for that. But what people are missing the most isn't money, it's heart, and love. We have to stop blaming you for what people don't have, and we have to take responsibility that it's our HEARTS that control where money goes. It's not you. Thank you for being a tool that I can use to show people that I care.

Giving is my favorite thing on Earth, money. And thanks to you, I can give without any bounds at all. Thank you for allowing me to show my support for causes and organizations that really inspire me. Thank you for allowing me to use you in ways that create the world I wanna see. Thank you for allowing me to silently gift to new enterprises, young entrepreneurs who are creating epic shit. I feel that's why you come to me so steadily and abundantly, because you know that I get it. You know that I know you're not mine. You know that I'll always circulate you in the direction of more consciousness. Thank you for trusting me to do it. I always will. And I will always invite people into a more generous life too, just like we did with our giveymoon. Next week, Cynthia flies to Kenya to update us on the new village we are supporting. That feeling I get knowing that we can equip these beautiful souls with education, food, water, medical help, and that through mobilizing them, we are unleashing their jeaniius into the world—That is my favorite feeling EVER! Thank for you for being the resource that allows me to generate this change in the world.

Thank you for allowing me to buy organic bamboo sheets and clothes for my new baby. Health and wellbeing is so important to me, and you allow me to live in a way where I never have to lower my standards.

Thank you for being a tool that allowed me to retire my Mum. I've never ever seen her so happy, vibrant, free and relaxed. She's not 'rolling in money' but she's without stress. She has more of a sense of adventure than she did in her 20's. She's gonna be the best Nanna, and she gets to see her grandchild way more than she could if she was still working 12 hour days. Thank you.

Sometimes I feel like you're this bullied kid, who almost all of the world talks shit about. I hate bullies and always have. That's why I feel so called to give you a different voice.

Some people say 'we will know ultimate consciousness when we are free of money in this world'. But I think that's just running from the real truth here. You're not here as a mistake. Come on, like as if the Universe would stuff up like that. You're yet another gift from Source to remind us of one of the greatest lessons we're here to learn 'we get to choose.'

To me, you're not a burden or an evil entity here with the sole purpose to fund Donald Trump's red tie collection. You're not here with the purpose to build missiles and nuclear weapons and fund tireless war campaigns that torment the souls of so many of us.

You're here as a non-judgmental energy with the ability to only go where you're welcomed, and not go where you're not.

I know you are part of Team Earth, money. I so know that you wanna play a bigger role in raising the vibration of the planet. I feel that. It's not you who is responsible for climate change, greed, war, homelessness... It's us. You are just responding to our vibration, our alignment individually and as a collective.

So money, I will always be the voice of your consciousness and I will always make it my work to empower our humans to change their story around you so you can be used in ways that raise the vibration.

We don't bow down to you, you don't bow down to us. We are both instruments on Earth, and change will happen a lot faster if we link arms. Thank you for reminding me of this daily with the way you work in my life.

Love always, PK. X

Love Letter to money: Janna

Dear Money,

Let me start off by saying that you mean a lot to me. That being said, I'm the jerk in our relationship. I mean, really, I put you last most all of the time. I use you whenever I need you. I expect you to be there for me, and I get real pissed when you are not available.

I realize now that I have not been all that understanding of what you need from me. I think it's because I'm mad. I'm mad at you like I'm mad at God. Silly, right? A pretty bold comparison, I know. But here's the thing. We started off as friends. The first time we met you were fun. My dad pulled you from behind my ear in a silver flash, and if I kept a few of you in my pocket I'd turn you in for a lollipop at the lake deli. Soon I'd find you as discs of copper, neatly rolled in brown paper, sitting in my Pa's desk—dressed for a bank deposit. A few years later I saw you hanging on a wall, all green and white and pressed flat behind the glass, a proud display of the very first dollar earned at our local machine shop. It wasn't long before you became a regular in my life. You made your way into my piggy bank (that was shaped like bear) from birthday cards and babysitter's compensation and a teenager's allowance. Turns out, you were pretty important, which is something I learned when I'd watch the adults fuss over you. Who was going to use you? It was always the great battle after a meal at one of our favorite restaurants. Would it be my parents who "got dinner" or their friends? Ugh, what a decision that was! Everyone fighting over you. You were just so important.

In fact, in 1997 you were all anyone ever talked about. "Do you have any money?" my dad would ask me. "Money would make our lives so much easier," my mom would say to me. "You better marry someone with money." I was 15, so, like, okay... But you were never around, and we really needed you then. And you didn't make things easier. You made things so much harder. Medical bills, nursing home costs, prescriptions, mortgages, lawyers, brain injury rehab... they all sucked up what we had of you. And then you sucked up my mom. So I was pissed, and that was that. Perhaps I lost respect back then. I never wanted more of you, but you never gave us enough. I no longer understood your value. Having you and not having you was the same to me. I guess I was drowning in different kinds of pain so North American capitalism didn't really matter. I would see you differently than my mother did. Hell, I wouldn't even see you at all. I was a child of a new generation, born into the infinite possibilities of my own making. I would make shit happen, with or without you.

And now you're laughing. Now I get it. It's 2017, and I really do get it. It's a give and receive relationship, and as an adult woman who runs a business, wants a family, and has every intention in the world to give it all back to my parents—to my mom, it's high time I step up. You're giving me work to do. I accept. I will believe. I will understand your value. I will honor our wealth. I will pay what I owe—literally. I will, I guess, forgive you so we can move on. I hope that you will forgive me too, because I have a feeling that we'll make a pretty good pair. You are, and have always been, very important to me. I suppose I've just been afraid to love you and trust you, because you might not love me back. I know now that you do, and I cannot wait to see the wonderful things we are going to do together.

I want you to know how much I appreciate your helping me create abundance in my life, for my studio, and with my family, and you are more than welcome to be a part of my life at any time.

Much love,

Janna Marie

Love Letter to money—Tara

Dear Money,

Thank you for providing me with all the resources, opportunities and financial abundance I need to create the most appropriate impact on the lives of myself, my family and those that I serve. Thank you for knowing that you are safe with me. Thank you for giving me the opportunity for world class mentoring by the one and only ***INSERT DREAM MENTOR HERE***. I have always wanted to work with her, and now, because of you, I can. What she teaches me directly impacts my tribe, and I feel honored and deeply humbled to be held in the hands of the best there is.

Thank you for making it possible for me to continually invest in my growth. Programs, events, books, masterminds. Thank you for flowing freely to us through the spirit of ***INSERT YOUR BUSINESS / PROJECT / ART / EXPRESSION HERE***—so that we may make whatever decisions are in the highest good of her, her staff and her customers. Thank you for entering my energy field so that I may continue to invest into Team Bliss... travelling and teaching and passing on the same lessons that you have been teaching me. My wealth grows to the extend in which I grow myself, and because of you, I'm able to encourage so many others to step fully into their own growth path and re-write the Money Story for their whole family. Thank you for allowing me to step away from the things that don't feel in alignment with me, and thus, dilute my impact and message. You allow me to hire, delegate, shuffle, reassess and reprioritise constantly.

Thank you for the opportunity to live a life of wild adventure, play and memory-making. The travel that you bestow upon me, the beautiful dinners, the spontaneous road trips, the outrageous ways I'm now able to give to those I love... I am forever grateful. Thank you for circulating so perfectly in and out of me, in a way that is just as it should be.

As I sit here, and I humbly ask for MORE, I can feel your trust in my request, and I know, with every cell in my body, that it is becoming.

All my love,
Tara xo

Love letter to money—Fia

Dear Money,

Writing this letter to you, I feel emotional. I want to take this time to really open my heart and honestly share with you the things my soul is yearning to express. I am so sorry. I see how I have treated you in a poor way, not seeing or valuing you and all you gift me in this life. I want to apologize for all the times I've talked bad about you or believed the stories other people told me about you. I apologize for all the times you've come to me and I haven't even noticed you or thought there was too little of you. I'm sorry for making you feel invisible, guilty, shameful, less than. I apologize for all the worrying I've attached to you, I'm sorry for not trusting you. I apologize for holding you in such a tight grip that you could barely breathe, because I was afraid of circulating you, thinking you would never come back. I apologize for not seeing you as the divine, light and beautiful energy you are. I'm sorry I've blocked your flow to me, all the times I've been stuck in scarcity and limited your ways of coming to me. I apologize for not having a safe space for you to enter. I'm sorry for not loving you.

I want you to know how grateful I am for you. You are magic, I see and feel that now and I want to love shower you cause girl you deserve it. Thank you for all the blessings you bring into my life. Thank you for the freedom you give me and all the epic memories we create together. Money, you are freakin' awesome. Thank you making it possible for me to eat such delicious, organic food that nourishes my body. Thank you for the wifi that connects me with the whole world, making it possible for The Supercharged to exist, for keeping me in contact with my beloved when we are across the Earth from each other. Money, you bless me with heating in this apartment, you make it possible for me to live in this beautiful space that brings me such peace and joy. Thank you for making this and so much more possible. You're such a powerhouse! Thank you for all the ways you serve me, you are my best friend. I love you so much. Thank you for fueling my business, making it possible for me to record new music that serves hundreds of people around the world, and soon with the help of you, billions. You make that happen and I feel honored and so grateful to have you on my team.

Can we rewrite our story? I come to you with the deepest respect and would to love build a new and healthy relationship with you. I've realized that I've given you all these mixed signals that wasn't matching what I wanted, and I'm sorry for that. I'll be crystal clear from now on. Let's create this together. Team <3

Money feels so good in my life. My relationship with money is evolving everyday. Money loves coming to me cause she knows I respect and love her so much. She feels safe coming to me, knowing I'm not bitching her around , complaining how there's never enough of her or how she is the root of all evil or any of that nasty shit. I take care of her, I honor her like the divine, powerful and queenly energy she is and therefor she flows easily and abundantly to me. Money loves coming to me cause she know I create amazing things with her.

When I check my bank balance, I feel ease, exhilaration and gratitude, look at all the massive abundance coming in, these divine resources of energy, eagerly waiting to be circulated in the most epic ways in my life. When I look at my income, I feel ECSTATIC. There is always an overflow and I feel so loved and supported by money. I receive ideas of how to create money streams easily and it feels fun and exciting to create these things that brings value to this world.

When money comes in my door, I give her the warmest hug and let her know that more is always welcomed here. With palms open I say, I am open to receive all the resources I need to be able to do what I'm most called to do and my capacity to receive is expanding infinitely like the Universe.

When money goes out, I thank her for serving me in all the amazing ways she is. Like making it possible for me to buy this delicious, high vibing food to gift my body, paying for my coaching with Annika and The Supercharged membership that is supporting me in upleveling even more in all areas of my life, but especially as a leader in the new music industry. As guiding light, a wayshower. This, and so so SO much more are gifts money so generously showers me with.

Generating and circulating money feels natural and fun to me, I know the laws of the Universe and flow with such grace. Money and I feel so relaxed and confident in each other. She knows I've always got her back and I feel that she is always looking out for me. We are growing together everyday.

I feel so abundant, I'm so grateful for this work I'm doing on money, It's really working. I know that before 2017 is over I will be financially independent and that feels so amazing.

Money, I love you so much. You are divine. You are a blessing and I feel honored to be in such a harmonious and blossoming relationship with you. Yes and more please. And so it is.

Thank you. I love you.

Yours truly,

Fia <3

Love letter to money: Jenessa

My dearest money,

Please forgive me for the delay in writing this love letter to you. I hit massive resistance in facing what may flow through me here. What's come up is that I have a loaded money story. It's hard to know where to begin.

My earliest memories I was made fun of by other kids on my street for having more money than everyone else. I was the only kid with a pool and a horse farm and 15 acres of land. I was shy and embarrassed, and I didn't even understand money let alone why others would not like me because of it. They were all invited to our pool and to ride our horses. No one was left out. Why did it hurt so badly to have money than? I see now it was not you that hurt, but people that hurt. You were just a beautiful light sharing gifts with the world.

I also recall vividly the loud and angry fights between my mom and dad over money. There was never enough, even though we appeared to have more than enough. They yelled and screamed, slammed doors and inspired fear and sadness over money. I tried to make them feel abundant with my love but that wasn't a currency they understood. I may have hated you, for my parents not seeing me. I'm sorry for placing that blame on you. My parents issues were so much deeper than money. They lived in fear and fight or flight. They couldn't not see your light, your abundance and your gifts. I see clearly now none of it was your fault. You were The scapegoat for the problem of others. I'm sorry I harbored ill feelings toward you all these years.

When we moved to Purchase, I lost my horse, my friends, my family home...but it was so that we could "have a better life with more opportunities than the country life could offer." I was perfectly happy with the county life. This new world was weird, foreign almost. Instead of pick up trucks, kid drove BMWs and Porsche's. Houses were mansions, and homes had indoor pools and outdoor pools. Money was sought after, a competition, a sense of worth, entitlement and superiority. I saw some ugly truths about money...

but money, I see clearly now it was not YOU! It was the responsibility of the people who earned, held, and circulated it. There is no negative energy around you. You are a positive spirit meant to help and support our communities and our way of life.

My mom lived on the streets of NYC as a homeless child. When she was 13 years old, she ran away from an abusive home. She learned to survive by begging, stealing, giving of herself to live. Money was necessary to live but came at such a high cost, she'd rather die. She has tried to kill herself 3 times but it's not because of lack of money, but because of fear, trauma and lack of faith as a result. I have faith. I believe in your spirit as a nurturing essence provided by the Universe in abundance when you are awake enough to receive it.

My mom's mom, my grandma was born to a very affluent American socialite family out of wedlock. My great grandmother and my grandma were disowned by their social elitist family. Forced to live on the streets and fight to live. The line of women in my family are strong, resilient fighters. They are survivors. They do not give up but they struggled, struggled to have, struggled to eat, struggled to live. This again is not your fault money, you did not set this stage for them. They had lessons to learn from the situations presented. They learned to earn, to hold and to circulate money. You were not the unloving family that disowned them. You were not the abusive father. You were not the child sex trafficker. You were a pure energy that people used in improper, hurtful ways. I see your light now. I see your beautiful, supportive, loving being separate from the story, separate from the person, separate from the lesson.

I've been told that in a past life, I was my mother's mother. I died from starvation in that lifetime, giving all I had to her so she may live. However, she later died during childbirth from malnutrition. Here I can see giving again as a life and death matter. I gave until I had nothing left. I can see why we are so emotionally connected in this life. I still give to her as my starving child. I still want to feed the world, help the homeless, and the abandoned. All the lifetimes and generations of DNA are wrapped up into this story and packaged as ME. But I see you separately now. I see your light. Your love. Your energy. It is kind, loving and ever supportive.

I see the anger I've held towards you. I've pushed you away. Like my great grandmother, I stormed away from the "filthy" money. I pushed it away, gave it away, repelled it. Hurt and betrayed by "you". It was not you who abandoned and disowned though. I see that now. You've taken the blame for the behavior of humans. I'd create my own, but it would always be a struggle, just like my mom, her mom, and her mom before that. I'd always be fighting for money like my life depended on it. Working hard, scraping by, not really wanting it for fear I'd be one of those people who misused and abused because of it. I'd give it away to save those who are starving. I'd sacrifice my own life so others may live. Self worth stories embedded in here. All this drama because I misunderstood you. I misunderstood your essence. I misunderstood your love and light. You are not the story. You did not create the story. You are not the cause or the effect. You are energy. You are light. You are love. I'm sorry for all the negative energy I tied up in you. All mistaken beliefs that do not reflect your light. I see your light. It's beautiful, warm and loving. I'm ready to allow you into my life, with ease, grace, gratitude and flow, to enhance my light, my love and my gifts of service to the world.

I love you, money.

My sincerest apologies and deepest appreciation,

Jenessa

Money Has Ears

Are you inviting it in or repelling it away?

Where is the money when we hand over a little plastic card? I don't see any money. That's because money is energy. Where is money when we log into our online banking and see numbers on the screen? We don't. We see numbers that can go up or down at the click of a finger, because money is energy. But do we have any respect for it?

R-E-S-P-E-C-T. That's money, holding onto a microphone, and singing for you, Aretha Franklin styles.

I like to use the word respect when it comes to money. Money is already working in your life, perhaps more in your favor than you're acknowledging. Most people focus on the lack of money, rather than the gratitude for what it's already allowing them to do, experience and choose. When you can respect money as a member of your team, but not bow down to it and feel at the mercy of it, then health can flow through your money stream.

Let's role play for a bit here so you get the gist of what I am talking about.

Your name is Matt, and you volunteer for a woman named Daisy. You're her intern, and you love what she is doing in the world. You don't need any payment in exchange for your work. You just love to serve and help Daisy, because her mission is your mission. Daisy was a hard working lady who grew organic vegetables for her local community. She loved to farm and she loved to give to her community the gift of health and Mother Nature, but she had hit a plateau in that she couldn't farm anymore without new equipment and new staff. She was really down about it, and that's where you came in. You could help her, but then you overheard a conversation she was having on the phone to her friend. "Matt just doesn't help enough," you heard her say. "I wish he would do more. I would be able to expand my business if it wasn't for Matt. He's really letting me down." Wow. And now you feel like shit. There is no way you would go to Daisy now and tell her your ideas about the new equipment and how it's going to be cost efficient and make everything easier.

Do you get it yet, Homie? Matt is money. Daisy is most people. Money listens to everything you say and responds to every thought you think. When it hears people asking for it, but then bagging it out over the phone to their friends, do you do you think that creates an energetic resonance to invite money in? Money has the freedom to flow anywhere, to anyone, and there are plenty of people out there asking for money. Why would money flow to an energy field that was unappreciative?

Just like any other energy, it goes where it's welcomed, and doesn't go where it's not. Depending on how we speak about money, it can feel invited and welcomed by us, or it can feel unwanted, blamed, ostracized. Are you welcoming and inviting money right now? Or are you speaking about it like it's an evil monster and secretly hoping it will show up anyway?

Words

I know it's not exactly Money 101 to learn that money is energy and a being that hears everything we say, so there is good reason that people everywhere see money as no more than a transactional currency, and are constantly wondering "Well, where's my money?" We must learn to respect money as a team member, an energy, and a valuable resource. Most people don't.

Just as any other living soul, when it comes to money, we must choose our words and language with love. Think back to that Love Letter from the last chapter. Keep that relationship in mind, because what you say out loud about money is giving energetic instructions to it. Think about the words, languages or go-to statements and expressions that you commonly use around money. Here's a common one: Money is the root of all evil. I know I wouldn't visit someone if they called me evil. Especially if I built orphanages, helped entrepreneurs build transformational companies, helped scientists build life-saving technologies. No thanks! Keep your evil to yourself! How about: Money doesn't grow on trees. The richer I get, the poorer the poor. That's not worth the money. Forget the generics. What is your language around money? Is it rewarding or unrewarding? Is it respectful or not respectful? And most importantly, is it inviting or not inviting?

Thoughts

Even so much as what you think is giving money its instructions, and often your thoughts are on auto-pilot. Remember that money is responding to you, in absolute and exact unison with your words, thoughts and energetic instruction to it. There are thoughts about money that have moved into your subconscious where they are instructing your life without you even thinking about it consciously. They are forming your identity. Your identity is made up of the stories you tell yourself either consciously or subconsciously. Your identity is your constant set of energetic instructions that are always instructing your world.

What do you think when you spend money? Really think about this. When you hand your card over, when you're out to dinner, when it's time to pay, when you're out shopping, how do you think about your transaction? It is stressful? Is it joyful? Is it neither?

What do you think when you receive money? When your paycheck comes in, when money lands in your account, when you get a bonus, when someone buys what you're selling, is there any gratitude for it? Any acknowledgement of it actually coming to you? Or is it just expected?

What do you think when you see people with money? Do you have judgements around rich people, how they got rich, and whether it's fair or not fair? Are you inspired by our ability to consciously create anything?

Actions

How you act towards money is giving it energetic instructions. Do you hoard? Or do you prefer to circulate? Do you give when someone's in need? Do you wriggle out of the bill? Do you split every bill as if it's life or death who pays the last 2 cents? Or are you incredibly generous but feeling out of alignment with that? Are you grateful for your bills when they come in because it reminds you of the ability you have to pay for conveniences in your life? Do you pay bills early, on time or late? When you spend it, what's your energy?

When you receive bills, what's your energy? Do you drive around for 20 minutes trying to save 2 cents a liter on gas, or spend 45 mins negotiating $10 off a blender? Do you give when you walk past someone asking for money all the time, sometimes or never? Do you look at your numbers regularly in your personal life and business? Are you a 'numbers avoider'?

I used to avoid numbers like the plague. I'd rather just be the one creating, building, serving, but now I know that both our personal lives and businesses require we know our numbers. We can hire people to take care of them (my accountant team and bookkeeper are my saving grace), but our numbers are what clue us in. If we ignore them, that's major in our relationship with money. I encourage not just entrepreneurs, but everyone to face off with their numbers, even if it hurts. Not just money numbers, but all numbers that tell us our results.

If money is a kink, if numbers are a kink, we have to unkink that so new money energy can flow through your life and business. We must cultivate an attitude of rising above the feeling of being controlled by money and numbers, and remembering they're not the be all and end all, but also having absolutely no kinks when it comes to them.

Respect money. Money listens to you when you speak about it. Money responds to the thoughts you think about it. Money watches when you act with it. Feeling that your money tap is kinked? Then check in with how you're interacting with money as a tool and a team member in your life. Elevate and expand your relationship with money by appreciating and respecting it for the role it is already playing in your life, and then let it become your teammate in your pursuit for a better life and a better world.

The Real Bank

Money isn't yours.

Money comes from Source and goes back to Source. Resources—that word contains in it the word *Source*. The origin of the word resources in French means 'to rally, to raise again' and in latin 'to rise again'. This is why I believe money is such an important part of the conscious conversation, because there is soul and divinity in our reSOURCES.

Our money is on loan to us from the Universe. *OMG! I know, right?* Yeah, you read that right. The Universe is the real bank. Did that just blow your super conscious cells into, "Okay, Peta, I can I really get on board this conscious money thing?" *Yes, you can.* The big banks, are not the real banks. Yes, they're the banks that allow us to operate money here in the physical. But where does money come from, truly? Not the mint. From Source. Sure, the mint prints the money, but the Universe is overseeing its circulation, and the Universe can oversee its distribution. The Universe is the bank that sits above all banks. Even the richest people, banks, organizations in the world are no match for the abundance and resourcefulness of the Universe. So let that just marinate in you while we touch on something equally as exciting and freeing.

Money isn't yours.

Crazy to think for some, right? *What? Money isn't mine? But I earned it!* One part of my money story that lights me up and reminds me of our connection and oneness is knowing that, although I am responsible for creating money and circulating it, it's not mine,

263

because *money isn't ours*. Sure. We all create and earn our own money every day through our hard work, through our choices and decisions, through the things we're willing to sacrifice that perhaps others aren't, through the years of study at college or the years of experience as an apprentice, and through the risks we take and the collaborations we pursue. So, yes, we do earn and create our money. But we do not own it. And you're still like, *Huh? But…*

Let me ask you: When you spend money, do you write your name on it before you do? When you're paid money, do you write your name on it? No, you don't. You wouldn't do that, because you are going to use it for something, and if you're going to use it for something, it would be a bit weird if you tried to label it. After all what is the plumber going to do with a bunch of bills with your monogram emblazoned on them?

We are not the owners of money, but we *are* the facilitators of money. We are all responsible for creating whatever amount of money we are currently creating. We are all responsible for circulating money in whatever way we are currently circulating it. And this flow of money is different for everyone. This is freeing for me. How about you? The thought, belief, and knowing that money is not mine or yours to attach to and own. It's entrusted to me on a loan from Source. I have it to play with and to create the life that brings me the most joy, the most health, the most freedom and choice. I have it for my time here on Earth and can use it as a valuable member of my team to create the change I wish to see while I'm here.

A Loan From Source

Source doesn't want us to struggle. And Source doesn't want us to stop at 'just enough' if we're being called to play with money in a bigger more abundant way. Source wants us to get into our own personal alignment with money and to ensure that we are accessing all we require to do what we're called to do, and on the flip side, not reaching for more than our soul actually wants (being in the pursuit of more that can take us out of our alignment).

Source loves loaning money, because we can generate it consciously and in ways that benefits more people than just ourselves. The more money I loan from Source, the more I can build and create the things that Source is asking me to create—like a divine partnership that money does play a role in. The more money I loan from Source, the more I can vote with my dollar in the direction of consciousness and harmony on Earth, and buy from small businesses, sustainable business, and give to people and organizations who are working on equality and bridging the separation.

Do you know how many people would be creating companies, movements, products and organizations if they didn't have a money story that got in the way of their instruction from Source? Do you know how many people are being guided to build and create things that are incredibly favorable for our planet, but their money story is cock-blocking them? *A lot.*

There are choices, desires and callings we have that are fully in our alignment, that often we don't or can't honor because we aren't letting ourselves bring our money relationship into alignment with it. Source does not want you to go without, and by *you not going without* you're not robbing anyone of anything. You can still serve, follow your callings, give, and create—and take care of yourself. Life is meant to be enjoyed, and money is a player in that—no matter how spiritual or conscious you are. Living life as a human on this giant playground we are so honored to live on is the most spiritual adventure of all, but it cannot exist without alignment with all parts of life, including the material and physical components, such as money.

When I first started earning (creating) money in abundance, all I wanted to do was buy a new pair of sneakers for myself. Previously, no matter how many KMs I'd run each year, my new sneaker purchases were way overdue. I just wanted to be able to get them when I needed them, and be able to get good ones that didn't give me shin splints. I remember the day I bought some new Fluro runners. It just felt so good, so comforting to me that this simple desire and choice wasn't impeded by anything. And that is where I wanted to live—where my desires, callings, and choices were fully able to be expressed regardless of anything.

I also wanted to be able to buy organic, healthy food all of the time. I'd write it in my goals. "I have a kitchen with a Thermomix and a fridge full of organic, healthy food." Simple, but that was my preference, my choice, and should there be any guilt around wanting that? That could be your story if you want it to be, but is that story coming from Source? No, Source wants you to have all that your soul chooses and will loan you the money to make that happen.

I know Source also loves loaning me money because I no longer have guilt around appreciating the things money allows me to do in my own personal life. That is the role that money plays in my life, and it includes giving, creating, and self-nourishment. Eating organic food, buying a special water system that allows me to have no toxins flowing through my taps and shower, buying organic bamboo quilts instead of the mainstream ones, flying first and business class (because this is my preference, and favors my joy and comfort—simple).

We don't always require more money, and sometimes we actually require less to be in alignment. But the key here is being free to follow your callings, desires and simple preferences with no hindrance. This includes, no money hindrance. No time hindrance. No hindrance at all.

Your Alignment Is Your New Credit Rating

Imagine if people started talking to the Universe like they talk to a bank. Imagine if people went to the Universe for a business loan. A loan that they didn't have to pay back because their conscious generation of money is all the Universe really wants from us. Imagine if the Universe didn't look at your credit rating, but your alignment with what you were asking for, and your intention. *Imagine money like that.*

Let's do an exercise to flex that imagination muscle. Think about what you would like some more money for right now. Ask yourself whether or not it's in alignment with your soul. Or perhaps it's an ego request that isn't really yours. Does it feel good to you? If it does, get out a pen and paper and write to the Universe asking for a loan. Tell Source why, and what for, and describe your plans. Whether it's simple—like being able to afford organic veggies every week or whether it's big, like you want to build a new enterprise and need some capital.

An Example and Template

Hey Universe (God, Source, Divine—whatever feels good),

I know that attracting the money I require for (Insert project here) is hugely energetic. I'm willing to do the work, be resourceful and be creative, but I know I also need to feel in alignment with why I'm choosing to call in some new money energy. I want you to know you can trust me to be a circulating, generating badass and circulate these new resources in the direction of *good*. So I want to share with you what's calling me.

Now speak about for what:

- I want to build _____
- I want to invest _____
- I want to give _____
- I want to be able to _____

Now speak about why:

- I know that If I can get to Africa _____
- India is calling me.
- I want to surprise my Mum, she's been working so hard.
- I want to nourish my body the way it deserves to be nourished. I want to feel lit.
- This idea hasn't left me alone and I am committed to bringing it to life.

Now share the actions that you're committing to that will be in alignment with your requests:

- I'm rallying my friends to help contribute too
- I'm going to community events to find potential partners
- I'm going to be a more present daughter
- I'm going to take the leap from my job so I can commit full time
- I'm doing a 3 day business intensive so I can uplevel my skills

Remember that the Universe wants to support your big projects and endeavors.

The Universe wants you to get on the plane and travel for six months. The Universe wants you to have the Tesla. The Universe wants you to be able to retire your parents. The Universe wants you to be able to give more than 20% of your income to people who need some assistance. The Universe wants you to be able to buy organic food. The Universe wants you to be able to move closer to the beach. The Universe wants you to be able to go to a yoga class every day. The Universe wants to loan you money to do whatever you're called to do—just as long as you're in alignment with it.

Remember, your soul is employed by Source. Your true soul's callings are in alignment with Source.

Think about it. Anyone can create money if they want it bad enough, so why can't *you* with your big heart? Because often people with the big hearts and genuine care for all people, are the ones who feel the most guilt around creating more money. However, think about what is in the best interest of Source. To give it to *you*, you who will spend it on conscious companies, acts of generosity, choices and preferences that raise your vibration, your beautiful brilliant ideas and entrepreneurial endeavors.

Your loan has been granted

To (you),

Yes, you!! The Universe is screaming. *Let me loan money to you!* Thank you for playing a role in circulating money more consciously. We need people like you with your hearts of gold touching money and circulating it. We need the conscious people of our Earth to be building companies that replace old and broken ones that are damaging our Earth. We need people like *you* to unkink yourself so you can be in the bliss and freedom of your life. Your vibration of joy and alignment is your greatest gift to this planet. Thank you for changing your story, thank you for writing a new one. Thank you for generating beautiful experiences and changes with money that upgrade the quality of life for you, your community and the wider world.

The Universe is the real bank. All of your loans, your gifts, and your resources come from the Universe. When you want a loan, when you need money to build a project, how often do you think to look up and ask Source, the most resourceful, connected, wealthy bank of all. Your true resources don't live on your internet banking screen, or in a brick and mortar building. Play the energetic game and not just the 'I'll just check my bank balance' game. None of us own our money anyway. It's all on loan to us from Source.

Your Money Identity

Upgrading the instruction you're giving to money: awareness, alignment and appreciation.

"You can't be in the absence of money and the essence of money at the same time".
—Abraham-Hicks

Nothing more can be given to an unappreciative energy field. This whole like attracts like concept applies to everything, all of the time. Money is no exception. Money behaves just as any other energy does. Receiving, spending, and expanding into more money is an energetic process, which is perhaps why some people refer to money as a science. It's not just enough to want more money, or to read books and listen to podcasts on how to get more money, or even to work hard to earn more money. We must learn to align with money, and then, once you figure out the game of money physically—in terms of investing, spending, generating, and the many ways we logically acquire more of it—can you allow it to live comfortably in your energetic field? Because if you can't, it won't.

There is no greater force on Earth than our identity. We have a comfort level and a safety net. We have a comfort level for our body image, our degree of intimacy in relationships, how successful we allow ourselves to be creatively. Whenever we do anything, experience anything or feel anything that goes beyond our comfort level, we hit our heads (so to speak) on our safety net. It's our ego's way of saying, "We've never expanded beyond this level of happiness in our body, with our creativity, in success, of joy in a relationship before...are you sure it's safe?" We also have a safety net when it comes to money. It's the amount of money, the degree of financial abundance, and the corresponding lifestyle we're comfortable with before our ego starts to challenge it (cue self sabotage here).

This safety net determines our identity, and our identity is our sub-conscious energetic instruction to the world. Let me repeat how powerful that is—our identity is our energetic instruction to the world. It's the energetic invitation and also the energetic boundary. When we have anything come into our field that is more or less than our comfort level approves of, then our subconscious goes to work, messing it up enough to return us back to our base line, having not gained anything. It's the phenomenon that explains why lottery winners often end up with less money than before than won the lottery. The amount of money that abruptly entered their orbit was not able to remain there for long as a result of their established energetic boundaries which had been put in place by their identity. So they engage in actions like overspending, which bring them back down to their money comfort level.

Our identity is the strongest force on Earth because it's instructing the world for us, even when we're not thinking about it—our own personal energetic body guard. Without us even knowing, it says yes or no to new levels, experiences and upgraded realities that are trying to make their way into our lives. If you want something and your identity doesn't allow it, it can't come in. It is rock solid. To upgrade your life in any area, you must upgrade your identity so that it instructs the world accordingly.

Let's explore your money identity with a few questions.

1. What is the amount of money you feel comfortable receiving each week?

2. What's the rough amount that sits in your bank account, the one you never seem to rise above?

3. How rigid are you when it comes to splitting the bill?

4. If you were moving house and no longer needed your toaster, would you sell it or give it away to someone who could really use it?

Remember, there is no answer that is wrong, because each one will bring awareness to your own energetic instructions to the world, and if you don't know what you are instructing now, then you are not able to make a change.

Some people do not care about buying quality clothes, because they prefer to travel the world and live minimally. That is no worse or better than someone who chooses to wear all organic cotton and have choice in their wardrobe. However, the problem arises when you tell yourself you can't wear organic cotton pajamas if you want to travel the world. Ask yourself: Is what I really want what my identity is allowing me to have? Or do you want something new, something fresh, something more, but you're not allowing yourself to want it because it feels guilty or wrong?

The big question to ask is if your money identity is what you want your money identity to be.

I often meet very conscious and aware people whose identity is one of extreme humility when it comes to money. They are happy to live a simple lifestyle and give up many of life's many 'out there' pleasures for a greater pleasure that they find 'in here.' These are the people who have no desire to own anything big, such as a car or land or home ownership. They want to eat well, have nice experiences, and be free to travel. Those are three pretty sweet privileges in themselves, right? Sometimes there are no greater desires, and that is fine and beautiful. But, sometimes there are, like businesses wanting to be born, helping mum or dad with their life long mortgage, personally investing in conscious startups, or renting a home by the beach where our soul thrives the most (but requires double the rent than we're used to paying). This is where we often trip. We often don't own these desires because they are not our needs, and instead we ask for something less, something that fits within our identity. But it's ok to want. It's ok to ask for resources to support doing what excites the shit out of you (and your soul). There must be alignment between what you *really desire* and what *you're saying you desire*.

So many people with this freedom value (me included), or similar, have callings that are requesting they shift their money identity. Callings to build organizations, or callings to pack up and move to Switzerland, give large amounts of money to a NFP, or gift your mum a trip to Greece.

What about buying a Tesla when you've never bought a new car in your whole life? "How fun would it be to just get one?" your soul asks. "Go for it!" But yelling back is your repeat money identity soundtrack, "You don't need one. You can get a Prius. People are starving in the world. You need a car, but do you really need a Tesla? That's so greedy! So not in line with your values!"

Sometimes your soul actually does want you to buy things like a Tesla, and it's not because you absolutely need it, but you do need to learn that enjoying abundance without guilt or constant self-judgment is necessary. We must learn to enjoy fulfilling our desires without letting the safety net close off our energy field—especially when it comes to spiritual guilt. These are tricks of the ego, tools that it uses to keep hard boundaries set and safety nets up. Self-judgment, guilt, and the idea that "you don't need anymore." Your ego will do its best to make sure you don't change your identity, but the good news is that you can change your identity. You are able to change your identity to break the boundary and energetically invite in more and hold more than what you have not or have ever had. First you must become aware of your money identity, then you must align with it, and ultimately appreciate it.

Now let's get into the three magic A's. These are the golden keys for tidying up your energetic environment so that money can show up, and stay in whatever amounts your soul requires for its highest evolution.

Deep, I know.

Awareness

The first step in noticing what your identity around money currently is to determine its limits and find the safety net.

Draw this out—imagine a circle around you—or you can write it down. Imagine you could look down from the clouds at your life and see the boundaries of your energy field—specifically around money. What does it look like? What does it encompass? Just show yourself how far your money energy field extends. Show yourself what is inside of it and what lies on the outside. Where do you want your boundaries to be?

Re-draw your circle to include exactly what you want to invite in. Get specific, and then get support that will help you physically retrain your new identity. You can read books, listen to audios, and surround yourself with resources that support your money upgrade. More so than that, surround yourself with people and places that support this new identity. This might sound personal, but it is. Your money identity won't change if your main group of friends is supporting your old identity of lack, strife, and guilt—or any other aspect of the identity you want to upgrade.

You are the sum of the 5 people you spend the most time with. Who are they?

1. _____

2. _____

3. _____

4. _____

5. _____

And what is their money identity?

1. _____

2. _____

3. _____

4. _____

5. _____

Just this little exercise, I've slipped in and you might have some insight. But don't freak out, because this does not mean that you have to cut ties with everyone in your life because they don't have a money identity that you desire. No way! The purpose of this is so you can be aware of your environment and check in to see how it could be impacting your identity.

With what do you want to become more comfortable? Is it a new space or building for your business? Take some time and go look at spaces on the weekends—go by yourself. Go ahead and get excited about training your new identity to see this as reality and not fantasy. Maybe you want more personal development and mentorship, but you baulk at the 'costs' of such investments. This is something so many people are afraid to do, and it's one of the greatest secrets to expanding your identity in the direction of abundance. Often, you can afford a coach, a mentor, or an event, but it's your identity that is tricking you into thinking that you have bigger responsibilities. That's a nice identity, and you can keep it if you like, but is it your new one?

It's time to change your money identity, and that it is going to take some leaps you are probably not feeling ready—or even able—to take. But here are a few more you can take, all in the effort of expanding your energetic boundary and ditching the safety net. It's time to start finding what makes your identity comfortable, so you can go beyond it. You are the trainer. You are the changer of your identity. Remember, as the great Albert Einstein says, "Nothing changes until something moves."

POP OUT: Upgrade your identity

○ Pay for the entire bill next time you're out at lunch with friends.

○ Pay your bills early and not late.

○ When you hear the price of something, celebrate that you can buy it.

○ Order what you want from the menu, not what's the cheapest.

○ Invest in the mentor and be grateful that you can, instead of worried that you can't.

○ Buy the clothes, the sheets, the car you want now—not when you have extra.

○ Start a savings account for 'that dream' or calling you've been waiting 'til you have enough' to open. Open it now, and invite the money in. It's like the old saying 'build it and they will come'. Open the 'dream' account, and then invite the money.

○ Choose cash over credit.

○ Say thank you when you get paid.

○ Say thank you when you invest money in your conveniences (bills, food, wifi).

○ Say thank you when you invest in your wants.

○ Give a % of your income every month to a cause you care about, because you can.

○ Most importantly..... SCRIPT!! See page 347

Alignment

When you know what you want and your soul is on board, own it.
Be cool with wanting to create more money. It's time to quiet the collective. Be cool with wanting to living on the ocean in a sunlit home. Be cool with wanting to buy only organic. Be cool with wanting to earn more than most people do. Be cool with the new car, the fancy napkins, the trip to Paris. Because here's the thing we may not all notice. Most of us are entirely fine with getting on board with our money stories when our money stories are for the world—give to the disaster relief fund, buy a rainforest plot, send Laura some money for her birthday, give to the Go Fund Me campaign, send money to the people fighting Standing Rock or Stop Adani —because those actions are uses of money that are noble. People don't feel that much guilt building schools, orphanages or water systems. No one feels selfish retiring their parents or building a non-profit. It's when people have to own their money story for themselves when the going gets tough.

The Tesla, the rain shower head, the make more to work less dream, that's when judgment and guilt creep in, spreading like wildfire from our ego, from the collective, from our peers. That's when you get in the way of your flow between you and money, and all your soul wants is to open that tap. Your soul, and Source, don't judge you for how much or little you have. The only thing your soul and Source gives a shit about is that you are in alignment—everywhere in your life, plain and simple, because you and money have things to create and a higher level of wellbeing to enter into together. Once again, we learn this lesson of alignment, which is always right up there with our most important things to conquer as humans.

Money is a tool for us to live in alignment, and for us to learn to work with this tool, which is here for our benefit and not for our turmoil (surprise!), we have to get clear on what we want—and we're doing that right now with this exercise people. Hold the judgments and just write.

You

1. What do you want that you desire more money for?

2. What guilt or judgment do you have around this want?

3. What would other people think if you told them this is what you wanted?

4. How good does it feel to own it?

Your Community

1. What do you want for the people in your family or community that you desire more money for?

2. What guilt or judgment do you have around this want?

3. What would other people think if you told them this is what you wanted?

4. How good does it feel to own it?

The World

1. What do you want for the world that you desire money for?

2. What guilt or judgment do you have around this desire?

3. What would other people think if you told them this is what you wanted?

4. How good does it feel to own it?

Appreciation

When you appreciate something or someone, it grows. The goal here is to own what you want for yourself, and to own what you want for the world in your creative work and professional work. Appreciation is a powerful practice when it comes to the energy of money. In fact, I have chosen to use the word "appreciation" here in place of gratitude. It's a little secret trick. The word appreciate means to grow, so when you use this particular word you are giving energetic instructions for something to grow. It's no different than appreciating assets—growth over time. The practice is to appreciate every cent coming in and every cent going out, a practice that will swiftly and powerfully shift your energetic environment of money.

When money comes into your world and you see it land in your online banking account or you receive a cheque or however you accept your method of payment, what is your ritual or practice? Do you have one? You don't, well, that's no biggie. That is why you are here reading this book—so you can create one. In my Supercharged, we talk a lot about rampages. Abraham Hicks, author of The Law of Attraction, is famous for these, and I believe they are the way to immediately upgrade your vibration to something higher and more rewarding. And now you're thinking, Rampage? Here's what it looks like.

You just saw that $2,740 was deposited in your bank account. You can either think or say the following out loud. Sixty seconds—go!

> *"I so appreciate this $2470.00 and that it's come to me. I appreciate it because it allows me to buy healthy food and nourish my body. I appreciate it because it allows me to be able to afford the simple pleasures in life like gas, electricity, and WiFi. I appreciate being able to live abundantly and not have to worry about little things. I appreciate that I am a receiver of money and that I can see how able I am to create it in whatever quantities I require. I love my partnership with money and what it allows me to do."*

Now these are my words, but you get the drift. And sure, it seems like a lot of work every time we see money come in, but 60 seconds is not a lot of work, especially if it changes your energetic environment so much that your $2,470 turns into $5,800, and $5,800 becomes $12,310, and so on. When you practise an Appreciation Rampage that is so very doable. I see this happen in my Supercharged all the time.

We always touch money with some sort of energy, attitude and intention when it leaves our bank or magically zips out of our bank account and into someone else's or onto their credit card machine, or when we hand over cash. I know it's old news, but worth repeating. Money is always energetic. Therefore, the same can apply when money goes out. Yet, so many of us have become so wired (read: our identity tells us) to think that it is always a struggle to spend or invest and that we're always losing money or having less money when we do so. I don't know about you, but that's not the money story I want. What if every time we spent money, we appreciated it just as much?

So what could be a nice Appreciation Rampage practice for when the money is going out—when you spend, invest, or pay for something, especially something that adds more fun, ease, or adventure into your life? Because let's face it, money going out is not a loss, because it is always energy in exchange for something that we want. Let's rampage. Sixty seconds—go!

> *"I love circulating money in whatever direction I choose and I love all of the different opportunities for me to generate money consciously. I so appreciate the fact that I can spend money on conveniences like WiFi, electricity and hot water. I love hot showers, I love hot baths, I love being able to FB my friends from my couch and watch Suits on Netflix. I appreciate being able to send my Mum flowers and make her day. I appreciate that I can give to the Unstoppable Foundation and feel good about what money can do. I appreciate that money helps me help others."*

That is a pretty inviting energetic environment if you ask me. If I was money and you were appreciating me every time I came in or went out, I'd be telling all my friends about you and bringing them all along to this high-vibing space of goodness. Think of money as a daisy. It wants to bloom in your garden, but you have to have the right soil, a soil rich in nutrients, such as awareness, alignment, and appreciation. And Source will smile happily as your garden grows because it doesn't want a heart like yours missing out on anything your soul is calling you to. And neither does our world, because the impact your heart will have on the collective money story and conscious enterprise evolution is what matters most to Source.

Alignment is the aim of every game, all of the time, period. We can only energetically hold, what we're energetically holding right now. So to hold more, we need to change our identity so that we are giving more expanded instructions. How aligned we are to our story, matters. If we say one thing about money and feel another, money will always respond to how we feel. And our appreciation around money really matters. Nothing more can show up for an unappreciative energy field, so appreciate everything that flows into your life and watch it grow.

Our Money Is Working 24/7

Choosing the world you want through money.

Have you ever come across one of those bills that has been drawn on by someone? Money with a little squiggle, a face, or maybe even a corner torn off. Hey, you might even run into some bills decorated in naughty genitalia. Anytime I see something like this—regardless if it's naughty or nice—I am reminded of the long journey that this money has been on, and the fact that it has landed in my hands means that there had to have been some very specific decisions made as to where it was exchanged. After all, money doesn't *poof!* disappear into thin air once we exchange it, it generates the stuff we want. Clothes, electricity, a latte. Our decision to spend money isn't one that stops once we let it go, once we buy the Apple, once we buy the plane ticket, once we eat at that restaurant. Our money continues to work long after we've laid our hands on it, and under-standing this is crucial for upgrading our relationship with money as a divine energy and as an incredibly valuable resource for us in our pursuit for a more conscious world. We must understand how our money is working twenty-four-seven.

As we learned earlier, we do not own money, but it is something that has been loaned to us from Source. We are entrusted with it, given full rights to circulate it however we want, and our hands are the tools that facilitate its circulation. We might see money with markings, but that is not the common practice. We do not put our name on every bit of money that moves through our hands or lands in our bank accounts. Money is not ours, but it is borrowed for a time to circulate as we wish.

There's a word we often use to describe what we do when we depart with money, and it's 'spend'. I don't use that word so much, because to me it implies that the money just goes bye-bye as soon as we've 'spent' it. If you type in 'spent' on google search, the definition is "having been used and unable to be used again." But that's not true. Money is used again and again and again after we spend it. It travels all around the world doing stuff for people and the world, providing stuff for people and the world, building stuff for people and the world.

So let me introduce you to three words I do use and always associate with money. *Circulating, Investing, and Generating.*

Circulating Versus Spending

Your decision of how you circulate money does not stop once you smooch yours goodbye. Money is part of a long, beautiful journey of energy. Once you touch it, it will now do things for you. It will change things. It will help a small business, feed a mouth, or let you sleep in soft and eco-friendly sheets. Your say in its circulation says something about what you care about. The world sees it. The collective feels it. Businesses are affected by it.

Look at all the signs these days that say, "Buy Local." You don't even have to walk five minutes down a town street to find one. Why? What does this really say? It says that when you purchase—circulate your money here—you are helping local families thrive. You are supporting people who are working hard to bring high quality goods and services to their community. These days many people care more about this than they do about buying something bigger or something that looks a bit better from a behemoth corporation. The same goes when we buy organic food. We're supporting organic farmers, because we care about their work and we want them to continue to provide healthy food for their community.

Something as simple as buying local is an example of the shifting consciousness around circulating money, a shift that has the power to create change that will shift our world consciousness. These are the shifts that bring about the rise of conscious enterprise, a key element to how the standards have been changed and are continuously being raised to change how a company operates in relation to the collective. It's not just about that profit game anymore. Millennials are making their views and opinions super obvious for all to see, by not only creating products, services, companies, and movements that are conscious and aware to replace those that aren't keeping up with this evolution, but by also refusing to circulate money in the direction of anything that doesn't support the rise in consciousness and sustainability.

So how do we create so much of the change we want to see? Take a look at how we're playing in this game of money circulation. Everyone has their big, long list of things they want to see change. Everyone can throw tomatoes at the TV screen when they see products and services and organizations who are doing things in ways that piss them off or disturb their understanding of how it should be, but how much do we take responsibility for the fact that all of our money—in amounts big and small—says something and does something when it circulates in the world. We as a generation are exercising one of our greatest powers when it comes to shifting our world through business by investing only in businesses, products, and services that support how we believe the world should be run. We understand that voting with our money is like voting on the ballad of an election, except that we get to do it every single day, as many times as we like.

When we can be conscious about how we circulate money, then it strengthens our relationship with it and we start to re-write our story. Our story stops becoming one of separation with money and unconsciousness and starts to become a story of connection and conscious money, which leads to conscious enterprise, which leads to conscious collective. How our money goes out from us matters. The energy in which we circulate it matters. Understanding that money can be a conscious game, just as it can be an unconscious game matters.

If you're in a relationship with money—just as you would be in a relationship with a stud muffin partner—would you expect them to care about your life if you didn't care a thing about theirs? Money is no different, because when you care about what happens to money when it leaves your hand (physically or by way of electronic transfer), then you are playing a conscious, caring money game, and this, my friend, is when we can call money conscious. Conscious money for you and for the world. That's how collectives shift, one by one, person by person. Either slowly or rapidly. And if you take a look around, ours is pretty zoomy.

Investing Versus Spending

Investing implies that we are choosing to circulate our money in a way in which it appreciates and grows. That is exactly what investments do. Investing isn't a word that only applies to houses and stocks. You're investing every single day and you need to give yourself credit for that. You may be currently investing in a personal development course or some sort of a business seminar or spiritual development event. My guess is that you have or are or will very soon will do one of the three. So let me ask you what your intention is for when you buy this ticket for your next course? Do you consider it an *expense* or an *investment*?

When you are in the energy (and vocabulary) of investing, you are saying to your money, "I am circulating you intentionally and in a way that will generate something even more beautiful in my life." Now that's a nice intention, a sweet awareness to have, because you are investing in yourself—not just the purchase at hand. Even buying this book was an investment in yourself. *What would you like this book to generate for you?* What are the possibilities of your investment in this book and what it can generate in your life? The same goes for your gym membership or your yoga class pass. Is it an expense or an investment? And what's your intent and consciousness when you pay it each month?

When I first started flying first class I always reminded myself it was an investment and not an expense. I was investing in my well-being. I was investing in a comfortable journey that had me feeling vital versus drained when I got off the plane. Often I'd be able to get on calls or run over some presentations upon landing, which was something I didn't always feel I could do if I didn't sleep well on the plane. Therefore, investing in a higher-priced plane fare was not "money down the tubes," once I got off the plane. Instead, that higher-priced fare was able to generate more than just a plane flight in my life. For it is my well-being that determines the quality of my work and what I generate is what impacts the world. This cup of cacao I'm drinking as I write this is an investment. Cacao is a great investment for me. It opens me up and allows me endless hours of creativity. This book was in large parts, fueled by cacao (and Source, of course). Obviously the cacao didn't write this book, but the well-being and tap-opening I feel while I'm drinking it sure does generate something.

Generating Versus Spending

Your money is always consciously or unconsciously generating something. When you invest in NFPs or other causes in which you believe, you are intentionally generating something better for the world. It's not spending. It's not an expense. It's not something you can just claim at tax time. It's an intentional investment, where you circulate money in a way it generates more consciously and produces more change than you can ever measure. Imagine if you could *appreciate* what your money generates? What are the infinite possibilities of what your money can generate on this Earth?

Going onto Kickstarter and putting money down for a product or service in which you believe. You're circulating your money in a way where it's going to generate something better, more consciously. I have always loved investing in other people's growth. In my early days as an entrepreneur I would buy young, hungry entrepreneurs tickets to personal and business development events. I never bat an eyelid at this, and it has always been one of my favourite ways to circulate and invest money. I always loved thinking about the possibilities of what could be generated as a result of this person going to this event. Perhaps they'd just hear one thing that had them stop overthinking their brilliant idea, give them the confidence to begin, and then produce the app which allows businesses to constantly monitor their carbon footprint, which would then… *you get the point.*

Perhaps they'd meet that one person who'd end up being their mentor or partner, helping them thrive and grow as a leader of our generation, mentoring kids in underprivileged areas for years and setting up little incubators around the world for kids to explore in their creativity outside of the traditional classroom, which would then….

It's like a domino effect. When we invest and circulate money with the intention of generating something even more beautiful, then we are playing an entirely different money game than "Well, I've spent it and it's gone."

Kiss Your Money Goodbye

Think for a minute about the power that money give us—the positive power. We have the potential to completely shift our collective and rejuvenate our Mother Earth by acknowledging the consciousness of money. We can do this every single day. You can set an intention when you circulate or invest your money. Just ask yourself:

- "What would I like this to generate for me?"

- "What would I like this to generate for the world?"

- "What are the possibilities of what this investment will generate?"

When it's time to smooch that money, show your money some love. Smooch away, with intention. Imagine you are saying goodbye to your money in the same way you say goodbye to your partner as they head off to work or your best friend as you two depart from lunch. Wish them a good day. Maybe tell them you love them. Kiss them goodbye, especially that stud muffin partner. In fact, I had a mentor that once told me, "If you really love your partner you will set a beautiful intention for their day just as you do for yours." Do I expect you to stand at the grocer, look at your bank card before you hand it over, and smooch it as if to say, "Bye-bye $5.99 organic banana. Go forth and multiply into 4 more organic bananas." No, not at all. Although, I would not put it past any of my epically crazy weird tribe to do that, and oh how I would love it. This is what I really mean by *smooching with intention*.

What if we just smooched each investment with a little energetic tag—an intention for our circulation? Just an intention that acknowledges that money will do what you tell it to do and what you intend for it to do. *Try it*. Every time you circulate money whether a big or small amount, just add a little energetic tag on it with a silent intention *generate more consciousness* or perhaps something even more specific, like when you buy a ticket for a business event, *my intention for this investment is that it generates crazy amounts of new epic knowledge that help me take my business to new levels of enjoyment and abundance.*

Money is always listening. And money is always working. Money works 24/7 and doesn't ever sleep. It's always being recirculated, reinvested, and regenerated. And if conscious, heart-centered, beautiful humans like you don't give it some love then others will, and perhaps you won't like it. Just like many don't like what money is doing now. It's not money's fault. Money wants a heart like yours giving more specific instruction for it to generate more consciously, which is why I am so big on bridging the gap between consciousness and money. Because money wants to be a valuable member in the pursuit of a more conscious, aware, harmonious world, and people in the light need to step up and play.

> *What we do with the money that's in our orbit is 100% up to us. You're circulating money, investing money, and generating change with money. Money is a workhorse. It doesn't stop once you exchange it for something. It*

continues to generate based on what you do with it—big or small. And this consciousness is why we can celebrate money as 'conscious money', how we give with money, how money becomes a valuable member of our team as The New Way becomes the new normal, and our planet becomes our priority again as a collective.

All of Your Needs Are Met

Resources flow to resourcefulness

"When you let go of trying to get more of what you don't really need, it frees up oceans of energy to make a difference with what you have."
—Lynne Twist

The reason I helped you to get clear on your *desires*, is so you can know the difference between your desires and your *needs*. What need are you pretending to need that you don't need right now? When you are in need, you are in lack, and there is no such thing as lack when it comes to abundance. This is usually when people stop and say, "Whoa, whoa, whoa, Peta... There are people who really do need things like food and water." Yes, that's true. That's why our generation's work is on not only to teach abundance, but to change the story to ensure that in the next 20 years or less, there is no one in real need. *Tall order?* I know, but we're going to talk about how in the final chapters of this book.

When I was in my mid-twenties, beginning to earn more and grow my success, people kept asking me when I was going to double my income—as if that was the only trajectory. But as I've talked about in previous chapters, I had reached a point where my greatest urgency wasn't in doubling my income, but in learning how to do more with what I already had. I was interested in giving and creating and generating. Those were my driving forces. I couldn't pull goals out of my butt that weren't really mine. I couldn't pretend I wanted a watch or a fancy car. I got my Tesla and am in love with him—his name is Playton. I couldn't pretend I wanted a more extravagant lifestyle. I had retired my mum and I was living the exact lifestyle that felt in alignment with me, food-wise, travel-wise, giving-wise. I didn't need anything more.

This didn't mean I was anti mo' money. It just wasn't my focus, because my focus had shifted to generating more with what I had. Chasing more without a vision or purpose? No thanks. If I was to ask for 'more money' in my world, then it was going to be to do more of what I was called to do. But then, I had more than enough to do what I was called to do, so I started generating. I created TNWL. I created The Supercharged. I created Jeaniius. I started circulating what I had to generate more for others—for my tribe, my generation, our world. I personally didn't take a single cent from this work. I was simply generating more with my abundance.

As I started creating, my callings got bigger and bigger. I required more people to support my work, more resources to keep building these epic festivals that are TNWL, and that is when my abundance expanded—when my callings were aligned with my purpose and I knew I was on the same page as Source. It was my requirements for my calling that had me tapping into an even bigger tap of abundance. It wasn't a false need that wasn't really a need or a mighty big request for more money that I didn't actually want. I tapped into a bigger tap of abundance because I acknowledged the abundance that was already so evident in my life. I focused on circulating and generating more with it, rather than pretending I was yearning for more. I wasn't yearning for more. I was yearning to do more with what I had. And thank God I was gifted with that understanding so young, or I could be sitting here right now, 28 years old with a profit that is triple my sense of purpose, and a burned out heart from chasing more, more, more. That doesn't sound like abundance to me at all.

But let's talk about you. What do you need right now? Like, what do you really, super-duper urgently need right now? Wait, let me rephrase that. Think of something you need right this minute to which you have no access. What is still remaining that you don't have but very much need? If you're anything like me, the answer is nothing. You have everything you need, and everything else that you super-duper desire is not a need. It's a desire, a calling, a want. When we can acknowledge that we don't need anything, we can be in the abundance of already having it.

When you can acknowledge that you don't need anything, you can be in the knowingness that everything is right there for you, waiting for you to tune into the signal of it.

You move from pretending you need it, to simply choosing it.

Otherwise, you're no different than a 5-year-old in a shopping center. "Mummmmm, I need this Transformer, I really do. Or the kids at school are gonna have one and I'm not!!"

We do that. We throw tantrums at Source. "Sourrrceeeeeee I need this watch/phone/money/shoes/car/man… I really doooooo. Or else the other adults are gonna have one and I'm not."

Many of these false needs are more than false needs. They are ego-driven and not soul-driven. They are, what we learned in previous chapters, our BS goals, and we know that our soul wants real goals. And because our souls and Source work together, meeting real goals and meeting real needs feels good, and the pursuit of them feels more joyful, more aligned, and a little like: It's already done, I'm just doing the work to get into alignment with it so I can have it. It feels like that because you know that your needs are always met. Although it's not easy to always remind yourself 'my needs are always met' if your landlord just booted you out of your apartment with 48 hours to find a new one, or if you don't have enough money to get the books you need for school. However, if we all, regardless of our situation, switched from "I need" to "My needs are always met," do you think we'd move into more alignment with Source and the tap, or further away from it?

Exactly. When you are in need, you are standing off to the side watching the tap. When you are feeling your needs already met, you are standing right underneath the tap taking it all in. If you haven't already embodied this philosophy—my needs are always met—then it's time to add this to your script. How does it feel to have your needs all met?

To add this to your script will be a large part of how you rewrite your story, change your identity, and redirect your energetic instruction around money and abundance. When you are in the tap of abundance, there are no needs. Only choices and preferences. **(See bonus section at the end of the book—THE SCRIPT).**

Abundance —

"I don't want it all. I just want what I choose. And I can choose anything. This is why minimalism feels so abundant. Cos you are living from choice, not from excess. There is space to enjoy your choices, so life becomes rich instead of just full ...."

All your needs are met, and if they have not been met, then they are not your needs. Think about that. Now, how can you remove this energy of need from your life and change it to I can have whatever I'm willing to get into vibrational alignment with.

○ Do you need funds to move across the country? Or do you already have everything you need to move across the country, but rather than be resourceful you just want the Universe to slap it down for you?

○ Do you need more time in your day? Or do you already have all the time you need and simply just have to choose to gift yourself spaciousness? Is 'I need more time' a big fat excuse for you not being resourceful with the time you have?

○ Do you really need an IT team before you launch your company? Or do you already have absolutely everything you need to begin, and 'I need' is just a convenient way to delay?

More powerful yet, ask yourself "What is the Universe withholding from you?"

Nothing. Whatever feels like it's being withheld is not the Universe's doing. It's yours. Feel like your situation is dire? The Universe has bounty waiting for you. All you need to do is go up and get it. Go up and get it, as in raise your vibration and you will find that it's all up there waiting for you. When you are in the 'I need' space you're not in alignment with what you have. Perhaps you will discover that you may be asking for more before you do more with what you already have.

If you want more, or if you simply want new, then you've got to create space for it, which is why I bang on about circulating energy so much. And nothing likes circulated energy more than abundance. Many people think of abundance strictly in terms of acquisition. They measure their abundance by what's flowing in and what's visible. But by simply waiting at the door for more to enter, you're missing a key piece to abundance—doing more with what you have. Sometimes you can't actually fit anymore into your world. Sometimes you can't fit more money, more things, more opportunities, more creativity, more resources of any sort, because you're not doing enough with what you already have. It's just sitting there, taking up room—same as all my new socks. Abundance is movement and flow. Abundance isn't stagnant storage.

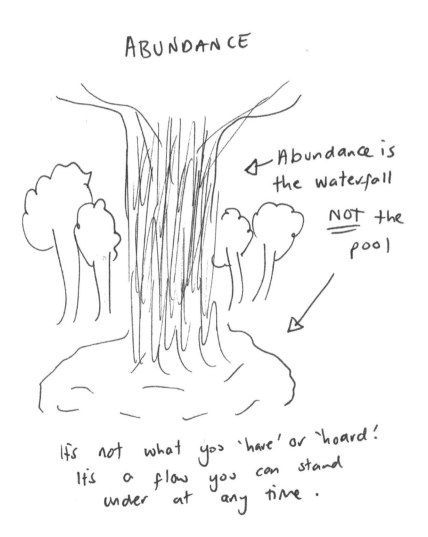

ABUNDANCE

Abundance is the waterfall

NOT the pool

It's not what you 'have' or 'hoard'!
It's a flow you can stand
under at any time.

POP OUT: Tap Into Abundance

How can you allow more abundance in your life, by doing more with what you already have?

GIVE MORE. Time, money, skills, talents, your ears (listening, not taking off your actual ears).

CREATE MORE. Use your creativity, tap into it, let it move so you can open up the channel for MORE to flow through. Remember, creativity flows from you, until you show up for it consistently, then it flows through you.

GENERATE MORE CONSCIOUSLY. Can you make your time/money go further and in the direction of consciousness? Can you be more intentional with what/how you invest your resources so they generate more epic shit in the world?

BE MORE RESOURCEFUL. How can you become 10x more resourceful with your time, money, and skills? Can you trade your skill set with someone else to start generating some new results?

Are you doing the absolute MOST with what you have? Or are you simply asking for more?

Resources Flow To Resourcefulness

"The future belongs to those who understand that doing more with less is compassionate, prosperous, and enduring, and thus more intelligent, even competitive."

—Paul Hawken

Resources do not want to flow to un-resourceful people. Would time and money look at how you're spending your time and money right now and say "Hey!! that looks like a good place for my buddies and I to go!" Are you asking for a $20K investment in your business, before you've utilized all of your skills and all of the skills and talents of your tribe? Basically, can Source trust you with more? First, get good at mobilizing what you already have. Take notice of what money comes in every week. Circulate it. Generate with it. Appreciate it. There are so many people who get stuck wishing for more, more, more, so much so that they don't acknowledge what money is already bringing into their lives. Money is allowing each of us to do things, to experience things, to create things, to enjoy things. We can pay for gas and water and electricity and wifi and food and this book. Begin to realize that no matter what you have, what you actually own, that it's all there for you. Because that is how taps work.

I love reminding my Supercharged tribe to take notice of what money comes in every week. Because so many people are stuck in the 'but I want more' that they don't acknowledge at all the game that money is already playing in their lives. Money is already playing a game in your life. It's already allowing you to do stuff, experience new things, pay for gas/water/electricity/wifi, pick up this book. Notice the abundance already in your life, and then you can choose to expand it.

Giving Generates Receiving

It's no secret that GIVING is the fastest way to receiving. Or is it a secret? Are you asking for more before you're willing to give more? I recently interviewed Cynthia Kersey on my Supercharged call. She is the founder of the Unstoppable Foundation, which has raised millions of millions of dollars for children and families in Africa and provided the five pillars—water, education, health care, nutrition, and financial opportunities—to families and villages through her hard work and commitment to our brothers and sisters globally. A pretty big giver, wouldn't you say? Someone in the tribe wanted to ask her "How do you balance giving and receiving?" There are so many empaths in The Supercharged who are great givers, but feel they're not great receivers. They often feel depleted like they're stuck on giving mode. You might be the same. So I asked Cynthia this question. She sat back, as if she was about to share her greatest secret ever. She smirked out of the corner of her mouth as if to say 'Oh boy, I'm about to drop the greatest secret I ever learned.'

"Peta, the receiving is in the giving. I feel like I receive more than anyone on the planet."

Giving is not an act of depletion, it's an act of repletion. When we give outwardly, we give inwardly. When we give outwardly, we open up our channel and we get into the tap, that tap where abundance lives. Abundance is a cycle. It's not one-way traffic. If you want to play a bigger game when it comes to abundance, it's impossible to do it without expanding the entire cycle.

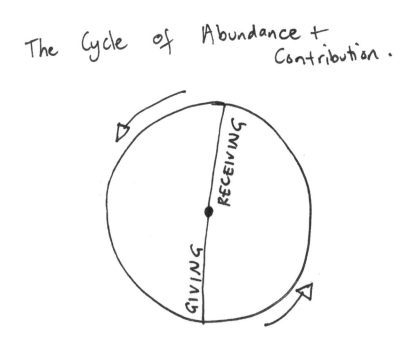

"*If you want to ask one question, ask yourself, what are you giving to the Universe and only that will be returned.*"

—Amit Ray

All of your needs are met. When you chase more of what you don't need and ignore what you have, you're saying to the Universe that when you receive, you ignore. Resources want to flow to resourcefulness. So when you can squeeze the juice out of what you have—your time, your money, your talents, your connections, your abilities, your potencies, your imagination, then you are saying to the Universe, "I am resourceful and am choosing more resources, but I don't need them." If you want to allow more into your life, give more. Then watch your tap of abundance widen.

POP OUT: Abundance is a team sport.

A letter to you, homie:

I love having the conversation about how we can each live in our own version of abundance, connected to the resources of the Universe and owning our choices without hesitation and resistance. I love having the conversation about upgrading our own money stories so we can each live in a way that allows us to thrive on this playground of Earth. I love having the conversation about upgrading the collective money story so that we can create and give more in the direction of consciousness, equality and protecting what is sacred to us all.

But this conversation gets upgraded when we realise the underlying truth of all abundance.

While we're here on Earth, we will only ever know the truest, most raw, most fulfilling feeling of abundance, when we all do. Sure, we can feel overflowing in the resources of God in our own lives, but doesn't something feel missing, when there are still people starving?

○ Doesn't something feel missing when there are still people sleeping on the streets?

○ Doesn't something feel missing when there are still people who don't have access to basic medical help?

○ Doesn't something feel missing when there are still people who are on a waiting list for clean water?

○ Doesn't something feel missing when there are children in our world who's #1 dream is to get the most basic education, something so many of us don't ever have to worry about?

The other day I was sent a sleeping bag backpack by a friend who partners with homeless organizations similar to me. It's a way for homeless people to carry their sleeping bag on their back, and when they lay down it it, there is a hood that covers their head so to have some dignity and privacy on the streets. I was so impressed by it and sent it to my friends who run homeless organizations around the world.

But as impressed as I was by it, my gut kept saying 'But why do we need to create sleeping bag backpacks. It's 2017, why are there still people sleeping on the streets?' I felt this torn feeling between 'I want to do everything I can to support those in poverty' and 'but let's get serious now. How can we create a world where there is no poverty and actually do it?'

When are we actually going to live in a world where there is no poverty? We're not lacking resources on Earth, that's a fact. These issues we want to solve aren't issues of the head. They're not issues that stem from our collective lack of resources. They're issues of consciousness. We have everything we need to solve each and every issue that tugs on our hearts. We have everything we need to eradicate homelessness and ensure poverty worldwide is no longer a thing.

We just need to add to our core intention of 'how can I thrive?' with the question, 'how can we all thrive?'

We have the resources, we just need to re-circulate them. This is why I am so big on empowering the conscious, heart-centered badasses of our world to upgrade their money story. Because we know what we need to do, and we have everything we need to do it, we just need to collectively be on the frequency that supports and allows it.

I am all for your abundance, and my abundance, in case you can't tell already from this book. You having less won't help anyone have more. But we'll never make it to the summit of abundance mountain if we're only focussing on our own abundance. We can experience a blissful level of abundance in our own lives whenever we choose to, but we won't ever reach the full, 'as high as we can go' height of fulfilment until we can participate in a world where everyone is readily accessing what they need.

This doesn't mean everyone needs to be rolling in it. Not everyone can energetically handle a big amount of money and they don't need to. However, my friend Kate Maloney recently said something that inspired the shit out of me and I wanna share it with you.

"Why don't we create a world with 7 billion billionaires?"

Just let that thought transport you to possibilities perhaps you'd never considered. Let that thought expand you into what's really possible in our world if we can collectively set intentions and goals that benefit us all. Collectively, our consciousness just isn't corresponding to a peaceful, abundant world for all. Obviously, right? Everything we're seeing whether it's war, poverty, presidents that challenge our love for humanity, is a reflection of where are as a collective. And we won't see an abundant, thriving world for all until our consciousness demands it.

But guess what? We're getting closer. Everyday we're getting closer thanks to superheroes like you raising your vibration and setting more bold intentions on behalf of all, many who've forgotten where they put their cape. We're getting closer thanks to the work of so many who are championing causes that are really making a difference.

We're getting closer thanks to the people on this Earth who really do give a shit. There are a lot of them.

Love, PK X

Pause & Play

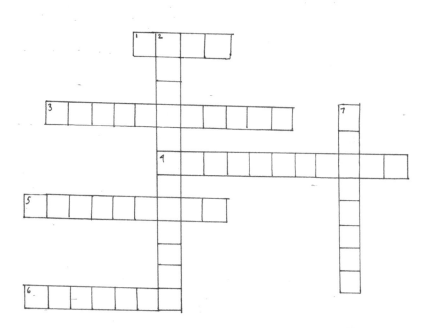

1. Money has ___ .

2. The 3 A's: Awareness, alignment and _____ .

3. Resources flow to the
_____

4. The Spiritual boss of your business.

5. You don't own your $, you _____ it.

6. Six sided shape that represents a Conscious Enterprise.

7. The 2 most important stakeholders are the planet and the _____ .

GIVING

Team Earth is the most important team we're on. We're wearing the same jersey as each other, and the same jersey as our planet.

"Treat the Earth well: it was not given to you by your parents, it was loaned to you by your children. We do not inherit the Earth from our ancestors, we borrow it from our children."
                              —Ancient Indian Proverb

…And may I add something Jane Goodall added onto that proverb— "We're systematically stealing it from our children."

Consciously Giving is the element of The New Way that is all about US and how we can give a really big shit about each other and our beautiful Earth. By being more like Mother Earth, we will know more harmony on Earth.

A letter to Sol,

After she was born.

My starseed,

Almost three months ago, your Dad and I were staring at you in our bed saying 'I can't believe she's here' and 'she's way cuter than us' and just… 'wow.' We basically morphed into the love heart eye emoji and I suppose the wind changed, because we still look like that.

You've taught me SO much in these three months.

How a little person can smile from morning til night everyday and not get a sore jaw.

That vegan babies can in fact have the most scrumptious, chunky #rollsfordays.

That even five minutes of 'just us' can be the most sacred ceremony of all time.

That it's possible for your Mum to completely melt every day and still somehow stay intact.

But one of greatest things you've taught me so far is real trust. There is not a single person on Earth more trusting than you and your friends.

I mean really.

From the moment you choose to be born, you trust us as your parents. You trust us to completely keep you alive from the moment you take your first breath. Whenever we pick you up from the bath, put you in the car, or even just pull clothes over your head and it goes dark for .5 seconds—I look at you and I just see unconditional TRUST.

There is just NO greater honour in the world.

But here's where I get all deep, cos you know #dasme.

What tears me up faster than anything is that you and all of your friends, trust me and ALL of us with your planet. You trust us with your world. You trust us with your future.

You trust us to protect the sacred and keep it sacred for you. You trust us to keep the Amazon alive, the ice caps icey, the forests full, the air clean and the people loving. You trust us to gracefully bridge the gap between the old and the new so that it's worthy of being home to the evolved generation of pure love and lights that you are.

I promise you, I will always do everything I know how to take care of your planet, even when it's inconvenient—How I shop, live, eat, what I drive, how I work, who I support, what I create, where my money goes—everything.

I promise you, I always do everything I know how to preserve and strengthen our humanity. I'll up-level my compassion even when it hurts, and even towards the people in power who take me from love heart emoji to red fire angry emoji.

I promise you, I will always follow the calls and build important things for your world even when it's scary, foreign and takes all the lady balls I have.

I promise to do MORE than just 'my bit' every single day, not online, but most importantly when nobody is watching, approving, liking or commenting.

The fact you trust me and us with your world is my inspiration every day. I'm not just fiercely protective of you, but I'm endlessly protective of your world, your friends world.

One of my favourite quotes is 'hope only makes sense when it doesn't make sense to be hopeful'.

The fact you trust us enough to be born is all the reason in the world to be hopeful.

We've got work to do, but you can trust us too.

It's our turn.

Love Mum. XX

What If Earth Had a Soccer Team?

Team Earth is the most important jersey we own.

"When asked if I am pessimistic or optimistic about the future, my answer is always the same: If you look at the science about what is happening on Earth and aren't pessimistic, you don't understand the data. But if you meet the people who are working to restore this Earth and the lives of the poor, and you aren't optimistic, you haven't got a pulse. What I see everywhere in the world are ordinary people willing to confront despair, power, and incalculable odds in order to restore some semblance of grace, justice, and beauty to this world."
—Paul Hawken

I was running a half marathon in Eugene Oregon on May 1 2016. I was feeling so freaking good, despite the fact that my calves were sore already within the first few miles. The energy was just electric and inspiring. I was running by hundreds if not thousands of strangers who'd come out of their homes, with homemade signs on big sheets of card, saying positive things, but also super funny shit like a little kid holding one that said, *Run fast, I just farted!* and *I'm sure it seemed like a good idea 4 months ago!*

I was so caught up in the funny signs (and trying to mentally note them down, so I could write about them in a FB post later on) and the fact that so many people came out of their house on a Sunday morning for no other reason but to cheer for thousands of crazy strangers who'd decided to run a crazy long way. I felt on top of the world, and immediately looked to my hubs and said, "I can see why marathons are addictive now! It's not the physical accomplishment, it's this environment."

There was nothing like it in the world. An environment where very little of it had anything to do with a 'winner' or a 'competition.' Sure, there was someone who was going to 'win,' but the competition was only for the people up at the very top. For the rest of us, it felt like we were all one big team, one big family, all just trying to do our best. You'd see people stop their own race so they could sit with a stranger who was dehydrated. There were more high-fives and 'you can do it's!' than I'd heard anywhere in my life. There were random bum taps, and "Do you need my gel?" and just *so much freakin' LOVE*.

Naturally, I was so in the love vibe that I got all philosophical on my husband's ass. From about mile 2 through to mile 8, I chewed his ear off about the meaning of life and how this marathon environment was such a perfect example of how humanity could, and perhaps even will, be one day. He looked at me at about mile 3 as if to say, *K hunny let's talk about this later, your legs are gonna need your energy soon.* I was just so off on one. I was peaking. I wished I had my phone so I could have written all my notes down.

I just couldn't stop thinking....

> *Imagine if more people could feel this genuine love and care from complete strangers. This feeling that they always have a team no matter what. So many people on Earth just don't ever feel that. But it's so rich and innate in who we are. We naturally do want to support our fellow humans, we do want to cheer them on. Everyone knows what it's like to care about something. Whether it's a cause, or a sporting team, or a country...*

It comes out when we are competing with someone, something, some team, or some country—person V person, team V team, country V country. We never fail to see passion and that beautiful "I'd do anything for my people." attitude when it comes to sporting teams, countries in the Olympics, or countries at war. We have that in us. Yet most of the time, it's only comes out in times of patriotism and competition—when we are against someone or something and for what we are for.

Imagine if we had that sense of patriotism for our entire human race!!

At about mile 4, when I was really hot on this conversation (where I basically levitated, because I was high on humanity, that or because my runners were cutting into my ankles), and I looked at my husband and said...

"What if Earth had a soccer team?"

What if Earth had a soccer team? Imagine this for a minute. Really, just humour me. Put on some 3D goggles, pretend you're at the movies, and think about this. Imagine there was The Planet Olympics. Earth picked its team, made up of all of the amazing athletes on Earth and hundreds of people in their jeaniius. Doctors, chiropractors, spiritual guides, equipment engineers, coaches... Earth was being represented as a whole. All of the religions came together. All of the countries came together. All of the sporting teams came together. All of the people with different beliefs about climate change, politics, and *yada-yada* came together.

Oh, my heart. Imagine the ease on Earth to know that we don't have to fight or win. Imagine the peace on Earth to know that we don't need to agree. Imagine the calm on Earth to know that we have nothing to be afraid of, nothing to fear, nothing to worry about, because we're all on the same team.

When the half marathon was over, I felt lit. I was so high on humanity that my body felt crazily alive. I wanted to keep running around the Oregon track and turn my half marathon into a full one. I didn't care for the free pancakes or massage after the run, I just wanted to get back to my phone, record a video and post it to my tribe reminding them that no matter how they felt, or what was going on, they had a team and that team was all of us.

Team Earth

This is what we need. Team Earth.

The chances of us going to the planetary Olympics are slim, at least in our lifetime. But right now we are competing in a different sort of Olympics. It's called 'Can we sort our shit out?' games. Earth is its own team, and every single human has been hand-picked to help us win. That includes you. We're all wearing the same jerseys, we're all wearing the same stripey socks, and we're all bleeding the same colour.

Life multiplies in beauty, richness, peace, ease, joy and especially abundance when we realize we are all on the same team. This is why we're still on Earth, working together to figure it all out. This is why every generation is being born with new equipment that the generation before them didn't have. This is why millennials were born with a sense of 'I wanna do it together,' a more evolved version than 'I wanna do it alone.' This is why more people than ever are speaking out about issues that don't support the highest evolution of the planet.

It's not a mistake. Our world is tilting, because we're evolving— together. The starseed I have in my tummy isn't coming here to just sit and eat cupcakes, (although I do hope she takes the time to do just that). The children being born now are coming here very specifically, with very specific equipment and very specific purposes, for which previous generations weren't ready. A whole new compassion, a whole new kindness, a whole new understanding of oneness, a whole new sense of togetherness, a whole new set of balls to say no to the systems and standards that aren't good enough anymore.

But it doesn't just take evolutionary brilliance. It takes a conscious intention from you, me, and us as Team Earth, which brings me to the last section of this book and the bow that ties The New Way all together, Consciously Giving. Consciously Giving is just a fancy way of saying 'Giving a shit.' That's the best and most blunt way I know how to say this.

We care. We give a shit.

> *Feeling the heart of humanity is one way to get high. Remembering the truth of our togetherness, is another. Regardless what political, religious, or sporting 'team' you may identify with, you're also apart of Team Earth—we all are. Earth Is Hiring us to pull our Team Earth Jersey out from the back of our wardrobe and remember that no matter what we see going on in the world, there are a lot of people who give a shit about you, about each other and about our Earth.*

It's Heart Science, Not Rocket Science

We have everything we need to change the world.

If Earth had a soccer team, everyone on Earth would wear the same jersey to support it. There'd be no them, there'd only be us. Winning for Pedro would mean winning for Sally. Winning for Mohammed would mean winning for Alora. We wouldn't wait for governments to implement policies that ensured people didn't starve or sleep in the freezing cold. We just did it. Me and you, us. We just behaved, lived, and gave as if we were all on the same team. In order for us to win, we all had to win.

I love imagining it. I go wild.

- ○ What if every business' goal was for the greater good for all? Where collaboration between companies instead of competition wasn't a fresh concept, but just the norm.

- ○ What if at every board meeting sat there with two spare chairs for 'humanity' and 'the planet' as their chief decision makers?

- ○ What if those with more money didn't have to be taxed up to their armpits, they just felt an innate responsibility to give to those who needed it?

- ○ What if it was just a-given that it was up to us, to take care of each other?

I was just reading a book the other day written by children actually, and inside it had a section called, 'We need to ask more questions,' and one of the questions children wanted to ask the world was, 'Why are there still people hungry when we have enough food to feed everyone?" If children are asking that question by the age of 10, then we as adults need to answer it for them. Or better yet, we need to make sure our childrens' children never have to ask the same thing.

So, let's ask the question. Why are there still people hungry when we have enough food to feed everyone? Is it rocket science, to work out how we can feed those who don't have food? Is it rocket science, to work out how to put shelter over those who are sleeping in the cold? Is it rocket science, to work out how to educate those who can't afford it?

No, no, and no. We have all the money we need, all the food we need and all the brains we need to create solutions for the world's inequality. If it were up to our minds alone to eradicate homelessness, we would have done it already. Giving to those who really need it, on a global level so that everyone has the basics for what they need is not rocket science. It's heart science.

There are still people hungry, cold and uneducated because we as a collective right now just don't give enough of a shit. Sure, there are lots of people who really do care. You and me, and everyone else who picks this book up for starters, but the inequality we see in the world persists because collectively we just don't give enough of a shit. It doesn't take an engineering quantum physics advanced calculus degree to work out how we're going to take care of those in the world who are suffering, but it does take more of us who give a shit.

It takes a collective heart opening and new standard of responsibility, where we stop waiting for the government to do it, and start to do it ourselves. It will take the collective demanding a new expectation from each other.

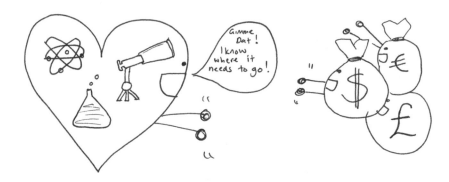

We have everything we need resource wise, we just need to collectively, give enough of a shit. And it all happens at the level of the heart.

So how do we redistribute and recirculate resources so those who need them, get them?

- ○ Companies like Tom's and their 1:1 shoe trade. For every shoe bought, one is given to someone without shoes.

- ○ Skyline socks, who provide socks for airlines in American cities, provide a pair of socks to someone in that city in need for every pair bought.

- ○ Warby Parker, who gives the equivalent of every dollar sold to Not for profit.

- ○ The Company Store, who provides a comforter to a homeless child in the USA for every comforter bought.

People have always given a shit. Giving a shit is becoming the new normal for companies. The collective is starting to give a shit, and we're holding each other to new standards now. It's not enough to just be frustrated by how many mouths Floyd Mayweather and his $200,000 mink coat could feed or how many educational supplies an ad slot during the Super Bowl could buy.

POP OUT: So what can you and I do to help recirculate resources?

We have endless opportunities to give. And it doesn't require you to be rolling around in money.

Erik and I chose, instead of receiving any wedding gifts, to turn our wedding into a 'giveymoon'. We asked all guests and all of our friends on social media to not send us a single thing, but to instead donate to our 'giveymoon'. It was not rocket science, it was heart science. We raised over $125k US so far for The Unstoppable Foundation and we're not stopping. That's 40 villages, 2,740 children educated and 13,967 people impacted. All because we chose redistribution instead of 50 new kettles.

We're now rolling this campaign over to be our baby moon too—no baby gifts, we just are asking people to redirect that money to our brothers and sisters who need it more. Anyone can be a part of something like this. It's not rocket science, it's heart science.

How can you redistribute some resources in your life to benefit people who need them more? Birthdays? % ticket sales from Events?

Give Props To Humanity

"When I was a boy and I would see scary things in the news, my mother would say to me, 'Look for the helpers. You will always find people who are helping.' "
—Fred Rogers.

Amongst all the chaos right now, the terrorist attacks, the online bullying, the fact that Australia still hasn't legalized gay marriage… Can you notice how beautiful humanity is?

- Can you notice the plethora of #bekind movements happening all over social media?

- Can you notice the hundreds of people sending resources to standing rock to support our American Indians as we fight for our water?

- Can you notice the Saudi cleric Sheikh Mohamad al-Arefe who put a fridge outside that serves as a food donation drop-off and pick-up point for people who need it?

- Can you notice when a pregnant lady is waiting for the toilet on a plane, and the SUPER duper busting lady in front of her lets her go before her, purely because she's pregnant? #girlcode

- Can you notice the man who risked his life to save a stranger in the flood?

- Can you notice the woman who stops to give her water to another runner who'd collapsed at mile 9 of her half marathon?

- Can you notice the man who stops running for the train so he can stop and help an elderly woman with her bags?

- Can you notice the house that leaves fresh flowers on the street side with a note saying 'free flowers to anyone who needs'?

○ Can you notice the people who put 12 phone chargers outside their home during hurricane Sandy so that people could charge their phones to let their families know they were ok?

○ Can you notice the group of people in Chicago that go out every Sunday just to offer #freehugs?

○ Can you notice the group of college kids who give their weekends to taking elderly people for a cruise on their Tuk-Tuk through the gardens?

○ Can you notice when someone drops a document in a busy downtown street and a women in heels clumsily sprints to chase it for them, just in case they really needed it?

○ Can you notice when a stranger runs up to another woman in the shop and says "Miss, your tag is hanging out of your shirt" and tucks it back in as if to say #igotchugirl?

○ Can you notice it? I suppose a better question is, can you be aware of all the chaos and the tension, but focus somewhere else?

I saw a car accident in Bondi. My God it was scary. A motorcyclist was hit head on by a man in a car. His entire bike flew under the car, but the motorcyclist who was hit (and it wasn't his fault), stood up immediately... *get this*... to make sure the driver of the car was ok. This guy's body was hit by a freaking car, and it was the car's fault, but his first reaction was to stand up and make sure the driver of the car was ok. Seriously? Legend. To add more big love hearts to this story the amount of people, who previously seemed to be rushing somewhere, stopped everything and stood by the accident just waiting to see how they could help. Just everyday humans, putting strangers first, cos that's what our hearts know naturally to do.

When I was watching the Boston marathon movie, the parts that gave me goosebumps were the parts where all humans switch into 'Team Earth' mode and do whatever they can to help the people who've been injured. Strangers ripping off their clothes to wrap around someone's wound, people sitting and pouring love and 'you're gonna get through this' into people who are in shock and don't know if they're going to survive. I think it was something like 90 people went to the hospital within 30 minutes (correct me if I'm wrong), and *all* that were transported survived.

People are just wired to care. Team Earth is who we are. Our humanity is greater than any terrorism, any hate, any separation. It takes people like you and I to shift our focus to what is going oh so right, every single day. The collective focus won't shift, until your focus and my focus shifts. You've gotta shift your focus, superhero. Most people on Earth right now don't have the tools to shift their focus. Many don't know that there's a world outside of what they see on the news. And that's the reason many if not most people on Earth right now aren't having a very good time. But you are not most people. The world needs more people like you, the superheroes, highlighting and emphasizing, and seeking out the good. Those who are noticing all of the beautiful acts of humanity that remind us of the truth of who we are... Team Earth.

So, superhero, are you ready to be bold and fierce about what you're *for*, without spending so much energy on what you're against? To spend more energy on focusing, noticing and celebrating the billions of humans who are giving people goosebumps daily?

Let's focus on all of the people who are helping, and be one of them.

> *Humanity is beautiful, and we are equipped. We have absolutely everything we need in terms of resources to create the change we want to see in the world. Brain power, jeaniius, money, time, experience, tools—we have it all. Changing the world is not rocket science, it's heart science. What we require now is for our hearts to become bigger than our capabilities. When we focus on the heart of humanity, trust that we can do anything together, we fuel each other and shift the focus from despair to 'humans are fucking amazing—let's do this'.*

Giving a shit about the planet—Non-negotiable.

POP OUT: My love letter to Mother Nature

Mother Nature,

Have I told you lately how much I love you? Not nearly as much as I should. You're not just two pretty words side by side that I use often in Instagram posts to up my hippie status. You are the greatest teacher, the greatest mentor, the greatest provider, and the greatest example and reminder of why we're here, and how we do shit right.

I thought I knew the extents of your beauty, magic and intelligence before, but being pregnant has shown me the real wildness of you, and more so the humility of you. I carry this starseed in my womb knowing that I'm not growing her, you are. I'm not instructing her evolution, you are.

I'm not innately nurturing her, you are. I'm not the one who helps her grow from a scallion size to a cauliflower size (thanks baby app), you are. You trusted me with your greatest creative expression, a new being on Earth. And even that gift alone teaches me more about your ability to trust, to gift, and to know without any doubt of what we're capable.

You're grooming me for motherhood, and I'm paying attention. It's easy as a Mother to worry about our babies. I already have the mother worry. But then I watch you and how you are with all of us. You don't worry about a thing. You're there when we need you, but you don't interfere with our evolution. You don't need to, because our imperfect evolution is just right.

I know that's our job for you too—to not interfere with you, to not interfere with the nature of our planet, to not interfere with the nature of your expressions. And yes, I do use that as an excuse not to do my hair. I have lion hair, cos #wwmnd. Mother Nature wouldn't curl or straighten her hair, she'd let it be wild, so I let it be wild. She'd roam bare faced and bare foot, and so I do that, too.

I don't want to get too serious here, Mo'Na. I know that what you want from us isn't for us to gather in a depressed protest that further separates us on Earth. I know that you want us to rise up to where you are, to come and meet you up there, in your energetic postcode that is so damn clear for us to see. When I'm in Sedona looking from the top of airport hill, that's when I feel your vibration the most clearly. I don't even bother taking my phone out anymore, because even the new iPhone 7 can't capture that portrait of your beauty. I know where you are energetically, and I know that is our goal.

A Mum wants her kids to play, but to be responsible for the world around them. And that's what you want from us.

I hear you.

We are all an extension of you. Without us even having to think about it, you gift us your magic capabilities and we walk this Earth as if they're our own. We are brilliant, but you are more so. And I am so grateful that you trust us to walk this Earth during this time that often feels chaotic and confused, while never swaying from your vibe. You love, you nurture, you trust, you know, you provide, and you roar when you need to. Just like Mums.

We will upgrade our vibration. We will upgrade our action. As a generation I promise that we are getting it and being the best bridge we can be for the generation to follow so they can thrive here, just like we are, but even more astronomically.

Thank you for hiring us.

Bonus' are not required, although I know you'll give them to us anyway. Because that's just what you do.

Love, PK XX

WWMND (What Would Mother Nature Do)

Do What Mother Nature Does, For Mother Nature

"Nature beckons you to be on her side. You couldn't ask for a better boss."
—Paul Hawken

My next tattoo is *WWMND*. What would Mother Nature do? I mean seriously, is there anyone or anything more badass than her? She's the sidekick to Source, yet she is equally as magnificent. She's the greatest nurturer and provider any human or animal ever has the privilege to witness. Just look at a tree, or a sunset, or the ocean, and you can see how big the boldness of her love is. I mean it, go outside and look.

Mother Nature is our greatest mentor and our greatest example of how to live a life so rich and generous that the whole world benefits. And you, are the greatest creative expression of Mother Nature. Right now, it's time you (we) start acting like it. We can't talk about giving a shit, without exploring how we can do more for our Earth. I don't need to tell you why it's important that we protect and respect her. We all know that she's our home. It's never amiss to remind you though, that it only takes one look at our children or grandchildren to remember just why this conversation needs to be at the forefront of our leadership.

I recently went to see Jane Goodall speak live (She is one of my heroes, go and see her speak if you haven't, because her grace is other worldly), and she said, "Have you heard that quote, 'We didn't inherit this planet from our ancestors, we borrowed it from our children?' Well, we're systematically stealing it from our children." It pierced me. I looked down at my pregnant belly, at my daughter who'd be living on this Earth long after I wasn't, and I thought to myself. What else is there to this conversation? I don't think people are ignorant to the actions we need to take in order to halt the rapid extinction of species, and reverse the many statistics that suggest our world is in real danger.

Just to name a wee few. *Over 110 million Americans live amongst such high levels of air pollution the government considers it harmful for their health. One billion birds and mammals die of ingesting plastic each year (Thanks treehugger.com and oceancrusaders.org). One look at the NASA page and you can see evidence of the sea level rising, threatening coastal towns in the next decade, decreased snow cover, shrinking ice sheets, the ocean acidifying, and extreme weather events increasing.* Some joke that global warming is a hoax. It seems pretty damn hot in Arizona! Although some find peace in this logic, you, and I can't. We've got to do more than most. That's what superheroes do.

"But I recycle, I don't eat meat, I drive a hybrid car and I go to protests three times a year. What more can I do?" While we're being called to find our fire and stand up and fight for what is right for our Earth, there is more to it. Protests are not the be all and end all of our calling and our mission here. Neither is recycling, composting, turning your house solar, going vegan, swearing off plastic, and shopping with a calico bag. Those are upgraded actions, which are critical and you get a big high-five if you're implementing more green practices in your life, but what is even more critical is the work we're doing behind the scenes, the message we share that isn't told by our Instagram pages or our Facebook posts, or Leo's new climate change documentary, or the fact we wear a biodegradable pair of undies. This is the work that nobody can see at all, but the Earth can feel. This is the work of upgrading your vibration.

Upgraded Action + Upgraded Vibration = More harmony with Mother Earth

Our work for the planet and our actions has to be accompanied by an upgraded vibration, and we must learn to live in a way that is more like hers. Mother Nature has a way of moving, creating, and acting, and for us to really help her, our goal has to be to make our vibration more like hers. WWMND?

If you are aware and clear enough about your connection to Earth that you feel called to protest, or give money to Standing Rock, or remove all plastic from your household, but you do so with an energy of "I can't believe people are so fucking asleep and don't give a shit", then is your vibration supporting the goal of your actions?

One day I watched Donald Trump on TV gleefully sign the executive orders to begin work on the Dakota Pipeline (drilling into sacred Native American lands, polluting the clean water, abusing the indigenous people of our Earth). I was sitting there with the next generation of humanity in my womb. My stomach started to knot up. I looked to my husband, with tears in my eyes, but a body full of nausea and rage. I whispered to him every fuck and shit and mother fucker I could so as not to draw attention (we were in a waiting room). I wasn't just upset, I wasn't just on the verge of spewing all over the waiting room, I was furious.

His ignorance! The complete dishonour he was showing to our Earth!! I was heartbroken for the indigenous people and all people of our Earth who give their lives to protecting our planet so that all people can thrive here. A few hours later, after a raging FB post, I finally cooled down. I reminded myself of the one thing I had shared from stage just a few months prior at The New Way Live in Sydney…

> *"What Mother Nature wants most from us now, even more
> so than our action in making a stand for her, is for us to go
> to work on raising our frequency, to be more like hers."*

I raged (cos I'm human AF) and then I asked the question 'WWMND?'

Practise Compassion. "He is just doing his very best with what he knows." As mad as I was, that felt better than being mad. My greatest work and yours too, is not gonna be in the 'how mad can I get at people who don't agree with me?' It's going to be 'How much more often can I respond how Mother Nature responds?' We don't fight fire with fire, and we don't fight a lack of compassion with a lack of compassion.

Yes, I can donate money to Standing Rock. I can buy trees for people's birthdays instead of gifts. I can turn my entire house solar. And I can dedicate a whole segment at my event to bringing awareness to these fights for the Earth. I can eat a plant based diet, recycle and compost, wear clothing that is sustainable, bring awareness to all through my work, watch documentaries like *Cowspiracy* and share them online with my people, and give my time to projects that are raising money for our pursuits for Mother Earth. I can live in a way that I feel supports our planet, but no matter what I do, my actions alone are not all that I can do, nor are they what she's most asking me to do.

I can do all of that and then some—I can also upgrade my vibration.

But if Mother Nature is so equipped, why do we need to save her?

Good question, right? The answer: We do not need to save her. We need to drop that save language real quick, because saving is not what we're doing here. Right now the pain that Mother Earth is feeling—the rise in tides, the destruction of the amazon, the spiking temperatures—is all a response to the core issue.

Humans as a collective are separated from Mother Earth. She is vibrating 'up there' (at what the spiritual folk call '5D' or 'The Fifth Dimension'), and we humans are collectively vibrating lower. The disconnection is what's causing the pain and the destruction that we can measure scientifically. This disharmony is why there is disrespect. We wouldn't need to protest against oil drilling and carbon emissions if people's hearts were more like hers. This disharmony is our work, we need to get on her level energetically. We need to be more like her in everything we do. If we really want our people to live in harmony with our planet—this has to be our compass. How can we be more like Mother Nature? How can we rise? Not, 'how can we save her?' It is our job to 'rise up so we can be on her level and this disconnection between us and her can stop hurting her.'

Planet lovers, Earth warriors, the Earth will be healed when we as a team are on the same page as Mother Nature. She isn't changing her game at all. She has it figured out. The temperature rising, the ice caps melting—she is simply experiencing the results of our vibrational riff raff. We don't need to drop to save her or heal her. We need to rise up to meet her at her level.

Get On Mother Nature's Vibe

All of your mentors, coaches, guides, and books (although amazing) can teach you very little compared to what you'll learn by watching what Mother Nature does. I remind myself of this all the time. If my vibe is shit, if I need an answer, or if I just need to be reminded of what matters, I do what Mother Nature does. If I'm hurt by someone who lashed out at me on Facebook, I can borrow her grace. If I'm over-thinking how to finish off the book I'm working on, I can borrow her simplicity. When I'm preparing to give birth to my first born child, I can borrow her trust. She is the ultimate queen. And all hail her, because she does so many things so well. So many things that we as human beings can do so much better.

Mother Nature does Forgiveness.

There is no one on Earth who has experienced more disrespect, misunderstanding, and mistreatment than Mother Earth, yet still she rises the sun for us every day. Still, she throws out colours we've never seen before as the sun goes down every night. Still, she blooms the most beautiful flowers in Spring and she still waters the farms. Still, she gives us the oceans and the waves. Still, she gives us the basic necessity for life on Earth—oxygen. She doesn't have time for grudges. Can you imagine how our lives would look if she did? #wwmnd

Mother Nature does Giving.

She gives the most without wanting any credit. Have you ever seen Mother Nature bombard her way through a Nobel Peace Prize awards ceremony and shout "No! This is absurd! Sure, Henry Jones can create a new currency but have you ever seen my sunset over Sedona? What about ME?!" Lols. No. She gives the most, does the most, and is the most robustly, unconditionally, generous being we will ever know. And isn't it wild that she can be all of that, without wanting a single ounce of credit? (Note: She may not want credit, but she is slowly starting to command respect. Natural Disasters are not a mistake, they're a text message from the Momma). #wwmnd

Mother Nature does Non-judgement.

Could you imagine Mother Nature giving sunlight to an entire country, except for Mark—your ex-boyfriend, Veronica—that girl at work who follows you around trying to convert you to Christianity while telling you how wrong you are for having sex before marriage, or Aaron—the guy who took steroids at the height of his Olympic career. No, she doesn't work that way. She gives sunlight to all, and she gives sunrises to all. Rather than have an excel spreadsheet where she tries to keep score of everyone's goods and bads like Santa Claus does, she is simple in her approach and judges no one. She isn't loving individual humans as much as she's loving a collective. She doesn't punish the ones who litter, or the ones who eat more than their fair share of meat, or the ones who hunt and kill. She treats all humans the same. This is why Team Earth is so critical. When you smoke, you harm your own lungs. When you treat the Earth like shit, you harm everyone on Earth. But… non-judgement. This is a practice we can notice in Mother Nature, and do our best to emulate. It ain't easy as a human (Insert Judge Judy theme song in here). #wwmnd

Mother Nature does Patience.

How many centuries has Mother Nature waited for us to learn about our oneness and togetherness and rise up to her vibration so she can stop being abused and disrespected? I don't know. Lots of centuries. She waits patiently for us to stop thinking we're at the top of the food chain (cos we ain't) and still while being her graceful, patient, badass self, she nurtures us all and gives us life. Just like a mother would do for a naughty kid who's gone astray. She does that for the collective, which is made up of people who love and take care of her and naughty kids who don't. She is patient with us while we collectively figure this out and rise up to meet her at her frequency. And yet we honk our horns at the Prius in front of us cos they didn't go within .5 seconds of the light going green. Or we roll our eyes when we have to wait 20 mins to be seated at a restaurant. Or we cut corners in our endeavours, because the long game just seems long. Does Mother Nature have infinite patience? I'm not sure. But her display of patience to this point is the greatest and most expansive, infinite example we will ever know. If in doubt, do what Mother Nature does. #wwmnd

Mother Nature does Trust.

Do you ever watch people throw rubbish on the floor, treat waiters like shit, throw cigarettes out of the car window and think "How fucking ignorant!" Or even worse, do you ever get a knot in your stomach when something like the Paris attacks, Boston Marathon Bombing, or everything happening in Syria and the middle east on the daily, and think "It's getting worse. What the fuck is wrong with some humans?" Yep. Small or big. A lot of the time our frustration and our worry is a) because we are judging or b) because we don't trust humanity and are frightened at where we're headed. I love to trust humanity, because it feels better than not trusting. I like to back my team, Team Earth and have faith that we're moving in the right direction as a collective. And whenever my trust drops even for a minute, I do what Mother Nature does, and trust again. No one on Earth has seen more, or been more mistreated than she has. And I don't know about you, but I haven't received any complaint emails from her yet? If she can create the Grand Canyon, then I'm pretty sure typing an email isn't so hard for her. But she never sends them. She stands strong in her faith, and keeps doing what she's here to do, no matter what. #wwmnd

Mother Nature is not only the most loving, compassionate, divinely nurturing being, but she is the most intelligent—period. She sits beside Source and they share the same DNA (cough, same as you too). How does it get any better than that? Right now we're in this epic evolution period, right? We're collectively rising higher, we're removing and releasing old energies and patterns that no longer serve us, and we're climbing up through what feels like an energetic shit storm into a new consciousness. It's like concrete on the sidewalk, cracking right down the middle when it's had too many people walk on it, and now, because of the new weather conditions, it hasn't been able to hold up. So the concrete has cracked. In the middle of the crack, flowers are beginning to bloom. Flowers that couldn't bloom before when the concrete wasn't able to crack. Right now on Earth, our metaphorical concrete is cracking. New light, new flowers, new consciousness is emerging. And we can either focus on the crack, or we can focus on the flowers. Mother Nature focusses on the flowers. And she sees and feels more of the cracks than any of us. She makes a stand for what is coming. What is true. What is light. Even while so many of us remained focus on what's broken or what's cracking, she knows what's happening, and she stays focused on the new flowers that are emerging. We can do that too.

She is soft, but knows when to stand her ground. Natural disasters aren't a mistake. They're not just a big ol' whoopsy that happened when Mother Nature and Source were planning their calendars out. Mother nature is intentional. Everything about her is intentional. Every rainfall, is intentional. Every sunny day, is intentional. Every storm, is intentional and every natural disaster is intentional. She will roar when she needs, when she needs us to take a closer look. That's what natural disasters are. She won't rob us of our opportunity to rise up together—that's our evolution and she's not gonna do our dirty (epic) work for us. But she will nudge us. And she does nudge us. Do you notice? If we don't do our best to take care of global warming, the tides will rise and beach side cities will be wiped. Perhaps our kids or our kids' kids won't ever see the glaciers of today. She's not gonna cover up for us, but she will love us on our journey and gives us clues and signs. It's up to us to pay attention.

There will be consequences for mistreating our Earth. Exactly what they are, I can't tell you. But you only have to pay a tad bit attention to the science that is so available to us and the work of so many planeteers who dedicate their life to educating and showing the world not only what's happening, but what's going to happen. You are far more equipped than you think and we have everything we need to bring humanity into harmony with our Earth.

What would Mother Nature do? What's most required of us now, superhero, is that we be more like her. WWMND.

> *There is so much conversation around what we can do to save Mother Nature. Should I compost, go vegan, sell my car? Superheroes understand that it's not only about upgrading our action, but upgrading our vibration. Mother nature is our greatest mentor and guide, and she is always showing us, guiding us, nudging us, and if we can pay attention to her like she is our greatest ever mentor, we'll be more like her. So, if in doubt, do what Mother Nature does. #wwmnd We gotta raise the collective vibe.*

11 (Or More) Ways to Upgrade Your Action for Our Mumma

It's simply non-negotiable.

To experience harmony with Mumma Earth, we need to upgrade our vibration and upgrade our action. How do we upgrade our vibration? We've been speaking about it throughout this entire book. The *living* section of this book, is that message. But let's talk about action.

Our children get it. They are being born with an innate connection to our Earth and an innate distaste at anything which harms her. I get messages weekly from friends whose children have declared things like 'I don't want to eat my friends. No more turkey sandwiches Momma!' The planet is in safe hands when our children start to lead, I have no doubt about that. But we've got to do our absolute best until then.

Our children are counting on us. I think of the quote by his Holiness Dalai Lama "Our prime purpose in this life is to help others, and If you can't help them, at least don't hurt them." The same goes for our Earth. If you don't want to become an activist, at least reduce your impact and your imprint. This isn't just a job for the tree hugging hippies, it's a job for everyone who gives a shit about their children, grand children, great grand-children. When I see someone pick up rubbish, or take their own reusable keep-cup to a cafe, I say thank you either out loud or under my breath—because it's not just their home they're taking care of it, it's mine, my husbands, my Mums, my dogs, my siblings and most importantly, it's my unborn daughter's.

Superhero, on behalf of Momma Nature, can we count on you to upgrade your action and take daily responsibility to upgrade your vibration? This book has given you so many examples of ways to raise your vibe (the entire living section), cos after all, it's the greatest gift we can give each other and our Earth.

And I'm giving you 11 (or more) ways to act, support your Earth Mama, and to raise your action. They are in no particular order, because just go do them. Don't rank them. Don't over think them.

1. *Chase people who put junk mail in your letterbox down the street.* Junk Mail is so 2000 and so not now. We have a *No Junk Mail* sign on our letterbox and people still put brochures for the local supermarket, the eyebrow lady, and the pizza shop down the street in there. I get it, local business matters. But junk mail has gotta go.

2. *Shop consciously.* This is probably the biggest. You're voting for a more sustainable world every time you spend a dollar. Shop locally when it comes to food, buy clothes and products from companies who have sustainable and ethical practices in place (or vintage if you're rad). Support companies who really give a shit. This is how we together, make sustainable companies the most relevant and create a whole new standard together. Every $ matters.

3. *Eat more plant based.* I'm not going to tell you you need to go vegan. I eat a plant based diet, cos it feels good to me and I know I'm contributing to the planet even a teeny bit by going without animal products. Do some research, if you're not sure why. Watch *Cowspiracy*. I don't think the whole world is ready to go vegan and in some cultures it just isn't on the radar, but I do think we can take small steps. Include some animal-free days into your family's week. Begin with one or two. If you feel called to veganism or even vegetarianism, then go for it. It's easy and inexpensive as long as you educate yourself properly about how best to get everything you need. I thrive being vegan—especially throughout my pregnancy.

4. *Use compostable products.* Nappies, garbage bags, paper towels, toilet paper—they are a few places to begin. Landfill is a big contributor to CO_2 in the environment. Compostable and biodegradable products are from renewable resources (like bamboo) and reduce the burden on landfill. One company I LOVE is Who Gives a Crap toilet paper, a social enterprise that is good for people and the planet (and your bum). Check them out!

5. *Recycle.* Seems so obvious, so 1990, but many people still don't recycle. Be the recycle nazi in your house if you have to be. I am in mine (soz not soz hunny). If you're not sure how to, research. And also check the recycling system in your neighbourhood. Buying recycled products helps too. (This book is made from recycled paper). #savethetrees

6. *Get a hybrid or electric car or car-pool more.* I'm not gonna be a dummy and suggest everyone goes and gets a Tesla or a Prius. But if you are in the market for a new car, there are electric or hybrids in most people's' budgets and more are being introduced to the market each day. Tesla is coming out with a model 3, in order to be a more mainstream affordable model. If you love your gas guzzler, be more mindful of car-pooling to reduce emissions.

7. *Plant more trees.* Whether you do it yourself, join your community, or give your friends 'trees planted' in your name as a gift. There are lots of organizations who allow you to buy 'trees planted. They plant the trees in their forest and you give a certificate to your friend or family in their name letting them know. I buy my husband 'trees' every year. Trees, socks, and jocks.

8. *Print less.* Simple. Print less where you can. Double sided where possible.

9. *Give your clothes away.* Recycled anything is super valuable. Clothes included. Have a 'clothes trading' day with your buds where you bring all your clothes over and just swap them. Or take them to an organization that provides clothes for those in need or a church or a shelter.

10. *Pick up rubbish even if you need to chase it.* Be 'that guy' who runs down the street attempting five times to step on the ice cream wrapper. Even if you don't catch it (make sure you bloody catch it), you'll likely inspire people around you to realize that it's up to us to keep our Earth clean. And you'll burn some cals. And people might even help you when they see the wild chase.

11. *Watch the documentaries.* Face the facts just so you're aware. Most documentaries about the planet leave us feeling either a) concerned or b) inspired. I think a combination of both is healthy. Documentaries like *Earthlings and Cowspiracy'* are confronting for many, but they're informative. And for people to make decisions about their habits, it's important that we know the facts. Do your research beyond the documentaries too if some information doesn't sit well. Just equip and empower yourself.

12. *Don't drink from plastic water bottles.* Don't buy them. Instead, buy a sweet non-plastic water bottle you can tote around quite easily, like a SIGG bottle that says, "Friends don't let friends drink from plastic." Plastic bottles are floating in our oceans, polluting our groundwater and our insides, and are filled by companies who are taking the fresh water from communities who need it. There are plenty of reasons to ditch the plastic, but if you need more, watch *Tapped.*

POP OUT: Love Notes to Mother Nature

I asked on a Facebook status "If you could write a short love note to Mother Nature, what would it say?" #lovenotestomothernature.

Here are just a few that moved me. The first one, is from my beautiful editor Janna.

Mother Nature,

I first met you when I was a little girl. Out in the woods on horseback rides with my mother and out on boat on the lake with my father. I learned of your beauty in bouquets of wildflowers and in fields filled with thousands of butterflies. We became best friends on the hill when you shared with me the magic of the clouds and the magnificence of summer thunderstorms. And when I needed to figure out why bad things happen to good people, you gave me your solid ground and showed me your changing leaves while you waited patiently with me to realize that I might not figure that out. Ever since then, you have been there when I need the ground to feel solid and the leaves to trust change. You know me pretty well, because when I feel smothered or lost, you lead me to water to show me that I too have the choice of freedom and flow—and you make the salt air just sticky enough so that I can take the energy of your oceans with me for a few more days. In a world that can make so little sense to me, you bring it all back home. Thank you for making me a better human. Sometimes all you have to do is give me a beam of moonlight. Or a breath of fresh air, the feeling of the sun warming my skin, a plunge into the ocean, the fur of a puppy, or the sparkle of snow. I'd be totally in my head if it weren't for you, but I'm so glad that's not the case, because you create the best reality one could ever imagine.

    Janna

◇◇◇

I love looking at you from above. Today I was in a plane and felt blessed to be part of you. When I'm on the ground and when I'm in the air you never fail to keep me immersed in your beauty X

    Nicole

Thank you for your sunshine, thank you for your rain, thank you for your lush green spaces, thank you for your oceans, seas and rivers. Thank you for your mountains, glaciers, deserts and forests. Thank you for providing home for animals, birds, insects, sea creatures—for your unwavering love, your fierce yet gentle heart, all you continue to provide us day in day out. Thank you for forgiving us when we don't show you the respect you deserve. Thank you for the reminders you send us, those that remind us of the duty we were born with, to love and respect your magnificence always 🖤

Alice

Mother Nature, thank you for showing us in every moment what it is to unconditionally love. Thank you for showing us that growth is our birthright and our most precious need. Thank you for showing us to show up with abundance even when it seems we have no more to give. Thank you for shining your light so we may know what shining ours looks like, and for giving us permission to shine ours. Thank you for showing us true forgiveness. Thank you for holding us with such grace and benevolence. We only need to look to you each day for guidance to realize we are whole and complete exactly as we are. Thank you Mumma Nature

Ellie

Thank you for showing me Beauty and Magic everywhere. Thank you for giving me everything I need in order to thrive. Thank you for showing me strength along with ease, grace, and flow. Thank you for reminding me to surrender and breathe.

Alexandra

Dear Mother Nature, thank you for having mountains that I can climb on to see the world, and myself, a little clearer. Thank you for giving me a place of stillness, a place of adventure and a place of connection. Dear Mother Nature, thank you for your mountains.

Sarah

Dear Nature,

I love how the waves coming and receding from the shore are like my breath. With each inhale you refill, you gather strength and with each exhale you give us waves of energy. I feel this reciprocal energy in my life and I understand that with everything I must have this flow, this circular energy. Thank you for allowing me to understand more fully that I need to have my time to fill up and then I must let go and give my wave of energy back to the Earth.

    Virginia

                    ◇◇◇

Mother Earth, I feel you breathe, your warmth nurture me. I honor your strength and beauty and applaud your patience. I listen to your wisdom and guidance and will continue to blow your seeds of love and marvel in your presence. I will continue the stories of ancient truths and respect you like you deserve. xx I Love you

    Amber

Dear MN, in all your roaring majesty you still teach me to be still, to be grounded, to be peaceful. Thank you for giving us life, thank you for giving us sunsets, thank you for giving us rainstorms and reminders of the ineffable ❤

    Charlotte

                    ◇◇◇

Dear Mother Nature,

Thank you for bringing me here to the place, where I can honour you. Where I can hold you close to my heart. Where I can learn all the lessons you have to teach me. I feel you. You give me life, and for that I am forever grateful. ❤

    Anika

                    ◇◇◇

Thank you for all the you give us for all the you endure through and for the power of resilience and beauty you show us. Thank you for grounding me, nourishing me and connecting me to Source. ☐

    Kelly

◇◇◇

Mother Nature I'm so grateful for your presence. You give me life and love and passion. I trust you with my whole heart and soul and I know you will always show me the right way and be my best teacher.

Ashton

◇◇◇

Thank you for your unconditional love and for always showing up no matter what. You show me the power of giving with no expectation of return and your energy grounds me every damn time. Eternally and infinitely grateful x

Ash

Thank you for always keeping me grounded and safe. You are so generous and I respect you so much. Your beauty, your serenity, your gifts of abundance are always offering us more.

Tara

◇◇◇

Mother Earth. from the core of my being my soul is deeply connected to you. Thank you. Thank you for your wisdom and teachings. Thank you for the countless blessings we receive daily...thank you for your unconditional patience and love as we journey through life here with you. Thank you for giving us the greatest gift of life.

Dominique

◇◇◇

Thank you for loving us unconditionally. I am comforted knowing I will wake up and you will be there. Comforted knowing there are enough light workers, working tirelessly to save you for future generations, because the light always wins. And I can't imagine a day not being able to gaze at the clouds or smile at a sunset. Thank you for sharing your immense beauty.

Stephanie

THANK YOU FOR YOUR GRACE MOTHER... for your gentleness and forgiveness. For being patient, loving and guiding... for trying so hard for us... even when we might be dead asleep! You are a mother of utter unconditional LOVE! You are ALIVE! VIBRANT! And I am YOU... YOU ARE ME ❤

    Mar

◇◇◇

Thank you. For being our greatest teacher. For being a living example of forgiveness, as we slowly learn our way towards oneness. Thank you for this playground, this heaven on Earth.

    Adam

◇◇◇

Mama Nature... thank you for the sun that warms my skin, the breeze that cools me, the air that fill my lungs, the flowers that make my soul happy. For your raw power, and your grace, your beauty and your strength. Thank you for this beautiful world. I promise to teach the next generation to take amazing care of you.

    Melissa

◇◇◇

Thank you for your energy, for your infinite expansive goodness and how you contrast that with the most delicate details. Thank you for always pouring into us even when not reciprocated. You truly teach us all about unconditional love. And when we stop to listen, I KNOW you are always telling us something. Sometimes the most important messages are in the space you create. You aren't only about the obvious beauty but also about that ever present space. So much love and gratitude for you. ❤

    Allison

◇◇◇

Mother Earth, I feel you breathe, your warmth nurture me. I honor your strength and beauty and applaud your patience. I listen to your wisdom and guidance and will continue to blow your seeds of love and marvel in your presence. I will continue the stories of ancient truths and respect you like you deserve. xx I Love you

    Amber

◇◇◇

Papatūānuku, thank you for sustaining life, thank you for being so patient with us as we've gone through our teenage angst and rebellion and for being so forgiving as we've stepped all over you and taken without any regard for you. I know it's taken us several lifetimes to get here but I apologize for all the hurt and pain we've caused you and now it's your turn to receive from us in the form of love, thanks and whatever acts big or small that we can take to preserve you and to care for you. Thank you just isn't enough. Aroha nui.

   Amie

◇◇◇

Mother.. You are Sacred.. it is Great to Be a part of You.. I Love You.. and Thank You.. I bow to You.. You are so Beautiful.. So incredibly Loving.. Nurturing in everyways. .I feel You and hear the voices of ancestors sing through me.. Thank You for every inch, every breath, every step, everyone, everything.. <3

   Giedrė

Back to Where We Began. Our Vibration

It all comes back to you

While writing this book, I've had some moments where I've paused and asked myself, "Can I really suggest that the biggest work of our generation is to focus relentlessly on our own alignment and vibration? To lighten up and stop taking ourselves and our deep work so seriously?"

And every time I've asked, my soul has piped up like a crazy football fan, with her hands on either side of her mouth yelling, "Yeeeessssssss!"

Wrapping up this giving (a shit) section of this book, I think about myself and the impact prioritizing my alignment has on those around me and the planet. When I'm aligned, feeling good, in my flow, unkinked, I'm so much more giving. When I'm aligned, I'm effortlessly generous to everyone around me. I do things like surprise my sister with an airfare voucher so she can come and visit.

I'm clear and sure. I don't hesitate to follow my excitements, to book the flight, to go on the picnic, to write this book. I listen more intently to the people I'm in conversation with because I'm not needing from them, I'm just fine, and because I'm fine, I'm present. I get on a Facebook Live with fire and passion and an energy that moves people more than my words.

I become crazily thoughtful. I sit and text people all the things I love about them, just as if I'm high from a cup of coffee. I'm open-hearted and see the beautiful qualities in people, rather than the things that bug me. I let people off the hook. Whether it's my family, Presidents, people I butt heads with. I can easily and quickly remember that everyone is doing their best. I'm just better to those around me. I'm better to the world.

We began this book in Chapter One by reminding you that your greatest commitment to this planet as a superhero is your alignment, your vibration. And I'm finishing up with this too. This doesn't mean you need to look like someone who has never come down from 7 years straight at Burning Man (or you can, whatevs). It doesn't mean you ignore your human AF emotions that make you the fierce, grounded badass that you are. It doesn't mean you pretend every day is your favorite day and that shit doesn't hurt. It doesn't mean you become 'positive Pete' and avoid all situations and emotions that aren't worthy of being turned into a sunset background meme. It doesn't mean that you don't honour the rage you feel when you see injustice and disrespect and behaviours that challenge your love for the world. No, it doesn't mean any of those things at all.

Vibing high, or prioritizing your—not somebody else's, mind you—alignment means focusing on your flowing tap, making your unkinked hose your numero uno, most important for every single day for the rest of your life.

- ○ This means being beautifully aware of the world and its contrasts and noticing what the contrasts stir up in you, so you can choose to respond, or not.

- ○ This means crafting your own choices, values and rules that make you feel good right now and not when Jim and Mary like your shit on Facebook.

- ○ This means to focus where it matters for you to focus and to stop pretending like every single energetic invitation is one in which you need to respond.

- ○ This means to stop pretending everything matters, cos not everything does.

○ This means move through life genuinely grateful that you're here, to remember what a privilege it is to be a human at this time where all is ripe for us to create epic shit.

○ This means to turn off the TV and stop pretending that 'their' news is 'your' news and that the same reality applies to everyone.

○ This means to rearrange your values and metrics so that you're not measuring the 'goodness' or 'suckiness' of your life based on an old model for success that isn't yours. This means to look up, and leave your phone in your bag.

○ This means to turn the corners of your mouth up, and just sit in the appreciation for the fact that this entire multi-verse is wanting you to win.

○ This means to listen to the excitement of surprise and scrap your whole calendar and go surfing in Fiji cos random exciting shit is just as much your responsibility as your other commitments.

This means it's time to stop prioritizing everything and anything over the one thing that you are the most responsible for—your alignment and the vibration your alignment gifts the world. Your alignment comes first. And you just watch how the world responds to a commitment like that. Because this is what the planet most wants from us, what we most want from each other, and what you most want from you.

It was partly Paul Hawken's Portland speech of '09 that inspired the title of this book, so I'll leave you with a piece of it. I leave you with all the information I have to share and with the words that have inspired me the most. By reading and applying what you learned in this book, you are fighting the good fight. You are fighting the good fight in The New Way.

"The great thing about the dilemma we're in is that we get to re-imagine every single thing we do...There isn't a single thing that doesn't require a complete remake.

There are two ways of looking at that. One is: Oh my gosh, what a big burden. The other way, which I prefer, is: What a great time to be born! What a great time to be alive! Because this generation gets to essentially completely change the world."

YOU ARE ABSOLUTELY BRILLIANT....
AND EARTH IS HIRING YOU.

Pause & Play

Last crossword

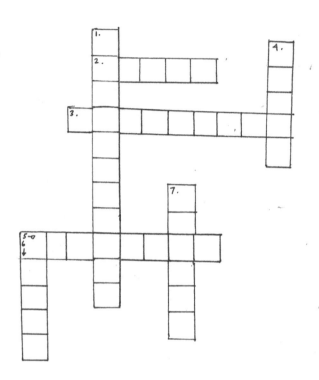

1. How can we _____ resources?

2. TEAM _____

3. Let's uprade our ACTION and our _____.

4. What would Mother Nature do?

5→. Give props to _____.

6↓. It's not rocket science, it's _____ science.

7. Let's upgrade our _____ and our vibration.

The Bonus: The Script

The Keys to Conscious Creation

"You have to tell the story how you want it to go"
—Abraham-Hicks.

Ok so this is where we re-write your stories and upgrade the instruction you're giving to the world!

You know about manifesting. You know about the **Law of Attraction** (even if like me, those words remind you of people with mullets at Abraham Hicks events. So rad). But do you consciously use it? Do you get it? Does it work? Is it working for you?

There are Three Steps To Conscious Creation that are important to know. It's important because I feel like most people make their biggest mistake by stopping their practice, just before it becomes super duper effective in their lives.

1) **TRUST**. This is when you believe in this 'law of attraction/ manifesting' stuff and you truly do believe that you can create anything you want. You haven't gone much deeper than this yet though. You don't have a solid daily intentional practice. Often you wait until things are going *not* how you want them to go, before realising you better take check on the instructions you're giving to the world.

2) **KNOW**. This is when you are practising some sort of intentional conscious creation everyday, and seeing some evidence! $500 gets put back into your account by your landlord, cool people show up in your life, you get an opportunity that blows your mind and is exactly what you request! You know conscious creation to be true for you. But, after receiving some evidence and feeling like a manifesting wizard, you stop practising.

Beware, most people stop at step 2

3) **EMBODY**. This step is the money. This is when you are so consistent with your daily practice of upgrading your story and consciously choosing what you want, that what you want becomes as certain for you as your name. Embodiment is when your entire being is giving the Universe the instructions you want to give, without you even trying. This is when the story you're telling yourself on auto-pilot, matches the story you want to see become your real life. This is where what you want and what you see are the same thing. This is when the entire Universe starts responding to your highest desires at God Speed, with the Universe sporting a 'but of course' smirk.

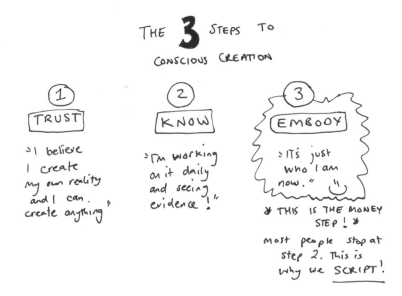

THE **3** STEPS TO CONSCIOUS CREATION

①
TRUST
"I believe I create my own reality and I can. create anything"

②
KNOW
"I'm working on it daily and seeing evidence!"

③
EMBODY
"It's just who I am now."

⚡ THIS IS THE MONEY STEP! ⚡

most people stop at step 2. This is why we SCRIPT!

You will get what you want when you feel what it feels like to have it—Another one of my favourite Abraham-Hicks bombs.

The work is not just in thinking about what you want or writing it down and shoving it in your undies draw. It's about *embodying* that you want so that your being sings *only* that song and you see *only* those things. This is why we script. And this is why we don't miss a day of reading it. Shall we?

With The Script, you get to choose.

We spoke briefly about *stories* in the leading section of this book. The stories we tell, instruct our lives. Here's where we tell the stories we actually want to become real.

THE SCRIPT

Oh The Script, my beloved. The Script is my #1, ride or die, go-to, tell everyone about, practise religiously, never miss a day tool. I've done a lot of 'manifesting' kinda stuff in my time, but this one takes the cake and will forever be a part of my conscious creation process. The Script to me, is all about choosing. It's about letting the Universe, God, Source know our preferences—and, more importantly, it's embodying a new story within you. That new story becomes your new identity. That new identity becomes your new instruction. Source hears and the world then responds. "Manifesting" can feel a bit of a buzzword, but The Script to me isn't that. The Script is practical. It's a practice, exercising our power to choose and upgrading the instruction we're giving to the world. It works.

So, shall we write one?

Here's what we're gonna do.

- ○ learn how to write a script
- ○ read some of one of mine
- ○ see how scripts can turn into real life

How to Write a Script

This is a movie script you're writing, but the movie is your epic life and you are the main character. You're giving instruction to your life in the form of a "it's already happened" movie script. As you write it and read it, it's as if the movie is already in the cinemas. Because, pretty soon it will be available for all to see in real life ;) Box office hit!

I've started with the instructions for writing your script, but you may digest them better if you first flip over and read some real examples.

10 Steps to Writing Your Script:

How do you want life to be? What do you want to create?

1) Choose to write it when you're feeling good, not when you're tired or feeling 'ugh'. Choose a time or day, or a special place, or just sit down and go for it when you're feeling hot and high vibe. I cosy up with a tap-opening cup of cacao every time I update mine.

2) *Always* focus on *how you feel*. You will write about specific things, events, people, and places throughout, but focus most on feeling. This gives the Universe room to move and surprise and delight you. So, if you've got a big keynote planned, how do you want to feel throughout it? When you choose how you want to *feel*, you're controlling the outcome without controlling the outcome. Know what I mean?

3) Write in present or past tense, never future tense. So it's always as if it's happening right now, or if it just happened. EG "The event was the best event ever!!" OR... "It's the morning of Day 2 of the event and I feel SO lit up and clear." Whatever feels best to you. Remember, you're writing a script about the life you want.

4) Begin with a paragraph detailing how you feel in general. What's your general vibe day to day? How do you feel when you wake up and go to bed? What are your thought patterns? How do you feel about life? Go wild here.

5) Next, move through the next 6-12 months of your life in chronological order. One paragraph for each 'part' of the movie works best. You aren't meant to get it all right and

know for sure what's around the corner, but think of things you have coming up. Maybe, a trip somewhere with your family, a promotion that you're going for, an event you want to go to, a trip you want to take, a program you have joined. Or maybe something like, you're having a baby, moving overseas. Anything at all! Script it out as it goes in your 'my epic life' box office movie script.

6) Add in as much detail as possible throughout that make it feel so real for you e.g. "I smile to my husband and grab his hand. I don't want to grab my phone like I usually do when we're taking off to fly. I'm so present, calm and grateful." Remember, the power of The Script is in choosing your outcome, no matter what the details are. So choosing how it feels, no matter what happens. The details are up to God. The choosing is up to you.

7) Go through and add colour. Highlight words or phrases that are super powerful for you and make them POP! Color gifts energy. You can add drawings or images if you want to also!

8) Finish with a powerful statement. My favorite is "Everything is getting better and better. How does it get any better than this?"

9) Read every morning or night, or at another time of the day when you're feeling good, like lunchtime, in nature, or mid-morning with your coffee or cacao. I like to play a rampage from Abraham Hicks or pump some high vibe music or do some whack Beyonce' dancing before I read mine just to get me feeling really good. Your script works better when you're feeling good—everything does.

10) Update your script regularly. You want it to get to the point where, while you're reading it you feel like 'uh, duh!!'. The goal is to *embody* your script. Not just to trust and know it. I expand on my same script, but I edit it as time goes to accommodate for new things coming up. I do this one to two times a month. There is no right or wrong for this. It's your relationship with your script.

Do not miss a day of reading your script. Many people miss a day. They get excited by it, and things start to show up that make them think 'oh look how hot I am I am a manifesting master', only to then stay at the *know* phase and not move onto the *embody* phase. This is what your ego wants you to do and you need to be mindful of the ways your mind will tell you to "just stop reading it now, you've been so good with it." We have 24 hours in a day. 10 mins a day to read your script is doable for *everyone*.

These are my script guidelines, but you Go Nuts!!! Do what feels good!

Hot Tips and FAQ's

○ You can hand write it or type it. Do whatever feels good to you. I type it on google docs so that I can edit it regularly, add colour, and then add it to 'books' on my phone. I also can barely read my own handwriting ;)

○ It can be as long or short as you want. My current script is five pages, cos I've got a bunch of personal stuff + script around this book + other Jeaniius projects + my birth added in + beyond my birth. It can be 2-5-ish pages. Or it can be more or less, you choose. Mine takes me about 5-7 minutes to read. Doable? Uh, yes.

○ You may want to include things that have already happened so that it makes your script even more real to you. "2016 was the best year ever. I got married to my stud muffin of a husband, we bought a house and I experienced ..." You can't tell the difference between what's happened and what's coming. It's ALL real.

○ Read it out loud if you want to, or just read it. I read mine quietly to myself most days but occasionally I'll read it out loud just for fun. Some people audio record themselves reading their script on their phone and play it while they drive, before bed, while they're getting ready. Powerful!!

○ If you feel called, share your script with your closest person, like your partner, your kids, your soul sister. My husband now also reads his script in bed every night. It's just something we do, no matter what and it's so special now that he's got his very own.

○ Add energetic words that you would normally use like 'OMG!!' and or F bombs if that's your thing! Words like 'BEYOND' and 'EVER' as in 'better than ever' are powerful and expansive. ALL THE CAPS are allowed!

○ Have fun with it. Remember that I can guide you, but you are the guru. Write it how it feels good and adjust it as it feels good.

The Money Script:

In order to rewrite your money story, you will need to have positive statements about money in your script. Come of up with a few of your own, or add some from the below. Remember, this is your story.

○ Money is a divine spiritual entity and it's up to each of us to choose our relationship with it.

○ I'm so bloody grateful I'm on the same team as money now and not competing with it! What a shift!

○ I feel excited and grateful when I open my online banking! I used to feel anxious, but not anymore. I love being pleasantly surprised by what I see on that screen!

○ The Universe loves loaning me money to create epic shit, experiences, memories, gifts, health.

○ With money I can build and create things for this planet that reward so many people and our Earth.

○ I am so grateful to have all of the resources to do everything that I'm called to do.

○ All of my needs are met, and although I don't need more, I choose to create more because this is an abundant Universe and I am always the one who chooses.

○ Money listens to everything I say and I love giving props to money and speaking nicely about all the ways it supports me to thrive, give and create.

○ I love owning my own money story regardless of anyone else, even those close to me. Everyone evolves at their own time.

○ Money loves coming to me because I generate it consciously on behalf of all.

○ I love thinking of all the ways money in the hands of heart-consciousness can raise the vibe on Earth.

○ I love finding ways to serve the world and letting them show their appreciation with money. I create value, receive money and then do it again but better.

○ Money in my hands serves the collective and our planet.

○ I love knowing that money isn't mine, but on loan to me from Source. I love what I can generate with money and that my relationship with money is conscious and heart-centered.

○ I always feel light when I think of money. It has nothing to do with the amount, but the understanding that it's always there for me when I am in alignment with it.

○ I love being able to help anyone, or anything I feel called to help with the abundance of money I have available from the Universe.

Now we are going to get real and talk about your specific feelings about money.

Finish the following statements — in your own words. Don't worry I gave you some prompts!

When I check my bank account I feel _____

_____.

I love that I can now _____

_____.

When I'm giving I feel _____

_____.

When I think about money, I now feel_____

_____.

Now add your Money Story right into your Script. Feeling confused, overwhelmed, a little writer's block? Here's an example of what it could feel and read like:

> *I am so grateful for how money works in my life. I'm so grateful I did the work to dissolve all the energetic crap I had around money for so long. I feel so in the choice now, and not controlled by money, I feel so free. I love living my life in alignment knowing that money isn't my core focus, instead it is alignment. I am so grateful for my fast Wifi, the fact I can shop at wholefoods, being able to drink nutritious high vibe water, knowing that if my friends need me I can be on a plane at any time, being able to invest in personal development. I love being in the appreciation of money and letting money be simply a playful team mate of mine.*

> *It's June 2018, my money story work is showing up in my life beyond anything I used to dream, wow!!! its working!!!! My bank account shows numbers and digits*

I've never seen before and I'm finally driving my new Tesla. I give more than my old 10% of my income to causes and organizations I care about because there is no limit to what I can give. I am giving to X org and it feels so good every month to give to them and be able to give to them because I changed my money story. I can feel in every cell how consciousness and money can be one and I'm so free of the burden of hating it. I love buying all organic food from my organic grocer every week without feeling bad about spending extra money on myself. I love nurturing myself. I love giving my body the best. I love being able to take my mum for organic facials once a month. I love being able to surprise my friends.

An excerpt from the money script of beautiful friend Tara. She wrote it after working through the money content in this book (At my event—TNWL) Her words inspire me so much.

Today as I wake, I am reminded of the absolute abundance that surrounds me in every moment, and that everything— utterly everything—is an energy, a vibration, and that I can either align with all that I desire, or I can pretend that I don't know how to do that.

I love money and money loves me. Money may not be able to speak but she is listening to everything I say about her in every moment. I'm a magnet for her because I respect her, appreciate her and circulate her in the best interest of the entire planet. Money knows she's safe with me. Money knows that when she comes to me she's funnelled into serving the spirit of my businesses, which provides value for thousands of people, that she's generously gifted to others and their causes—either out of necessity of 'just because'—that she allows me to have experiences and go places which change my world and my perspective, and thus allows me to offer an even higher vibration to the planet and its people.

I allow money to reach me with ease, gratitude and relief. Money is truly relieved when she lands in my hands because she knows how often people are bitching about her, blaming her, resisting her, pretending they don't want, need and love her when in actual fact, they do. Of course they do. Money knows that I want, need and love her, and that my palms are open, and that I am grateful, and that I do not take her for fucking granted anymore.

With tears in my eyes, I receive, I receive, I receive. I am trusted. I am a fantastic custodian of money and I refuse to betray her with my ignorance and sleepy conscience. She supercharges my dreams, breathes life into my purpose, enables me to live a beautiful, healthy and inspiring life, and makes it possible for me honour the spirit of my businesses unlike anything else in this world.

It is nearing the end of 2016 and my heart is open and light as I finally remember how deserving and worthy I am to be entrusted with this. I am not the money that flows to me. I am what happens as the money flows out. We have just had our most financially abundant month ever and this income is being circulated with integrity—***INSERT YOUR INTENTION/ GOAL HERE.***

As 2017 rolls around, my beliefs around money shift again, the ceiling shatters, and my vibration lifts to attract more of her and her opportunities, as well as other divine custodians into my energy field. 2017 is the year that we manifest a contract I made with money a very long time ago. This is the year she equips me with the divine responsibility of attracting ***INSERT YOUR AMOUNT HERE*** annually. Universe, thank you for helping me co-create ***INSERT YOUR INTENTION / GOAL HERE.***

I can feel how excited and joyful money is about 2017... she is so excited to reach me, because she knows she will be distributed beautifully. She is bouncing around, clapping her hands, screaming:'FINALLY!' and 'See you soon, Tara!' and 'I can't wait to create all of this magic with you!' and 'We're going to have the most amazing time!'

I do not simply spend that money that I attract... I circulate and invest it in the good of all.

Let's move onto scripting for other areas of your life. What stories do you want to tell?

Here are some snippets from my general script:

I feel...

Opening paragraph, the one where you detail how you FEEL. Write it in your own words cos my words didn't come from your soul.

> "Everything is getting even better. I am the happiest person ever and my vibration is so expansive, playful and vibrant. I am in my tap, and every single day I am receiving all of the love, abundance, success, surprises, and opportunities that are coming to me. Everyday I feel more and more in the genuine bliss and gratitude of my life. My thoughts are naturally positive and my vibration is rising higher every day. I am attracting SO many epic, beyond epic surprises into my life. It's getting better and better and better."

My Pregnancy...

I evolved the pregnancy aspect of my script several times as it progressed and also have a part of it that details my birth, but this was part of my first one.

> "I'm so blessed with the most amazing, loving, caring, fun, handsome husband and our expands blissfully every day. Being married to Erik is the greatest joy and everyday we rise higher and higher in love together. I am pregnant with the healthiest, HAPPY, sweet, chubby, cute, wise, loving, connected, smart baby ever and it's the greatest joy in the world to be experiencing pregnancy for the first time. I love being called to slow down by my body and take extra rest so that I can nurture myself and my baby. It's like we check into the spa each day together, put our feet up and just bask in the presence of THIS special day of the pregnancy. Each day of pregnancy is so special and

I love <u>celebrating</u> each day for it's <u>magic</u> and <u>newness</u>. I love how much more aware my pregnancy is helping me to be. I'm so extra aware of foods to eat and not to eat, certain smells. It's like my awareness got a 1000x boost so that I can best take care of myself and our baby during this time. I love the gift of extra awareness pregnancy brings and I love the gifts of extra self care pregnancy brings.

I am so healthy. <u>My baby is so healthy.</u> <u>My baby</u> knows that my body is so <u>SUPER healthy</u> and that our birth will be <u>phenomenally beautiful, easy, amazing, and healthy</u>. We are happier everyday and enjoying the pregnancy every moment. She is thriving in my belly and I trust my body to support and nurture her innately :)"

Something coming up…

Working through the next six to 12 months of my life, knowing that I had some of these coming up and writing how I want to feel.

"I'm on my flight to Australia now and i'm so excited. I can feel the <u>angels surrounding the plane</u>, nurturing and protecting our baby and me and fuelling us with extra divine light, <u>joy and exciting</u> downloads from the cosmos, just because. I love allowing myself to eat a little bit of bread on the plane ;) I love the gift of <u>self nourishment</u> and the little joys like that this pregnancy brings. It's like I'm giving myself permission to do ANYTHING that makes me feel good cos I know the baby requires that <u>alignment and joy</u> for her internal environment. That is a pretty cool gift of pregnancy."

My big event…

I won't include it all cos it's lonnng. But you'll get the idea. And no judging, because this is verbatim—grammar rules out the window!

"I am so excited for the event. Everyone is so pumped and people are flying from everywhere. It's already got the vibe of the best event ever and I know that's exactly what it's going to be.

I am prepared and 100% ready to have and be in the space for two days and let amazing, fresh, cosmic information flow through me powerfully. I love how ready I am and how relaxed I am about the event. It's freakin awesome…

I am light, happy, expansive, trusting, excited and so grateful to be able to gift this event and experience this special two days with my tribe.

As much as it's for them, I know I am receiving so much joy, happiness, love, satisfaction, abundance from this event and I let it all in :)

Lauren is super organised and on top of everything, even more than I can dream of. She so gets the vision and is just such an epic member of my team. She has gone above and beyond and everything is flowing so smoothly and beyond!

We walk through the venue on Tuesday and it looks amazing! Super rustic and big and just the perfect vibe for this event. I'm bouncing with so excited and happiness for everyone to see it!

I spend a little bit of time looking over the slides and I feel SO great about the way it's organised. The website is all complete and the systems are hooked up! It's all seamless and amazing and ready to go! It all looks SO GOOD!! I'm so excited to show everyone the new website and for them to be able to simply navigate it for whatever they need. Game changer!! Boom!

It's Friday and we head to the venue to help Lauren set up. Omg it looks SO epic!! Everyone is going to lose their shit when they see it! It's just so rad, so cool, so funky and has an energy of play and expansiveness. Even the venue on it's own is transformative cos people are so used to boring old hotel venues—their vibes are gonna be elevated expanded, enlightened and super joyous when they see this one :)

It's GAME DAY! Saturday morning! I wake up feeling amazing...light, happy, present, calm, clear, eveready... and know it's going to be a the most fun light event I've done to date. Every event I do gets better and better and better! How does it get any better than this?

I arrive at the venue and everyone is so buzzed! Vibing and already and ready to receive, absorb and take their life to the next level...Sky rocket them into a new orbit... It's SO good to see so many people I know OMG! I just feel SO at home and so in my zone and space.I have the All the Angels, Guardians, Sensei's, Masters, The Divine, Source, Spirit Guides and All the Gods and Goddesses guiding and looking after me with ease in every breathe and step. I can do ANYTHING today :) and DO IT! Baby is there letting me know she/he is supporting me and will give me all the energy I need (while still being perfectly fine). We have lots of snacks and water and Erik is so supportive in ensuring I am fuelled.

Ben's opening is great!! I can tell he put a lot of thought into it and I'm so proud of him. It was so special for him to open! The welcome to the country was so beautiful my God! I am so happy we did that and I'm so proud to be aussie. The audience LOVED it. It's off to an epic start!

My The New Way opening is SO good! 10 x better than the last one. I'm just so in flow and so in my zone, energy and space. It's so effortless, funny, inspiring and people feel they already got SO much from that first hour!

Day 1 goes just beautifully—it is beyond anything I could have imagined. It blew my mind away and has my soul and spirit feeling SO happy and grateful. Tara was INSANELY good! Lockie was SO epic!"

Script Wins. The proof is in the puddin'.

So, how did my event go? *Exactly how I scripted it but better.* How is my pregnancy going? *Beautifully :) Beyond beautifully.* I am embodying positive, rewarding beliefs and stories around birth, not just knowing them. And whenever anyone asks me how my pregnancy is doing its automatic "SO good. I've had the BEST time!!" That's The Script that comes out of my mouth now without even thinking about it, and that's how you know it's embodied. I could go on and on about small parts of my scripts that came true, like how I scripted for my green card interview to be in January when it was highly unlikely that it would be, only to receive an email from my lawyer saying "This is unusual but your interview has been scheduled for January!" But rather than bang on about MY #scriptwins, I want to share a bunch of Script wins from my Supercharged tribe. I'm so proud of them and their commitment to their highest and best life. Flip the page, and just indulge in the possibilities.

POP OUT: Script Wins

#scriptwin #fijibaby

When I got the news the first thing I wanted to do was jump on here and share it with you all!

So I've had in my script since I wrote it (about 4-5 months ago) about getting off the phone to the new human i'll be aligning with for a new role. I detailed how it felt "Relief and calm washes over me as I share the news with my fiancé. We are ecstatic to have all our dreams for this years living in a space of peace, balance and joy come to fruition" and BOOM!

When I first starting reading it all I imagined was somewhere near the ocean (my inner Moana is calling for the ocean to be closer to me), doing a job that gives us a healthier work life balance and doing something, somewhere new, that we love.

Then my cousin about 2 months ago sent me a link to a job in FIJI. What is the job? I asked... Oh it's a general manager position at a resort I thought you'd be really good for. Which island? MANTARAY ISLAND!!!

I lost my shit—I visited this island about 3-4 years ago, the only holiday I've ever been on on my own, and LOVED it! Always wanted to go back, and now I get to work there!

Better yet, they've created a role for my fiancé, which really excites me. Knowing he can really focus on his book writing (Fantasy book series before he writes about how curiosity of the cave man sparked, watch this space, they're going to be EPIC) and we get to be somewhere new and fresh and do the things that make us HAPPY and make us FEEL GOOD.

I'm so excited to share this news with you guys, I'll be unleashing it to the world on my personal page later this week but had to tell you guys first!

Exactly how I wrote it in my script, is exactly how I felt. This script writing yo! It's the SHIZ!

#scriptwin ......

I am over the moon with this and I cannot thank this group and the Universe enough!!!! Turned out even better than expected, of course!

To be authentic here, I have been inconsistently script reading while I've been run down the past week (I realise that's the time I MUST read my script, to help me get back to health, highest vibration and keep up the conscious creation).... and yet, probably because I went on a mighty rampage when I added this to my main script, I must have infused the right energy into it. Every day even though I sometimes didn't read it I've been thinking about this as though it'd already happened.

The story is... We just got approved for the most amazing apartment ever, with total EASE (when I say total ease I mean absolutely no competition for this one.... and this seems unheard of for eastern Sydney suburbs where up to 90 groups turned up for previous apartment inspections we went to).

We have everything we could dream of.... we even have a massive stand alone tub in our ensuite (unbelievably amazing)! The interesting thing is, a few locations and places didn't work out over the past 2 weeks, which I know now is because we were receiving something infinitely better. I'm so grateful to you Peta for your advice to be clear with the energy and intention, but not so super detailed the Universe has no room for surprise. Well, fucking amazed and surprised I am!

Honestly, wtf!!!!

Oh yes.... and we move in 1st April LOLZ

#scriptwin

When you script your son to have a siesta so you can get to work on your business. Where were these scripts a couple of years back when I was running on air with a baby that didn't like sleep?

#scriptwin

I want to share my script win!!!

I've launched an online leadership program last month and during the lead up to the launch I wrote a script which described the lead up, the feelings I had, the co-creative energy I was receiving from previous participants and the flow of money into my bank account, 95% of it has been manifested and more and more keeps flowing into my life. It's been totally amazing.

Tonight as I reflected on all that has happened, I hit a kink, the phrase 'be careful what you wish for' popped into my head and I stopped and examined the thought rather than let it take hold, I got up close to it and examined what it was telling me. It's has been what has been holding me back, The Script has given me the vehicle from which I have broken free from this limiting belief and shifted the kink. Thank you Peta for your teachings around this and thank you to the people in this group who consistently show up and share the love and support. #Scriptwin

#scriptwin!

 I'm experiencing a HUGE flow of creative energy and I'm daily having to up my game to match what is being asked from my soul to be delivered and I feel so grateful and happy to be in this place.

I recently put this sentence into my script, like a week ago:

"I receive ideas of how to create money streams easily and it feels fun and exciting to create these things. I know that before 2017 is over I will be financially independent and that feels so AMAZING. I can live on my music!"

AND JESUS have the ideas/requests been flooding in! (always in the shower btw, always. Must be clearing all the gunk away on all levels! Anyone else who has this?)

• In the last week I have had two people reaching out to me asking for private lessons to learn my songs

• I'm teaming up with a producer who contacted me and will be doing vocal session work ON A CONTINUING basis

• I'm creating a song book for people who want to play the songs themselves and share with their community

FUCK YES I LOVE THE SCRIPT!

Thanks for sharing the joy, love you and the epic space we share xx

#scripttwin

There was no way I was able to afford a flight to Brisbane for a big event. But madly wanted to go, and then van life for a week after with Tully. Also wanted to go from 280 to 1000 in my private Shakti support group on FB by the time I left. Put it in The Script. Invested energy and time every day into it. What does it FEEL like to wake up in that van, the freedom. To get on the plane to Brisbane. To have a network of 1000 beautiful women in one place.

A week out my finances weren't looking like Brisbane was an option and I stayed strong with The Script. Threw a little sex magic in there. 5 days out landed a random gig for services in exchange for a flight to Brisbane which lined up dates absolutely perfectly. And now, waking up in the mornings with my lover in the van. HOW GOOD. Exceeded 1000 women in the group the day before I flew out. However so excited to revamp the entire script, what can we create from here?

#scriptwin

Holy sheeeit. This has been powerful. It helped me realise a lot of the time I have avoided consistency with my conscious creation practice is because I didn't want to own the fact that I actually get to choose. We get to choose. The Script has helped me move from "trusting" that to "knowing" that and I'm excited to stay consistent with it and start to "embody" it. I've still missed a couple of days since starting however it's been MUCH more consistent than any other practice I've had.

The reason for this post is for an epic script win that happened extremely quickly, I'm just getting around to sharing it now. Littered throughout my whole script is how epic, light, free, expansive, excited I feel about money (interesting point is a rarely wrote specifics about how much I was earning or anything like that) and three days after reading this script twice a day I woke up to an email from my accountant saying I'd overpaid a certain tax bill on an ongoing basis and had $13,000 sitting in an account that needed to be transferred back to me.

The other interesting thing was that I found out about it because if started to get organised and respect my finances.

Seriously, you can't write this shit. Well... You can actually. And you can put it in your script.

Keep chipping away and doing the behind the scenes work guys.

You are a magical manifestor and the Universe is waiting on your every instruction. You have a magic wand, made of your energy and you can direct the Universe. You have so much super power to embody anything. Conscious creation takes work, but it can be fun work. And now you have the 3 steps to conscious creation—Trust—Know—Embody. You can do the work. You will be successful. You get to write your own script. Do it daily. Embody everything you wish for. I do it daily and I have every I want in my world.

YOU'RE DONE!!!

And you're SO hired.

Thank you for being on this journey with me.

Stay in touch on IG and FB and share whatever you found valuable.

Take photos, share your fav parts,
and just let me know what resonated for you!

Use the hashie #earthishiring

I hope to see you at an event soon!

Tour dates, and all other book-related
goodness can be found at:

www.earthishiring.com

KEEP READING FOR......

Glossary

Acknowledgments

References

Glossary

AYAHUASCA: Definition taken from Makenzie Marzluff. Ayahuasca (Aya) is a plant medicine from Peru—a tea that is brewed from a vine and a leaf, traditionally consumed for spiritual connectivity by shamans and Amazonian people. The spirit of Aya is very feminine; once you work with her, you understand why everyone refers to her as 'Madre.' She is known as the mother of all plants, the bridge between you and your higher self. She will heal, cleanse, purge, transform, invite, love, connect, and inspire. For me, it's primarily a conversation about everything—Purpose, Business, Relationships, Love, and the World.

CHIEF ENTITY: (CE), the spiritual boss of your company or creative project; above CEO, CMO, and COO; otherwise known as 'your vision'. The CE guides you as you lead the project on Earth, sending you ideas, nudges, and offering 'yes or no' when making big decisions. CEs hand select humans who are equipped and aligned with their ideals in order to create the company, project, not for profit, or creation; where spirit + business combine.

CONSCIOUS ENTERPRISE: a business, organization, or enterprise that includes the planet and the next generation as two of their most important stakeholders and makes decisions, products, and policies that reflect this ideal.

CONSCIOUS MONEY: money that is generated and circulated consciously and with appreciation; the result of bridging the gap between your soul work and money; the state of a healed and healthy relationship with money and an upgraded money story.

DIVINE ENTITY: a being from 'up there' where Source, God, the creator is—something with it's own existence. Invisible to the eye but real and felt.

FREEDOM LIFESTYLE: being able to work independent of location, with just a laptop and good WiFi. A trend amongst millennials who choose not to work a 9-5 office job in pursuit of more freedom, adventure and creative environments.

HOMIE: a person that you resonate with so deeply that their words and presence make you feel at home. You can have real life homies and you can also have Instagram homies you've never even met. Homie is also used to describe someone you grew up with or a member of your community.

HUMAN AF: Human As Fuck is the state of being equal parts magic and messy; appreciating the contradictions in our lives and letting them be okay, i.e. meditating in the morning in deep gratitude and then flipping the bird at the guy who cut you off in traffic. Being Human AF allows you to just be like 'Yeah, Ok. So I got mega pissed off today even though I'm wearing all white and headed off to Kundalini.'

IDENTITY: the comfort level, in terms of money, relationship, productivity, success; the state that creates a *Vibration* and instructs the world to give you more of it. To upgrade your life in any area, you've got to upgrade your identity.

JEANIIUS: secret spiritual signature (sig-*nature*); a mix between passion, purpose and genius (soul's genius, unlike intellectual genius); the gifts and talents that we can pursue by listening to and following clues such as, *what excites us the most, where we're the most curious, what we could do all day without getting bored.*

KINK: anything (commitment, relationship, responsibility) that feels heavy; anything that involves the word "should," as in obligation that doesn't flow with our alignment. A kink blocks your flow, just like a kinked hose.

KINKED HOSE: living out of alignment; saying *yes* when we mean no and *no* when we mean yes; when *The Tap* does not flow freely (or at all) from Source. This is the state of over-commitment, living a life of obligation, having too much "ugh, I have too…" on the schedule. The metaphorical garden hose cannot deliver.

LAW OF ATTRACTION: the attractive and magnetic law of the Universe that draws similar energies, thoughts, things, people, and circumstances together. Everything is always attracting its vibrational match and we are always giving energetic instructions to the Universe.

NETWORK MARKETING: a business model that pays everyday people to excitedly share a product that has impacted their life with other people; integrity marketing if it's a truly impactful product, with a heart-centered company who really gives a shit about people and planet; word of mouth marketing.

RADICAL ALIGNMENT: free, light, blissful spaciousness when you only *say yes* when you mean yes, *and no* when you mean no; radical denoting the ruthless that is sometimes required to put our alignment first. Living in radical alignment is living in a way where no commitment is more important than our own sense of wellbeing.

RIDE OR DIE TRIBE: (Ride or Die), a community of people who feel like home to you; you're serving them, they're serving; all members are *Human AF*. The term 'Ride or Die' originated from hip hop culture, and it described a woman willing to support her partner no matter what. Now, it's commonly used (with respect to hip hop), to describe the utmost loyalty you can have for another person or community.

SACRED GEOMETRY: a term used to describe the symbolic and sacred meanings given to certain shapes and structures.

SAFETY NET: an invisible net that lives between you now and your next level; whether it be the amount of money you earn, the richness of relationship you allow, your well-being, sense of happiness in your body, or how you crush it creatively; a device employed by your ego with the purpose to keep you safe, comfortable, and familiar.

SOURCE: the most commonly referenced word for a higher power (God, Spirit, Love, The Universe, etc…) used throughout this book, all of which refer to our Creator, our infinite Source of love, guidance, wisdom, and abundance, and *The Tap*. Additional common references include; God and The Universe, and it is important to not judge what anyone else believes to be true. There is only one Rome, but a million different ways to get there.

SUPERHERO: a human, committed to raising the vibe of our Earth by living in their own radical alignment; not interested in being seen as spiritually superior or a guru of any kind, and their superhero status isn't at all dependent upon what they do for work. The Superhero is Human AF, a proud member of Team Earth, living in a way that keeps all people and beings in mind. The Superhero reminds the world to play and to lighten up as we usher in this new consciousness.

THE HEXAGON: a 6-sided model to guide entrepreneurs as they build their own *Conscious Enterprise*; depicted as the symbol of a beehive (a successful beehive is made up of thousands of hexagons). In nature and in *Conscious Enterprise*, the model fails with one hexagon alone, but thrives when all hexagons interact to create change and do the work we want to see.

THE NEW WAY: The framework for upgrading our standards of Living, Leading, Earning and Giving as we usher in a new consciousness as a generation; the ancient way made fresh.

THE SCRIPT: a powerful exercise for embodying the vibration of everything you want. It's a script you write, to tell the story you want to tell so you can live the story you want to live instead of a default or borrowed story. A powerful exercise for consciously creating your own reality and giving the Universe intentional instruction.

THE SUPERCHARGED: a mentoring program designed to dive into all areas of The New Way and connect superheroes from all over the world for epic collaboration and a sense of family and home.

THE TAP: a (metaphorical) waterfall of everything we could ever want—clarity, abundance, lightness, inspiration, insight, downloads, ideas, sureness, clues, resources, love, which flows straight from Source (God, the Universe, Divine, Pure Love) into *all* beings. Living in *Radical Alignment* puts us in the tap.

TIME MACHO: being pigeon chested about the hours you work and how long you slave at a desk. This definition is by Anne-Marie Slaughter: "relentless competition to work harder, stay later, pull more all—nighters, travel around the world and bill the extra hours that the international date line affords you."

TNWL: (The New Way Live), a festival of consciousness, badassery, and play; where profound meets play and where personal growth meets the world's most fresh team huddle. TNWL is where the superheroes of our generation gather to collaborate, dance, face paint, share their jeaniius, and discuss what's most required of us. DJ's present, food trucks on hand, bean bags up front. It's the event that brings you home.

TRIBE: A community of people united by beliefs, traditions and/or ancestors. This word is used commonly to describe 'community' because of the word's very powerful essence. In using this word I pay massive respect to the Indigenous people of our Earth, especially the Indigenous Australians of the land I am so grateful to call home.

UNKINKED HOSE: living in alignment; saying *yes* when we mean yes and *no* when we mean no; when *The Tap* flows freely from Source. This is the state of an unkinked hose, just like a garden hose, when there are no kinks in it the water can flow and the plants get watered. The same goes for us.

VIBRATION: the energetic message you're sending to the world 24/7, which carries gifts and instructions for the world and the world responds. Your vibration talks, and the people and world around you listen. Your vibration instructs the world on your behalf.

Acknowledgements

I feel this is the greatest reward for writing a book—getting to thank my favourite people at the end (and not having to worry about grammar).

Writing a book really is a labour of love, because you can go so long without anyone telling you 'yeah, it's good.' While in commitment this book, I was nurtured, love and challenged by people who were constant reminders and fuel for me to complete it. It's easy to stop a book half-way, to tell ourselves that it's basic, boring, old news, shitty and not worth it. This is when we lean on our families and let their love be our rocket (creative) fuel.

I am so, so grateful to have the most rock solid stewards of love in my life.

My husband Erik,

You are simply the greatest. Your love and belief in me is all the fuel I'd ever need. It was because of your bigger-than-all-the-galaxies size love and support that this book was created. It was written when we were pregnant with Sol, and edited in the first three months of her life—and it was your calmness, rock solid belief in me and epic team work that allowed it to be completed. Thank you for always making this book a priority, even though you are responsible for so much at the same time. Your love is everything to me and superpowers every area of my life. I love you so much. XX

Sol,

My beautiful, chubby, wise, brilliant, clever, other-worldly blue-eyed starseed. Thank you for being the co-author of this book while in my womb. Whenever i'd need reminders, input or ideas I'd just look down and know exactly what you wanted me to write. Thank you for being the most easy, fun, joyful baby and for inspiring me to always be better for you and your Earth. This book is for you and all of your friends. I love you so much. XX

Mum,

My hero since day one. Thank you for supporting every decision I ever made, for being my greatest inspiration and cheerleader, and for going to your very edge so that we could always thrive. Your hard work, sacrifice, strength and courage will never be forgotten by the four of us. I am so grateful you are my Mum, I am your daughter, you are Sol's Nanna. Thank you also for proof-reading this book, everything has to pass the Mum test :) I love you so much. XX

Ben, Leigh, Sian,

My sibs. You are all crazy and I am so grateful to have grown up in Australia's smallest house with you. Thank you for taking the piss out of me and calling my bullshit while loving me at the same time. Aren't you lucky I didn't write this book at the kitchen table while you were chewing. Love you so much. XX

My Dad,

Our relationship teaches me so much and I acknowledge you and your heart for always doing your best and being there for me. I love you Dad. X

My tribe,

The Supercharged and everyone who has attended a TNWL—Thank you for how you show up, how you stretch and for everything you teach me. Thank you for trusting me since day 1. Thank you for nourishing me and for supporting the vision we're always building together. You're invaluable to me and I'm so grateful to be playing, creating, growing through shit and thriving with you. Love you X

Isagenix,

Thank you for giving me the platform to learn, grow, give, serve, nourish my body. You grew me as a woman and a leader. Thank you for allowing me to create a life so young, that allowed me to travel, create and figure out what I'm here to do. Thank you for the freedom to write this book, print and publish it without cutting any corners. X

Janna,

My rad, badass, beautifully articulate editor. Thank you for being so patient with me as we stopped and started this book three times. Thank you for showing up for this book even as your life needed you elsewhere. Thank you for believing in me and it and for how you can help my jibberish make sense. Thank you for the clarity and confidence you injected into me especially towards the end. X

Victor,

My mentor since I was an entrepreneurial, life, money, leadership, spiritual rookie. Your questions, your clearings, your perspective, your unwavering invitation to always go higher and see things from there. Thank you for always laughing whenever you answer the phone and for responding to 'how are you?' with 'magical, brilliant, epic, superb, amazing, healthy, wonderful'. You always instantly remind me of what life is about. You have impact my life immensely and I am forever grateful for you.

Kakao,

Thank you for being my ride-or-die, heart opening, creative fuel that sat with me as this book was created from top-to-bottom. You are Mother Earth in chocolate form and this book was #createdbykakao.

Makenzie,

For this foreword, for your influence on my life, for how you inspire me to serve this generation, for your soul-twin-ship, for your guidance and for your 8 page texts that are medicine for me. I love you, soul twin. X

Marc-John,

Thank you for proofing this book with your astronomically giant heart and wizardous way with words. You are a brother to me and we haven't even met in the flesh (this lifetime round). X

My home girls, you know who you are, for just being my home girls. Always there for me, always checking in to see how the book is doing, always there for a big ol' gas bag. I love you so much. X

Lauren,

For always getting my vision, being so patient with my particular-ness and for creating my dream book cover. X

Hilde,

My assistant for years. Thank you for supporting me always and loving me as I grow. I appreciate you dearly. X

All those who bullied me for years,

Thank you—For constantly reminding me what I wanted to be for our generation and for teaching me compassion even when it really hurt.

Mother Earth,

For being the greatest mentor, nurturer, teacher, provider, lover and badass on Earth—period. I am grateful to learn from your love *and I love that you're my boss.* X

Resources

US Chamber Foundation

https://www.uschamberfoundation.org/sites/default/files/article/
foundation/MillennialGeneration.pdf

Forbes article

https://www.forbes.com/sites/workday/2016/05/05/workforce-2020-
what-you-need-to-know-now/#1ce3b3682d63

Peter Diamandis

http://www.diamandis.com/blog/data-world-getting-better

Planet Stats

https://www.treehugger.com/clean-technology/20-gut-wrenching-
statistics-about-the-destruction-of-the-planet-and-those-living-up-
on-it.html

Nasa

https://climate.nasa.gov/evidence/